# EVOLUTION & THEOLOGY

# EVOLUTION & THEOLOGY

*Augustine Pamplany cst (Ed.)*

**SERIALS PUBLICATIONS**
NEW DELHI (INDIA)

First Published - 2011

ISBN: 978-81-8387-451-9



*Published by*

**SERIALS PUBLICATIONS**
4830/24, Prahlad Street, Ansari Road
Darya Ganj, New Delhi-110002 (India)
Phone : 23245225 Fax : 91-11-23272135
E-mail: serials@sify.com

# Contents

# Acknowledgments

This book carries a special debt of gratitude to a number of persons. I am deeply grateful to the eleven authors who have contributed articles to this volume by painstakingly employing their hermeneutical skills in extrapolating the theological implications of the theory of evolution. I am grateful to Dr. Job Kozhamthadam who went over the manuscript and made several valuable suggestions. My special thanks are due to Very Rev. Mathew Kumpuckal, Superior General, Little Flower Congregation; Very Rev. Thomas Anjilivelil, Provincial Superior; Dr. Johnson Puthussery, President of the Institute of Philosophy and Religion; Joby Edamuriyil, George Mullukodickal, Shibu Kuliraniyil and Joseph Purayidathil, my colleagues at Little Flower Seminary. I thank Alwin Padinjarekkutt, Arun Nelliyaniyil, Jino Pongampara, and Arun Madathiparambil for their valuable help. My sincere thanks are due to Serial Publishers, New Delhi, for their quality printing and publication of this book.

# Introduction

Throughout the history of the interaction between science and religion, evolutionary theory found itself in a paradoxical situation whereby the proponents as well as the opponents of the science-religion dialogue exercised their hermeneutical skills to adapt the theory to their theoretical positions. It is not long since the academic and scientific community celebrated the bicentennial of Darwin's birthday and sesquicentennial of the publication of his epoch-making work, *The Origin of Species by Natural Selection*. Apart from the constant subservience by the scientific community, what has sustained the evolution theory as a hot academic topic is its overarching existential outreach, or its imposing appeal to the horizons of humanity's meaning-world. The philosophical and religious ramifications of this theory have been so foundational that the proponents and opponents of this theory were destined to wrestle with it in one way or the other. The 18th and 19th century intellectual and religious world had difficulty in accepting Darwin. And even now many thinkers are devising ways to domesticate or ignore it. Andrew Dickson White had stated that theory of evolution was something like a plough into an anthill, annihilating the very delicate fabrics of religion and faith. As for Richard Dawkins, the pitiless indifference of the natural selection enables one to be an "Intellectually Fulfilled Atheist." Daniel Dennet found the impersonal, algorithmic, blind, purposeless processes of the universe of the evolution to be too dangerous an idea for believers to defend their faith.

Owing to the plethora of theological and philosophical accommodation that the theory of evolution has enjoyed over the decades, the voice of these ultra Darwinists is now almost a cry in the wilderness. Atheism on Darwinian grounds, now, rather than yielding to intellectual fulfillment, testifies to the intellectual bankruptcy, philosophical mediocrity, epistemic fixation, and the sabotage of almost every logical axioms and rational standards. These claims will be substantiated by the eleven articles of this volume on evolution.

The series of articles in this volume engage themselves with a positive and explorative dialogue between evolution and religious belief. The opening article by Peter M. J. Hess highlights the sacramental value of a dynamic and evolutionary world. Post-modern Christians need to absorb the reality that we inhabit a very ancient, dynamic, and evolving universe. The sacramental value of the world can be rediscovered in an evolutionary matrix. He argues that the incarnational perspective serves both as the zenith point of the inherently sacramental character of the universe and of the unity of knowledge.

K. Babu Joseph, having presented the most up-to-date features of the Darwinian formulation of the theory in terms of natural selection and its validation in the wake of developments in genetics, challenges the stereotyped image of the science-religion conflict on evolution. Evolution theory has the limitation of not being able to explain the advent of life, justifying indulgence in meta-scientific reflection. Making use of a picture of God as Energy and Information or Probability, he opens up a novel way of reconciling evolutionary and religious perspectives on creation.

Pamplany argues for the transcendence of the entire creation from an evolutionary point of view. Thus the evolutionary theory gives a new theological framework for cosmological reflections. The inward and onward dynamisms of the evolutionary world is the urge for a restful comfort, which may be termed as cosmic transcendence, the culmination of which is the glorification of the entire creation as envisaged in the Pauline vision. A world that exhibits clear qualitative transcendence in its emergent evolutionary stages can be depicted as a pilgrim movement towards the heavenly Jerusalem; towards a new heaven that will appropriate its urges, and, a new earth that would be full of actualities.

Patrick McDonald's paper is a theological reflection on original sin in the context of evolution. Although there is good reason to believe humans have evolved, and that this may raise very serious questions about one account of original sin, it does not impact the central dynamic of the emergence of sin in human history and the need for healing and redemption. Accepting an evolutionary account of human origins does not undermine belief in God, belief in Christ, belief in the Bible, belief in a soul, belief in the salvation of that soul, nor belief that the means for such salvation have been offered to us. However, holding all of these together consistently and plausibly might require some rethinking of what these beliefs mean and how we understand the sources of such beliefs.

Jacek Tomczyk and Grzegorz Bugajak contend that although in the course of the last 150 years discussions between proponents of the theory of evolution and advocates of the creationist view of the origin of human being have been frequently fraught with mutual hostility and accusations, it was all unwarranted. Viewing this period with hindsight, it becomes clear, however, that the theory of evolution prompted both scientists and theologians to address anew the phenomenon of the human. This challenge seems to remain actual still.

In spite of the many controversies that Christian faith had to face, some eminent theologians now argue persuasively that Christians can indeed, with integrity, connect their faith in God with a scientific understanding of evolution. They point out that evolutionary science can actually be taken as an invitation to enlarge our sense of the divine. Sarojini Henry examines how theologians like Teilhard de Chardin, Wentzel van Huyssteen and John F. Haught maintain that the theory of evolution exposes a fresh view of the reality of the sacred and an astoundingly meaningful universe.

Kuruvilla Pandikattu focuses on the impact Darwin's theory had on contemporary society, including religion. After exposing the grand idea and the response it has generated in terms of admiration and awe, the author looks at the relation between science and religion specially among American scientists to study the impact of the theory of evolution on religion. Finally the plea is made for a reasoned and creative response by believers and scientists alike, which will respect the autonomy of both science and religion and at the same time plead for a creative interaction in shaping human understanding and the evolving society at the moment.

John Britto analyses and evaluates in detail the various Christian responses, especially the Catholic position, to evolution in their historical dynamics. Beginning with the mid 20th century, Catholic attitude has been one of great acceptance, with Jesuit scientists, Catholic scholars and many high-ranking clerics rejecting both literal biblical creationism and intelligent design. Today, the Church's unofficial position is a fairly non-specific example of theistic evolution, stating that faith and scientific findings regarding human evolution are not in conflict, though humans are regarded as a special creation, and that the existence of God is required to explain both monogenism and the spiritual component of human origins. The auothor showcases how the proclamation of later Pope John Paul II has been instrumental in promoting a substantive dialogue between evolution and theology.

After considering the various theories of creation and evolution Francis Xavier reaches at a constructive hermeneutical synthesis where evolution-theory and creation-faith converge into 'creation in evolution.' Both evolution and creation are processes; the former, on the physical level explaining how one being becomes a higher being, whereas the latter stating where the dynamic force for becoming comes from. God is the initial dynamic force that set the evolutionary process in motion, as he created time, and He still continues the work in the universe - and this process we understand as evolution.

Binoy Pichalakkattu deals with Creationism, one of the mostly debated ideologies contrasted with evolution. He dwells in detail especially on Intelligent Design Creationism which believes in the cosmological, astronomical, mathematical, evolutionary and chaotic models of divine design. It is shown that creationism is non-scientific, and intelligent design creationism is a methodological error from a scientific perspective. The paper concludes by addressing the methodological concerns in creationism to affirm that the claims of creationism are not anything scientific, but scriptural claims which are unfounded theologically and exegetically. The test of creationism is to use the criterion of reasonableness.

The last paper by Chris Montoya, David Montoya and Graeme Mackay, is an eye-opener into the transdisciplinary model of approaching the fact of the universe. Throughout the article they make a comprehensive attempt to carry out an enquiry into a transdisciplinary harmonization of science and religion from religious epistemology and psychological analysis. Taking the example of pro-lifers and pro-choicers, the authors claim to articulate the problem of the beginning of human life and conclude that a soft fusion of scientifico-religious enterprises would agree that conception is the time when human life begins. The grand distortion of the Darwinian truth of the affirmation of a creator God is explicitly brought out in the second phase of the paper where phylogeny is invoked to answer the problem of the science-religion duel. They argue that the distortion of the original Darwinian theory by mincing the creator-part of the theory led to the penetrating inconsistency of theories and want of clarity in conceptualizations regarding the origin and development of the universe.

The thrust of this entire volume, in general, is that the clichéd notion of science-religion conflict is now no news to any informed person. And, in particular, we emphasize that rather than tampering evolution with fixated and parochial soliloquies, an open and explorative approach can open up deep depositories of truth and knowledge at stake in it. The papers here argue that evolution should be sustained on the horizons of our religious and existential meanings for there is much more that has to be harvested from the hidden potentials of this theory.

**Augustine Pamplany**

# The Sacramental Character of an Evolving Creation

# 1

PETER M. J. HESS[1]

*"The heavens declare the glory of God, and the firmament shows forth his handiwork."*
***Psalm 19:1***

*"Through him all things were made, and without him nothing was made that was made.... And the word became flesh and dwelt among us."*
***John 1:3, 14.***

## Introduction: God, Creation, and Sacramentality

Among the world's great religions, two traditions presuppose and articulate with particular clarity the sacramental character of the cosmos. Hinduism and Christianity testify in contrasting ways to the presence of God within creation. With appropriate caution for generalizing about a collection of sacred writings that is perhaps more diverse even than the Judeo-Christian scriptures, it can safely be said that in Hindu philosophy creation reflects the very being of God:

> Desiring that he should become many, that he should make of himself many forms, Brahman

> meditated. Meditating, he created all things. Creating all things, he entered into everything. Entering into all things, he became that which has shape and that which is shapeless; he became that which can be defined and that which cannot be defined; he became that which has support and that which has not support; he became that which is conscious and that which is not conscious; he became that which is gross and that which is subtle. He became all things whatsoever: therefore the wise call him the Real.
>
> (*Taittiriya Upanishad* 2:6:1c)

Emanating from the One, or Brahman, the world unfolds over time into the myriad forms of biological nature. In a literal sense the whole world is a sacrament, a visible manifestation of God. Vedantic texts testify both to the specific manifestations of the divine in nature, and to the universal that transcends the particular. Inquiring into which among the avatars of God is most properly the recipient of supreme worship the *Shvetashvatara Upanishad* asks,

> Who is the master of the gods on whom the worlds rest?
> Who is the Lord of the two-footed and four-footed here?
> To what god shall we reverently give offerings?. . .
> It is the protector of the world in time,
> the master of the universe, hidden in all creatures.
>
> *Shvetashvatara Upanishad* (3)

To summarize, in Upanishadic Hindu thought, God or the originating principle is manifest in and through nature, and indeed, is one with nature, and humans ultimately are one with all nature and with the divine.

The monotheistic metaphysic of the Western traditions stands in marked contrast to this, distinguishing as it does between God and the works of God's creation, expressed in Genesis 1-2, and in the psalms:

> How many are your works, O LORD!
> In wisdom you made them all;
> the earth is full of your creatures.
> There is the sea, vast and spacious,
> teeming with creatures beyond number—
> living things both large and small.
>
> Psalm 104:24-25

In its theology of creation—solidly rooted in Hebrew tradition—Christianity rejects pantheism, the identification of God with the multiple elements of the world. However, Christian theology affirms not only the infinite transcendence of God, but also the divine immanence. In an inverse of Hindu sacramentalism in which God is manifest in nature, Christian thought locates nature within the all-encompassing matrix of divine reality. Christian theology can quite appropriately be expressed in terms of panentheism, the philosophical framework in which God is both immanent within nature and infinitely transcendent to it.[2] Because it exists within God, nature is capable of manifesting the divine through bread and wine, oil and water, fire and light, as we find expressed in scripture, liturgy, and theology.

How does the Christian sacramental principle inform the thinking of religious believers in a world dominated by and organized according to the categories of modern science? We inhabit a very different world from that of the biblical authors and first theologians of the Early Church. The picture of a young, finite and static cosmos has fallen away before our conception of an ancient, dynamic and evolving universe. Physics informs us that the universe is governed by quantum mechanics, and cosmology tells us how it may have begun 13.7 billion years ago. Astronomy discloses to us the processes of stellar evolution and the formation of rocky planets by accretion from nebular discs. From chemistry we learn about the nucleosynthesis of heavy elements in stars and of pre-organic compounds on planets, and from evolutionary biology we learn the details of the history of life on earth. Neuroscience and psychology allow us to explore the development of human rationality, including the emergence of moral awareness and spiritual sensitivity. Even if science by itself is intrinsically incapable of discovering God, a Christian believes God to be immanent in the processes that are the subject of science.[3]

Through centuries of changing explanatory frameworks of science, Christianity has retained its essential sacramental orientation. Pope Benedict XVI has noted that "only in the mystery of the Word made Flesh does the mystery of man truly become clear."[4] In the Incarnation, God enters into an ancient and dynamic creation, communicating divine truth through the capacities of the human creature. We can express this truth in complementary ways. From the perspective of evolutionary biology or anthropology, *Homo sapiens* represents the mostly fully developed terrestrial manifestation of emerging primate rationality. From the theological perspective, humans as *imago Dei* embody the moral and spiritual response called forth by God from creation. The Incarnation is the supreme expression of this response: in the person of Jesus God took on the quarks of the Big Bang, the dust of supernovae explosions, the DNA of dinosaurs, and the long history of the primate genome. In an evolutionary paraphrase of St. Gregory of Nazianzus, God assumes creation by becoming incarnate at its heart in a human person, Jesus Christ.[5]

A sacramental perspective carries important implications for theologically understanding our evolving universe. The Hebrew account in Genesis declares that God saw the world was good, and the Christian tradition has always affirmed the goodness of creation against denunciations of the material world as evil, launched by heretical sects such as Gnostics, Manicheans, or Cathars. Karl Rahner noted the significance of this affirmation:

> The point at which God in a final self-communication irrevocably and definitively lays hold on the totality of the reality created by him is characterized not as spirit but as flesh. It is this which authorizes the Christian to integrate the history of salvation into the history of the cosmos.[6]

Indeed, in Catholic perspective creation is necessarily the domain of God's redemptive work, capable of bearing the incarnation and of being transfigured in turn by that creation.

A second important implication of the sacramental perspective is the principle of the *unitas scientiae,* firmly held in Catholic tradition from Augustine to Albertus Magnus and Pope Benedict XVI. This is the principle of the unity of knowledge or truth. Because God is present in and through creation, the truths revealed by science and by religion ultimately constitute two sides of the same coin. The first Jesuits understood and maintained this unity with great competence at the dawn of the scientific era,[7] but in our era of compartmentalized knowledge negotiating the *unitas scientiae* is increasingly a challenge. Pope Benedict argues for an architectonic vision of truth rather than a simplistic biblical literalism:

> Holy Scripture in its entirety was not written from beginning to end like a novel or a textbook. It is, rather, the echo of God's history with his people. The Bible is thus the story of God's struggle with human beings to make himself understandable to them over the course of time; but it is also the story of their struggle to seize hold of God over the course of time.[8]

The unity of truth is challenged not only by compartmentalization, but by the bewildering pace of change affecting scientific knowledge, social institutions, and even established moral truths. A critical faculty that recognizes all experience as being evolutionary or developmental in character is essential to interpreting this changing knowledge. If we appreciate this-as did Newman with respect to doctrine more than a century ago[9] - we will understand why theological models are subject to periodic reinterpretation, and why this should pose no threat to the core of our faith tradition.

## The Perspectival Shift in the Third Millennium

The Christian tradition has enjoyed long and fruitful engagement with science, or "natural philosophy" as it used to be known, dancing an intricate ballet characterized alternately by harmony and conflict, by indifference and mutual engagement.[10] Christianity naturally has reflected the worldview assumed by its believers, and over the course of half a millennium the physical worldview of the Christian West has been dramatically altered. The geocentric cosmos that until the Renaissance had served as a backdrop for the biblical drama of human salvation began to disintegrate in the face of discoveries in the natural and life sciences. The loss of the Aristotelian-Ptolemaic cosmology in the seventeenth century worked a progressively dislocating affect on the modern psyche, exemplified by Pascal's statement that "the eternal silence of these infinite spaces frightens me."[11] The classical view of the world would suffer yet further erosion with the eighteenth-century excavation of geological "deep time" and the nineteenth-century discovery of the evolving nature of life.

The close partnership enjoyed by faith and reason in the Middle Ages became more fragile during the period known as the Scientific Revolution.[12] The English Jacobean divine and poet and John Donne (1572-1631) illustrates the ambivalent response to the shifts in world view during this period. A man of deep pastoral concern, he engaged with more than a passing curiosity new currents of thought in natural philosophy, but ultimately he subordinated questions about science to his more urgent theological interests:

> I need not call in the new philosophy, that denies a settledness, an acquiescence in the very body of the Earth, but makes the Earth to move in that place, where we thought the Sun had moved; I need not that help, that the earth itself is in motion, to prove this, that nothing upon Earth is permanent; . . .[13]

Genuinely curious about the new science, Donne's judgment that we will not improve our understanding of scientific matters by clinging to the spectacles of the "old philosophy" offered a startling critique of the seventeenth century canon of scientific authority:

> How imperfect is all our knowledge! . . . Young men mend not their sight by using old men's Spectacles; and yet we look upon Nature, but with Aristotle's Spectacles, and upon the body of man, but with Galen's, and upon the frame of the world, but with Ptolemy's Spectacles.[14]

The relationship between Donne's critique of science and his wider theological concerns is instructive: even should the "new philosophy" (non-Aristotelian science) provide us with a closer approximation to truth in the physical sciences, this would remain as incidental as all other merely human learning unless it guided us in the direction of spiritual salvation.

The vast shifts in perspective spread across three centuries- in cosmology, physics, chemistry, medicine, geology, and natural history - were in some respects intellectually and spiritually traumatic.[15] The disintegration of the long-established medieval world view sowed seeds of doubt and of mistrust of science in particular, illustrating the risk of too close a dependence of theology upon a specific natural philosophy.[16] However, for every disintegration of a world view there is a corresponding reintegration. With varying degrees of caution and success, religious communities in the early modern period responded by absorbing the most cogent models and ideas of the relevant sciences, including heliocentrism and atomism, pulmonary circulation of the blood and the existence of a vacuum, geological change and ecological relationships.

The pace of revision of our scientific outlook accelerated in the twentieth century, creating new flashpoints of controversy. The Enlightenment emphasis on reason gave birth to methodological naturalism, which now often slips surreptitiously into metaphysical naturalism. A spate of recent books has launched an all-out attack not only on religious practice, but on the coherence of religious belief itself.[17] These arguments have in turn received rebuttals, sparking a vigorous debate that can be constructive for both religion and science.[18] Daniel Dennett has asserted that the theory of evolution by natural selection is a universal acid that "eats through just about every traditional concept, and leaves in its wake a revolutionized world-view, with most of the old landmarks still recognizable, but transformed in fundamental ways."[19]

This is hardly news to a theologian familiar with the theory of evolution, and may in fact be considered salutary for the critical rethinking of religious concepts. Indeed, John Haught welcomes the evolutionary perspective as "Darwin's gift to theology."[20] Evolution forces the theologian to integrate religious belief into cosmic history, and offers a context for a doctrine of God as compassionate, suffering with, active in, and fully related to the world.[21] A theology that is not challenged and transformed as the scientific culture changes around it is not really a living theology at all, but only the fossilized relic of a once-living tradition. Here we look at five global developments in scientific and cultural perspective that place us now in a very different world from that inhabited by our medieval Catholic forbears.

1. *Space:* our perspective has shifted from that of a relatively small cosmos to that of an unbounded universe. Cosmologies inevitably evolve, as happened when the Old Testament view (adapted from the Babylonian[22]) was replaced by Greek astronomy. The medieval Aristotelian-Ptolemaic cosmology - in which concentric spheres bearing the moon, sun, planets, and fixed stars revolve about an earth sitting in the least honorable position of "cosmic sump"[23] - has given way to the modified Newtonian system of planets that revolve around the sun, itself one of a hundred billion stars in one of three hundred billion galaxies in the known universe. Echoing Nicholas of Cusa's metaphor for God, the universe is unbounded in every direction, with its circumference nowhere and its center everywhere.

2. *Time:* the static medieval vision of a cosmos created in six days has given way to that of a dynamic universe with a history far longer than the 6,000 year biblical timeline. The Newtonian view has in turn been modified by Einsteinian relativity, quantum mechanics, and Lemaitre's proposal of a Big Bang model of cosmic origins. During 13.7 billion years of cosmic inflation, hundreds of billions of galaxies of stars formed from gaseous nebulae, heavier elements were cooked by nucleosynsthesis within stars, and individual stars and planets formed from accretion discs of interstellar dust and gas. It is now generally assumed that the universe will continue expanding into the indefinite future, probably until it suffers an entropic heat death tens of billions of years from now.[24]

3. *Evolutionary relatedness:* the "Great Chain of Being" has metamorphosed into an ecological web. Our terrestrial view of the hexaemeral creation story of Genesis - in which plants and animals were created in their unique habitats on days four, five and six of creation week – has given way to a perspective in which life on earth is shaped by a long history and a shared genealogy. The eighteenth-century discovery of deep geological time and animal extinctions, led to the proposals of evolution by Lamarck, Wallace, and Darwin, and these to the Modern Synthesis that forms the core of contemporary

evolutionary theory, supplemented by later developments such as molecular genetics, endosymbiosis, and evolutionary developmental biology. Western science has incrementally arrived at a unified account of the history of life on earth, from the first eukaryotic cell to the branching bush of life, of which primates form one branch and *Homo sapiens* one leaf related to all others through their shared inheritance and common ecologies.[25]

4. *Personhood:* the Christian perspective on the human person has come almost full circle. The Hebraic vision of the human as a psycho-somatic unity created in the image of God was at the core of the earliest Christian theological anthropology. This was submerged in the Patristic era, however, by a Platonic dualism that separated soul from body, spirit from matter. In the Middle Ages the Aristotelian metaphysic adopted by Thomas Aquinas held for a closer relation between body and soul, but the influence of Platonism persisted in Cartesian dualism. After the Enlightenment, dualism had to share the stage with materialist reductionism and a monist epistemology. Catholic theology since Vatican II has moved back in the direction of a Hebraic psycho-somatic unity of the person,[26] a view supported by various theories of emergence.[27] *Homo sapiens* is now understood as intimately bound up with the universe, from the atoms or "star dust" that are our matter and the genetic information that is our form, to the self-reflective awareness that drives us to try to understand ourselves, the universe, and God.

5. *Cultural development:* a final transition may be identified in the move away from a perception of culture as having been imparted in the early chapters of Genesis, toward a more evolutionary understanding. In the last few centuries, ideas of development have influenced studies of such diverse topics as language, culture, morality, ritual, and spiritual consciousness. It is clear that language and culture have pre-human roots, that proto-morality thrives among non-human animals,[28] and even that religion and theology have evolved,[29] as humans with their cultural evolution have developed greater philosophical sophistication and deeper metaphysical understanding.

These great changes pose some significant questions for religious believers in the third millennium. Post-modern Christians must absorb the reality that we inhabit a very ancient, dynamic, and evolving universe, and yet at the same time maintain our fidelity to foundational beliefs and traditions. The sacramental Christian perspective allows us both to embrace tradition and responsibly to engage the expanding worldview of modern science. Faith and reason are not natural epistemological opposites, aligned respectively with religion and with science. The two terms in fact play complementary roles in both the scientific and the theological enterprises. Faith is central to any religious tradition, for without it, scriptures are indistinguishable from other literature, and rituals are emptied of transcendent meaning. In Christian thought, faith as "the assurance of things hoped for, the conviction of things not seen" (Hebrews 11:1) stands in complementary relationship to reason, which is essential to articulating and defining theological discourse:

> Since the same God who reveals mysteries and infuses faith has bestowed the light of reason on the human mind, God cannot deny himself, nor can truth ever contradict truth. Consequently, methodical research in all branches of knowledge, provided it is carried out in a truly scientific manner and does not override moral laws, can never conflict with the faith, because the things of the world and the things of faith derive from the same God. [30]

Reason has been regarded since the Enlightenment as paradigmatic to the scientific method, serving as it does to assess the sufficiency of theories in explaining evidence. However, faith plays an equally significant if under-appreciated role, for a key component of a scientist's work is faith that the world is in fact comprehensible, that truth about it can be discovered. The conviction that science is an enterprise to which it is worth dedicating one's life is a matter of faith. In religion, the *traditio fidei*, or handing on of the faith, continues today as it did before the Scientific Revolution, and now (just as then) the believing community celebrates the mutual support of two ways of knowing. Pope John Paul II noted that although "faith is not based on reason, it can certainly not dispense with it. At the same time, it becomes apparent that reason needs to be reinforced by faith, in order to discover horizons it cannot reach on its own."[31] My working assumption is not only that faith and reason do coexist, but that they are necessarily partners in every act of human knowing.

## The Sacramental Perspective and the Challenge of Science

The great shifts in perspective we have traced above - that the universe is unimaginably large and very ancient, that the earth has a history and all life on earth is related through common ancestry, and that human language, culture, art, morality and religion have all evolved from capacities in pre-human animals- these now inform all dimensions of human reflection. Our thinking in spheres as distinct as science, theology, ethics, culture, and aesthetics no longer assumes a young and static world, but rather presupposes one that is ancient, dynamic and evolutionary.

Indeed, perhaps no intersection is affected more profoundly by evolution than the issues arising at the interface between science and religion. Such issues include questions about creation and eschatology sparked by cosmological investigation into the origins and far future of the universe, questions evoked by biology about evolutionary suffering and human origins, and questions raised by neuroscience about human cognition and the nature of spiritual experience. Let us look at how three representative questions might be approached in a way both that is responsive to the truths revealed by science about the evolving world, and that is faithful to the Christian theological affirmation of the sacramental character of the universe.

### *The God of Creation and Evolution in a Sacramental Universe*

Creation and Evolution are not contradictory but complementary terms, in the same way that "sphericity" and "orangeness" are complementary descriptions of a fruit. "Creation" is a non-testable metaphysical claim, the belief that the universe depends for its existence upon something or some being outside itself. It makes no assertion about how or when the world came to be, or even whether or not creation was an event or an "act" in time. "Evolution," by contrast, is the biological theory that all life is related through "descent with modification." As a theory it is testable, and in fact it is as well substantiated as the theories about gravity, atomic structure, or continental drift. Properly interpreted, evolution makes no claims about God's existence or non-existence, and is compatible with theism, atheism, and agnosticism. Regrettably, the ancient and venerable terms "creation" and "creationism" were hijacked by Fundamentalists in the early years of the twentieth century,[32] and are only slowly being won back for appropriate theological use. Christopher Kaiser has traced in meticulous detail how the Christian doctrine of creation has been of seminal importance in the development of western thought, and particularly of its science.[33]

In the last year we celebrated the bicentennial of the birth of Charles Darwin, and of the sesquicentennial of the publication of *The Origin of Species*. It is as important to consider the theological implications as to celebrate the scientific significance of theory of evolution. Pope John Paul II acknowledged in 1996 that evolution is "more than a hypothesis,"[34] and Pope Benedict XVI has said that "since it has been demonstrated that all living organisms on earth are genetically related, it is virtually certain that all living organisms have descended from this first organism."[35] The scientific model of an evolving creation raises some intriguing questions for Catholic belief. Aristotle held that the world had been shaped by God out of preexisting matter, whereas in Christian theology the idea of God speaking the world into existence *ex nihilo,* "out of nothing" has long enjoyed currency, although the biblical support is ambiguous.[36] Pope Pius XII' identification of George Lemaître's "Big Bang" with the primordial event of creation *ex nihilo* was premature, and Lemaitre himself cautioned the Pope against reading theology into a scientific theory.[37] There is now considerable speculation in cosmology about the preconditions of the Big Bang, and there seems to be nothing to indicate that such an antecedent state would be antithetical to the theology of creation.[38] Even if we inhabited an "oscillating universe" (an infinite sequence of Big Bangs and Big Crunches) - and the evidence now seems to show that there is not enough dark matter to drive such a gravitational collapse[39] - this model would still be compatible with a God who sustains creation. Ilia Delio finds in an evolutionary understanding of the universe and of life on earth rich resources for theology, particularly so for re-envisioning Christology for the third millennium.

## *Evolution, the Soul, and "Original Sin"*

One of the thorniest problems raised by evolution is the nature of the human person and the implications of an evolutionary account for the theology of "original sin." Following the publication of Darwin's *The Descent of Man* in 1871, it became progressively more difficult to deny both the evolutionary history of *Homo sapiens* and the genealogical relationship between humans and other animals. Mainstream churches (both Protestant and Catholic) managed a gradual theological accommodation of evolution. In *Humani Generis* (1950), Pope Pius XII cautiously endorsed evolution even of the human body, but he drew a protective belt around the soul, which he declared to be uniquely created by God.[40]

To be sure, by definition, the purely spiritual lies rightly outside the province of science, but what the parameters of the "soul" are is a profound question. Moreover, to seal off forever from scientific study the most interesting and important dimensions of what it means to be human seems both scientifically and theologically misguided. *Humani Generis* categorically ruled out "polygenism" or the view that humans did not descend from a single pair:

> For the faithful cannot embrace that opinion which maintains that either after Adam there existed on this earth true men who did not take their origin through natural generation from him as from the first parent of all, or that Adam represents a certain number of first parents.[41]

The problem is that science has now shown that monogenism - in the sense of the descent of our entire species from one set of parents, Adam and Eve - is genetically impossible. In-breeding reduces population viability because the resulting lack of genetic diversity makes the population more susceptible to disease and trauma. When a species falls below a certain threshold of breeding pairs, it reaches what is called a "genetic bottleneck," carrying the risk that the population will suffer irreversible genetic degradation.[42] Humans appear not to have suffered catastrophic bottlenecks within the last ten thousand years,[43] although the climatic results of Sumatra's Mt. Toba eruption were severe enough to reduce the population significantly.[44] It is estimated by some that the minimum population during the tens of thousands of years of it took hominids to evolve into full human consciousness was between 3,000 and 10,000 breeding pairs.[45]

What does this imply about the story of Adam and Eve in Genesis? It means that the author(s) of Genesis were employing richly symbolic theological language, as is true of the other cosmogonic stories in Genesis 1-11. "Adam" (Âdâm, "dust, humankind") and "Eve" (Hawwâ, "living one") do not denote individuals, but symbolize rather the whole human race. Their names may appropriately be applied to *Homo sapiens* as a whole as the species was evolving into rationality, moral consciousness, and spiritual sensitivity. In the story, the breathing of God produces a *nefesh hayya* or "living being," but it seems pointless to pursue even a modified literal interpretation that seeks to map Genesis 1:26-28 or 2:7-25 onto a prehistoric infusion of souls into some tribe of suitably prepared hominids tens of thousands of years ago. *Prima facie*, this would seem flatly to contradict *Humani generis*, and to reject established dogma about Original Sin as caused by Adam's and Eve's disobedience, and as transmitted to their descendants through the "carnal begetting" frowned upon by Saint Augustine.[46] However, it is by no means evident that Augustine's is the only theologically viable model of original sin, and Jerry Korsmeyer, Ilia Delio, and numerous others have articulated models of original sin that are more reflective of what we know from science.[47]

How should we conceive theologically of the nature of the human person in light of evolution? Traditional dualist conceptions carry the usual problems of defining what the soul is and how it is connected to the body. Recent reconsiderations range from defenses of a modified dualism[48] or a dipolar monism[49]to various forms of non-reductive physicalism and philosophies of the soul as an emergent property of what is essentially a psychosomatic unity.[50] Theology has been able to accommodate evolution of the human body from pre-human ancestors. Therefore, once we have accepted a symbolic, non-literalistic interpretation of the Genesis creation story, theology seen from a sacramental perspective should also be capable of accommodating evolution of the "soul," or of "soulishness," the moral and spiritual capacities that set our species apart. A theology in which God works in, with, and through creation can conceive of the soul as being transmitted integrally through the evolution of human physical nature and its increasing neural endowment. This is consistent with a Hebraic understanding of the person as a psychosomatic unity, and addresses a number of important theological problems:

(1) It preserves the sacramental idea of the universe as transfigured by God. It rejects a Platonic dualism in which all and only human souls are "saved," a position that in itself renders unintelligible the Pauline notion) that "all creation is groaning together" (Romans 8:22). "Salvation" involves the whole of creation, not merely human souls being somehow "raptured" out of bodies.

(2) It solves the problem of a radical and genetically unintelligible disjunction between pre-human hominids and *Homo sapiens.* Since all life on earth shares a common ancestry, and *Homo sapiens* represents the one twig on the great terrestrial bush of life that so far has evolved into rational self-awareness, it is impossible to draw a sharp dividing line between creatures that possesses an immortal soul and those that do not. Depending on how we calculate it, humans share close to 98.4% of genes with chimpanzees,[51] and our basing ensoulment on whether or not an entity carries human DNA seems little more than genetic chauvinism. All beings are possessed of

soul, at an intensity appropriate to their level of neural complexity. In the evolutionary model we avoid the irrational conundrum of having a generation of non-human parents giving birth to human children, or of one single breeding pair as progenitors of the entire human species.

(3) It makes sense to an ecological theology that regards all God's work as the subject of a new creation, including the whole spectrum of life from the evolution of the first self-replicating molecule to the evolution of rational life wherever suitable conditions are found in the universe.[52]

(4) It maintains the integrity of both scientific and theological perspectives on reality. Theology does not need to assert a soul infusion that is in principle undetectable by science, because there never was such an infusion. In evolutionary history in sacramental perspective, the soul evolves concomitantly with the capacities of the body, at a rate commensurate with it. If God works "in, with, and under" evolution (to use Luther's Eucharistic terms), evolutionary biology, genetics, and neuroscience need not fear treading on theological claims about personhood.

### *Imago Dei* and the Range of Personhood

Related to the difficulty of justifying a sharp demarcation of immortally ensouled from non-ensouled primates is the problem of the range of manifestations of "personhood" within the human species. It is deceptively simple to look at "normal" human beings as carrying the *imago Dei*, and on that basis to ascribe to every human - and *only* to humans - an immortal soul. Some experts estimate that up to fifty per cent of human conceptions result in miscarriage because the zygotes or embryos have a chromosomal abnormality incompatible with life, or because they are otherwise so genetically compromised that they cannot develop to mature gestation and a normal birth.[53] If immortal souls are imputed to these zygotes, fifty per cent or more of humanity will never have lived conscious lives on earth, but rather will have entered immediately into eternity without ever having been able to make any decisions at all, moral or otherwise. The eternal destiny of more than half of humans, therefore, will be independent of any ethical decision making or moral life. While we are certainly not in any position to pass judgment on the status of these embryos, the implications of this disconnect are not insignificant.

The doctrines of both "soul" and *imago Dei* are complicated yet further by the twinning continuum. When a conception results in conjoined twins who are easily separable, or who have discrete brains, the theological conclusion appears to be straightforward: each twin is an ensouled person. The situation is more complicated with parasitic twins, however. When a twin embryo fails to separate fully, one embryo can cease to develop but remain as vestigial tissue attached to the otherwise healthy and fully formed twin. In the well-publicized case of Lakshmi Tatama (born in 2005) in Bihar State in India, Lakshmi's parasitic twin could not independently move the extra arms and legs that projected from Lakshmi's body, because the twin had no head or brain. It could experience nothing, feel nothing, learn nothing, and make no moral or aesthetic judgments. Without a developed personality or conscious life, the personhood of Lakshmi's twin remained entirely and solely *in potentia*, and its eschatological state would presumably be independent of its truncated organic life. In contrast, like that of any other normal person Lakshmi's eschatological state would presumably depend, at least in part, on her moral state during her life and at the time of her death.

On the extreme end of the twinning spectrum lies another perplexing phenomenon. "Tetragametic chimeras" carry the genetic contribution of four gametes (two eggs and two sperms) resulting from the fusion of two fertilized ova at the blastocyst stage.[54] Each ovum or population of cells in the developing blastocyst retains its own character, resulting in "mosaicism" or a mixture of tissues. One pair of gametes supplies the genetic information for part of the body, and the other pair supplies the information for the rest. Mosaicism might explain baffling phenomena such as gender dysphoria, in which an XY gametic pair forms the head, and an XX pair forms the genitalia. Most tetragametic chimeras appear outwardly normal, however, and have a unified psychological sense of self. Prior to the era of genetic testing, they would have gone through life without ever knowing about their dual origin, and thinking of themselves only as "I," not as "we."

In the case of tetragametic chimeras, if we insist upon the doctrine of the infusion of an immortal soul at the moment of conception, theologically speaking do we end up with two souls living side-by-side in one body, one of them perhaps lying dormant for the entire life of that body? Or is the soul whose gametes did not supply the brain removed by God at the moment of fusion? Could we imagine two souls and thus two *images Dei* in one person? The case of the tetragametic chimera is one in which science compels us seriously to rethink our theological anthropology. Jose Mario Francisco has warned in another context that the term "soul" is too easily drawn into a radical dualism, and that it might be better simply to use the pronoun "I."[55] Considering the ancient religious and cultural valence of the term "soul" this proposal may not be realistic.

However, in light of the sacramental character of an evolving creation, perhaps we can rethink the entire concept of *imago Dei*. God has become incarnate within creation, illuminating it from within. The whole created order in this sense is in the image of God, and its many elements reflect that image with a degree of transparency commensurate with their degree of evolution toward moral responsiveness and spiritual sensitivity. Perhaps we should reckon personhood or ensoulment or reflection of the *imago Dei* as depending less on a presumed ontological state at the moment of conception than on how that image is developed throughout the life of the individual. Noreen Herzfeld has maintained that the capability of sustaining authentic relationships is a sounder criterion for what it means to mirror the image of God than is intelligence or some other genetic endowment.[56] I make the case that consciousness of personal identity, the ability to sustain relationships, and the capacity for graced perfection should count for more toward determining the presence of the *imago Dei* than the number of fertilized ova at conception.[57]

**Conclusions**

We began with the question of how post-modern Christians can remain faithful to their foundational beliefs while at the same time absorbing the reality that we inhabit an ancient, dynamic, and evolving universe. When we study the Christian worldview as it has unfolded over many centuries, we see that it has retained its integrity through countless changes in our understanding of how the world actually works. For much of that history no particular conflict was perceived between religion and science. Galileo remained a faithful Catholic until his death, seeing no contradiction between his religious belief and his confidence in the truth of heliocentric astronomy. And however estranged they may appear to be today, faith in scientific reason lies on the same continuum as religious belief.[58] Theology and science are natural partners in an astonishing enterprise of knowing.

Reflection upon the sacramental character of an evolving creation can enrich our theological vocabulary by rendering it more responsive to our deepening knowledge of the universe we inhabit. For two millennia Christians expressed their theologies in the terms of the prevailing philosophical language and scientific models used to describe the natural world, whether Platonic or Aristotelian, Newtonian or Darwinian, pre-scientific or post-modern. As they have done in every revolution in worldview in the last twenty centuries, Christians in our century can make peace with the scientific perspective that we inhabit an ancient, dynamic, and evolving universe. So long as our biblical interpretation, our doctrinal formulations, and our other foundational beliefs are not irrevocably wedded to one particular perspective on nature, there need be no conflict between scientific and religious perspectives. The sacramental perspective is consonant both with biblical revelation and theological tradition, and with a science that recognizes the limits of methodological naturalism.

For scientists the nature of the evolutionary universe is quite properly a puzzle to be unraveled by means of the scientific method.[59] For theologians and religious believers the universe is both this and something infinitely greater: it is a mystery before which we fall silent. Pope John Paul II has noted that

> Scientists are well aware that "the search for truth, even when it concerns a finite reality of the world or of man, is never-ending, but always points beyond to something higher than the immediate object of study, to the questions which give access to mystery."[60]

Theology written from an evolutionary perspective, which takes seriously the antiquity of the world and its dynamic processes and its long ages of suffering, has an apophatic character - it has nothing to say when it confronts the blank wall of mystery. Christians believe God to be the author both of nature and of our act of knowing, and in Karl Rahner's words "in every act of knowing a person has an innate grasp of God, not as an object, but rather as a horizon of mystery.[61] Let us give the final word to Pope John Paul II, who noted that since "the things of the earth and the concerns of faith derive from the same God" a vital interaction between science and theology "leads to a greater love for truth itself, and contributes to a more comprehensive understanding of the meaning of human life and of the purpose of God's creation."[62]

### Notes and References

1. Dr. Peter M. J. Hess serves as Faith Project Director with the National Center for Science Education (NCSE), and as adjunct professor at Saint Mary's College, Moraga, California. He is a member of the International Society for Science and Religion, and has worked for both the Metanexus Institute and the Center for Theology and the Natural Sciences. His scholarly work focuses on the historical interaction between religion and the sciences.
2. Philip C. Clayton, Barbour's Panentheistic Metaphysic," in *Fifty Years in Science and Religion: Ian Barbour and His Legacy*, ed. R. J. Russell (Aldershot, Hants, UK: Ashgate Publishing, 2004), p. 116.
3. Peter M. J Hess, "Creation, Design and Evolution: Can Science Discover or Eliminate God?"*The Journal of Law and Public Policy* (forthcoming in 2010).

4. Pope Benedict XVI, Address to Catholic Educators, Catholic University of America, 17 April 2008.
5. Gregory of Nazianzus, "What is not Assumed is not Redeemed," from "To Cledonius the Priest Against Apollinarius", found in *Nicene and Post Nicene Fathers*, Vol. 2, #7, p. 648.
6. Karl Rahner, *Hominization: the Evolutionary Origin of Man as a Theological Problem* (Freiburg: Herder, 1958; London: Burns & Oates, 1965), p. 55.
7. Mordechai Feingold, *Jesuit Science and the Republic of Letters* (Cambridge, MA: MIT Press, 2002), pp. 1-45; Marcus Hellyer, *Catholic Physics: Jesuit Natural Philosophy in Early Modern Germany* (Notre Dame, IN: University of Notre Dame Press, 2005), pp. 1-4, 240-244.
8. Joseph Cardinal Ratzinger, *'In the Beginning...': A Catholic Understanding of the Story of Creation and the Fall, trans. Boniface Ramsey*, O.P. (Huntington, IN: Our Sunday Visitor Publishing, 1990), p. 18.
9. John Henry Cardinal Newman, *Essay on the Development of Christian Doctrine* (London, 1888).
10. This engagement is sketched in Peter M. J. Hess and Paul L. Allen, *Catholicism and Science* (Greenwood, 2008), chapters 1-3.
11. Blaise Pascal, Pensées, ed. and trans. Roger Ariew. Indianapolis, IN: Hackett Publishing. Co., 2005), p. 205.
12. The term "Scientific Revolution" is still serviceable, although important caveats about it are registered by Margaret Osler and others in Margaret Osler, ed., *Rethinking the Scientific Revolution* (Cambridge University Press, 2000).
13. John Donne, *The Sermons of John Donne*, ed. Evelyn M. Simpson and George R. Potter, 10 vols. Vol. 7, sermon 10, 1626, (Berkeley: University of California Press, 1954), p. 271.
14. Sermons, vol. 7, sermon 10, p. 260.
15. Marjorie Nicolson, *The Breaking of the Circle* (New York: Columbia, 1960), pp. 100, 106-7. Marjorie Nicholson has suggested that the scientific discoveries which "hastened the breakup of the circle of perfection and the celestial harmony of the world...heightened the perennial drama of human mortality" for Donne.
16. Max N. Wildiers, *The Theologian and His Universe: Theology and Cosmology from the Middle Ages to the Present* (New York: Seabury Press, 1982), pp. 158-60.

17. Richard Dawkins, *The God Delusion* (London: Bantam, 2006); Sam Harris, *The End of Faith: Religion, Terror, and the Future of Reason* (New York: W.W. Norton & Co., 2004); Christopher Hitchens, *God is Not Great: How Religion Poisons Everything* (New York: Warner, 2007).

18. John F. Haught,*God and the New Atheism: a Critical Response to Dawkins, Harris, and Hitchens* (Louisville, KY: Westminster John Knox Press, 2008), and David Berlinski, *The Devil's Delusion: Atheism and Its Scientific Pretensions* (New York: Crown Forum, 2008).

19. Daniel C. Dennett, *Darwin's Dangerous Idea: Evolution and the Meanings of Life* (New York: Simon & Schuster, 1996), p. 63.

20. John F. Haught, *God after Darwin: a Theology of Evolution*, 2nd ed. (Boulder, CO: Westview Press, 2008), pp. 49-60; *Deeper than Darwin* (Boulder, CO: Westview Press, 2003), passim.

21. Discussed by Archbishop Józef-yciñski in *God and Evolution: Fundamental Questions of Christian Evolutionism* (Washington, D.C.: The Catholic University of America Press, 2006), pp. 181-194.

22. Guy Consolmagno, *Brother Astronomer: Adventures of a Vatican Scientist* (McGraw Hill, 1991), p. 82.

23. Dennis R. Danielson, "The great Copernican cliché." *American Journal of Physics*, 69 (10) (2001), p. 1030.

24. Joel R. Primack and Nancy E. Abrams, *The View from the Center of the Universe: Discovering Our Extraordinary Place in the Cosmos* (Riverhead Press, 2007).

25. Richard Fortey, *Life: A Natural History of the First Four Billion Years of Life on Earth* (London: Vintage, 1999).

26. Karl Rahner, "Natural Science and Reasonable Faith," in Rahner, *Theological Investigations*, Vol. 21, trans. Hugh M. Riley (New York: Crossroad, 1988), p. 42. Citation from Mark F. Fischer, "Karl Rahner and the Immortality of the Soul," *The Saint Anselm Journal* 6.1 (Fall 2008), p. 2.

27. Philip Clayton and Paul Davies, eds., *The Re-emergence of Emergence: the Emergentist Hypothesis from Science to Religion* (Oxford; New York: Oxford University Press, 2006).

28. Marc Bekoff, *The Emotional Lives of Animals: A Leading Scientist Explores Animal Joy, Sorrow, and Empathy and Why They Matter* (New World Library, 2007).

29. Joseph Bulbulia, et al, eds., *The Evolution of Religion: Studies, Theories, and Critiques* (Santa Margarita, CA: The Collins Foundation Press, 2008).
30. *Catechism of the Catholic Church* (Vatican City: Libreria Editrice Vaticana; Washington, D.C.: United States Catholic Conference, 2000), paragraph 159.
31. Pope John Paul II, Encyclical letter, *Fides et ratio, of the supreme pontiff John Paul II: to the bishops of the Catholic Church on the relationship between faith and reason* (Washington, DC: United States Catholic Conference, 1998), paragraph 67.
32. Ronald L. Numbers, *The Creationists* (Berkeley: University of California Press, 1993), pp. 37-53.
33. Christopher B. Kaiser, *Creational Theology and the History of Physical Science: the Creationist Tradition from Basil to Bohr* (Leiden: Brill, 1994), p. 8.
34. Pope John Paul II, "Message to the Pontifical Academy of Sciences on Evolution" (1996).
35. Pope Benedict XVI, "Communion and Stewardship: Human Persons Created in the Image of God" (2002) *http://www.vatican.va/roman_curia/congregations/cfaith/cti_documents/rc_con_cfaith_doc_20040723_communion-stewardship_en.html*
36. It seems implied by 2 Maccabees 7:28; Genesis 1:1-2 is ambiguous.
37. Hess and Allen, *Catholicism and Science*, pp. 104-106.
38. *Michael E. Lodahl, "Creation out of Nothing? Or is Next to Nothing Enough?" chapter 9 in Bryan P. Stone and Thomas Jay Oord*, eds., *Thy Nature and Thy Name is Love: Wesleyan and Process Theologies in Dialogue* (Nashville: Kingswood, 2001).
39. The Supernova Cosmology Project, <*http://www.lbl.gov/supernova/* >; S. Perlmutter et al., "Discovery of a supernova explosion at half the age of the universe and its cosmological implications," Nature, 391, 51 (1998).
40. Pope Pius XII, *Encyclical letter Humani Generis* (Vatican, 1950), paragraph 6.
41. *Humani Generis*, paragraph 37.
42. The European bison, the cheetah, and the giant panda are all animals with very low heterzygosity, and thus are suffering severe bottlenecks. See Ridley, *Evolution* 3rd. ed., (Blackwell

Publishing), 151 - 153; Menotti-Raymond and O'Brien, "Dating the Genetic Bottleneck of the African cheetah," Proceedings of the National Academy of Sciences 90, 3172-3176, (1993).

43. John Hawks, et al. "Population Bottlenecks and Pleistocene Human Evolution," *Molecular Biology and Evolution* 17:2-22 (2000); Xiong et al, "No severe bottleneck during human evolution; evidence from two apolipoprotein C II alleles', Am J Hum Genet 48, pp. *383-389*.

44. Stanley H. Ambrose (1998). "Late Pleistocene human population bottlenecks, volcanic winter, and differentiation of modern humans," *Journal of Human Evolution* 34 (6), pp. 623–651.

45. Alec MacAndrew, "Misconceptions around Mitochondrial Eve: A Critique of Carl Wieland's AiG article on Mitochondrial Eve," at *http://www.evolutionpages.com/Mitochondrial%20Eve.htm.*

46. Allen and Hess, *Catholicism and Science*, p. 102.

47. Ilia Delio, *Christ in Evolution* (New York: Maryknoll, Orbis Books, 2008), pp. 53-65; Jerry D. Korsmeyer, *Evolution and Eden: Balancing Original Sin and Contemporary Science* (New York: Paulist Press, 1998).

48. Philip A. Rolnick, *Person, Grace, and God* (Grand Rapids, MI: William B. Eerdmans, 2007), pp. 248-255.

49. Terence L. Nichols, *The Sacred Cosmos: Christian Faith and the Challenge of Naturalism* (Grand Rapids, MI: Brazos Press, 2005), pp. 127, 153-181.

50. Warren S. Brown, et al., eds, *Whatever Happened to the Soul? Scientific and Theological Portraits of Human Nature* (Minneapolis: Augsburg-Fortress Press, 1998); Philip Clayton and Paul Davies, eds., *The Re-emergence of Emergence: the Emergentist Hypothesis from Science to Religion* (Oxford: Oxford University Press, 2006).

51. "Initial sequence of the chimpanzee genome and comparison with the human genome," The Chimpanzee Sequencing and Analysis Consortium, Nature, Vol. 437 | 1 September 2005, pp. 69-87; *http://www.genome.gov/Pages/esearch/DIR/Chimp_Analysis.pdf*

52. *Ted Peters and Martinez Hewlett, Evolution from Creation to New Creation: Conflict, Conversation, and Convergence* (Nashville, TN: Abingdon Press, 2003).

53. One study testing hormones for ovulation and pregnancy found that 61.9% of conceptuses were lost prior to 12 weeks, and 91.7%

of these losses occurred subclinically, without the knowledge of the once pregnant woman.[3] Edmonds DK, Lindsay KS, Miller JF, Williamson E, Wood PJ (1982). "Early embryonic mortality in women," Fertility and Sterility 38 (4), pp. 447–53. PMID 7117572.

54. Claire Ainsworth, "The stranger within," *New Scientist* 180.2421 (Nov. 15, 2003), pp. 34-37(4).

55. Jose Mario C Francisco, "Too much "soul": points and counterpoints from culture, theology, and science," in *Science and Religion... and Culture in the Jesuit Tradition: Perspectives from East Asia* (Adelaide: Australian Theological Forum Press, 2006), pp. 135-156.

56. Noreen Herzfeld, *In Our Image: Artificial Intelligence and the Human Spirit* (Minneapolis: Augsburg Fortress Press, 2002), pp. 94-95.

57. The author gratefully acknowledges the counsel of Patristic theologian Hamilton Hess, D.Phil. Oxon., on this and other points.

58. Michael Heller, *Creative Tension: Essays on Science and Religion* (Philadelphia: Templeton Foundation Press, 2003), p. 161.

59. Francisco J. Ayala, "Darwin's devolution: design without designer," in *Evolutionary and Molecular Biology: Scientific Perspectives on Divine Action*, ed. Robert J. Russell, et al. (Vatican City and Berkeley: Vatican Observatory Publications, CTNS, 1998), p. 113.

60. Pope John Paul II, Fides et Ratio, paragraph 101. "I would urge them to continue their efforts without ever abandoning the sapiential horizon within which scientific and technological achievements are wedded to the philosophical and ethical values which are the distinctive and indelible mark of the human person."

61. Anne M. Clifford, "Creation," 195-248 in *Systematic Theology: Roman Catholic Perspectives*, vol. I. ed. Francis Schüssler Fiorenza and John P. Galvin. (Minneapolis: Fortress Press, 1991), p. 236.

62. Pope John Paul II, *Ex Corde Ecclesiae: Apostolic Constitution on Catholic Universities* (Rome: Vatican, 1990), pp. 17, 20.

# Evolution: Science and Meta-science An Introduction

# 2

K. Babu Joseph[1]

## Introduction

The theory of evolution offers a more or less convincing explanation of the origin of biological species. Available data seem to suggest that life appeared on the earth some 3-4 billion years ago and has been evolving ever since. Although several thinkers have proposed the idea of evolution early on, it was Charles Darwin who presented its first scientific formulation. Natural selection, according to him, is the key to evolution. It favors the emergence of higher life forms from lower ones. He visualized it as a very slow process taking thousands or millions of years in contrast with creation, as taught by various religions. Evolution occurs through a sequence of steps called adaptations. If one regards evolution as science and creationism as an artifact, then there need not be any conflict between science and religion.

There are some open problems in the biological theory of evolution like the origin of life and the so-called missing links. The current opinion[2] about the latter is that in the fossil record there are indeed several links between the common ancestor and man, while there are gaps between the common ancestor and chimpanzee. As for the 'origin' problem, science doesn't give a unique solution, and for that matter, there is no unique theory of the origin of the solar system or the Milky Way. The evidence for the Big Bang, an event at which physical laws break down, is based on an extrapolation of galactic motions back in time as well as a couple of predictions that have been verified. Incompleteness is the hallmark of science, but it need not restrain one from pursuing science, because scientific theories are open-ended and falsifiable. The evidence in favor of evolution is so strong that it is naïve to imagine that the theory will be overthrown someday and replaced by creationism. Nevertheless there is ample scope for interpreting religion's role vis-à-vis that of science. With its traditional emphasis on revelation, religious experience is ineffable, euphoric and not falsifiable. Despite the difference in approach, religion and science can co-evolve without mutual acrimony. Science has its singularities such as Black Holes and Big Bang, and direct verification of any prediction under such extreme conditions is impossible. Do we not see a parallel between science and religion in this regime where falsifiability is absent? In a sense this justifies the transfer of the jargon of one discipline into the other. For example, in the language of physics God may be characterized as Infinite Energy and Infinite Information. Compare this description with the common portrayal of God as Infinite Power and Infinite knowledge. The faithful look upon God as a person who can be cajoled to yield favors. Prayer or no prayer, God responds in an unpredictable way and can, therefore, be described in probabilistic terms.

The purpose of this article is to appropriate to evolution theory the distinction of a scientific discipline, and to religion, that of a cultural conundrum, and to work out a synthesis of the two under the banner of science. Since science relies ultimately on observation, religion should not contradict it but attempt to conform to it. This is not scientism because separate areas of relevance are delineated to both - the world of senses for science and the world of the spirit for religion. Whenever anything having scientific connotation arises, the last word shall be science's.

The author has published two articles[3,4] and prepared a report[5] on a concept of God inspired by quantum physics. In the present article, an attempt is made to briefly outline evolution theory in its modern version and to link it with a simple description of God sketched in Ref.3. It is hoped that this approach comprises the best of 'both worlds' and will satisfy scientists as well as religious thinkers.

**Evolution in a Nutshell**

Jean-Baptiste de Lamarck[6] was the first biologist to seriously propose evolution in place of a sporadic process of species extinction, to account for the existence of fossils. He argued that species got modified through adaptation to the environment. His theory was based on the principles of use and disuse, and inheritance of acquired characters, both proved incorrect later. Darwin, in his path–breaking work *On the Origin of Species*, published in 1859, defined a mechanism called natural selection which turned out to be acceptable to biologists. Alfred Wallace also had simultaneously arrived at this idea, in an independent manner. Both Darwin and Wallace were influenced by Thomas Malthus, a British economist, who pointed out that while a population increases in geometric progression, the food supplies increase only in arithmetic progression, causing a struggle for existence especially among the poor. Those who have access to more food will reproduce more. In the biological theory of evolution, this struggle is generalized as competition among the members of each species. Those who survive are the fittest individuals whose offspring outnumber those of others. Thus gradually, the species improves. Darwin restricted natural selection to sexual selection by individuals. By adapting itself to the local environment in a long span of time, a geographically separated species can become another species. In his book, Darwin quotes from a paper read by W. C. Wells before the Royal Society in

1813, in which he distinctly recognizes the principle of natural selection:

> Of the accidental varieties of man, which would occur among the first few and scattered inhabitance of the middle region of Africa, someone would be better fitted than the others to bear the diseases of the country. This race would consequently multiply, while the others would decrease; not only from their inability to sustain the attacks of diseases but from their incapacity of contending with their more vigorous neighbours. The color of the vigorous race I take for granted, from what has already been said, would be dark. But the same disposition to form varieties still existing, a darker and darker race would in the course of time occur: and as the darkest would be the best fitted for the climate, this would at length become the most prevalent, if not the only race, in the particular country in which it had originated.[7]

The strongest evidence in favor of evolution came from fossils of extinct organisms that lived in older geological strata, that is earlier epochs in the history of the earth. While the fossils found in the most recent geological strata often closely resemble species still living, those of the older strata display remarkable differences from their living representatives. This observation was interpreted as supporting Darwin's hypothesis that organisms of the earlier periods gradually evolved in their descendents in the later periods. There are, however, many gaps in the fossil record, the reason being the possible loss of fossils in natural catastrophes such as earthquakes, floods and volcanic eruptions in the past. Occasionally, a rare fossil is found that fills the gap between ancestors and modern descendents. Since birds are believed to have descended from reptiles, there must be at least one transitional creature separating the two classes. The discovery in 1861 of the Archaeopterix, half-reptile, half-bird, that lived about 145 million years ago, was hailed as a remarkable proof of Darwinism. The current thinking is that since at the genetic level there is so much overlap between different species, it is absurd to try to trace lineage in the living world!

Humans belong to the mammalian order called primates, creatures having a tree-living ancestry. Monkeys, apes and humans are classified as anthropoid primates, characterized by a highly developed brain, protracted infancy and increased parental care. Contrary to all pre-Darwinian schemes that envisage a linear process of descent, Darwin proposed the revolutionary notion of branching evolution. According to this view, all organisms on earth have common ancestors and it is possible that all life emerged from a common source. This is known as the theory of common descent. Branching is the consequence of formation of new species. Common descent explains the observation, among different classes of vertebrates, of common characteristics including anatomical features. All such species must have come from a common ancestor. There is enough reason to believe that man (Homo sapiens) and Chimpanzee (Pan triglodytes) had a common ancestor, but have evolved along different branches. The bonobo (Pan paniscus) or pygmy chimpanzee is another chimpanzee-like species which manifests the so-called human emotions of love, pity, jealousy and hatred. Up until now, not a single uniquely human trait has been identified that is not found in non-human primates. Characteristics such as tool use, reasoning ability, excitement, learning of words and meaning, consciousness, self awareness, enjoyment of humor and so on, which are usually rated as human, are shared by these animals too. Features such as the upright gait, the greater manipulative skill of the fingers enabling precision grip, the location of the vocal chord enabling free sound-making, and the presence of a very large number of neurons in the brain, distinguishing man form other primates, are the gift of natural selection.[8] There is a difference of about 5% between the human and the chimpanzee genomes which is equivalent to 100 to 1000 genes. All efforts to identify a patently human gene have failed so that it has been suggested that the similarity in the two genomes implies that all genes of humans and chimpanzees are on an average 95% similar and 5% different.[9]

Hominid is the common name given to humans who differ from apes and monkeys by having the greatest number of adaptations helpful for terrestrial locomotion. The common ancestor we share with chimpanzee lived about 6 million years ago. One of the oldest fossils discovered till recently is that of a girl referred to in the literature as Lucy. Her biological classification is Australopithecus afarensis. She was small but smaller still was Homo floresiensis, mockingly called Hobbit whose fossils were spotted in a cave in Indonesia two or three years ago. Among the other human species identified are Homo erectus, Australopithecus africanus, Homoneanderthalensis and so on.[10] The latest find is Ardipithecus ramidus, hailed as the breakthrough of the year 2009 by the journal *Science* in its column, Science News This Week,[11] who is said to have walked on the earth 4.4 million years ago. Ardi's anatomy is unlike that of living apes or later hominids such as Lucy. So she belongs to a transitional species (link) between the common ancestor and the humans.

Each gene is a portion of DNA and the genome is the totality of all genes.[12] The DNA of a given species is a polymer molecule made up of billions of permutations of the four letters A, C, G and T which stand for the nucleotides adenine, cytosine, guanine and thymine, respectively. Each event in the evolutionary history of a species is recorded in its DNA. Any change or new trait in an organism, called mutation, is traceable. Mutation appears as a sequence of changes in the DNA. Some mutations are favored by nature and are preserved. This explains why certain genes have been preserved in the living world for billions of years, while others have been rejected through natural selection. Though random, natural selection acts on what is useful. Not all mutations result in biological change as there is a *tolerance* range of variation. Such variations are the secret of why each human is a unique individual biologically.[13] Natural selection operates through adaptation to the environment. For instance, a moth species with background-matched color can survive the attack of predators better than that with color mismatch. Thus the species with matched color becomes selected over that with unmatched color. Several cases of co-selection in which some trait of one species is beneficial to another species and vice versa have been discovered. Competition and co-operation are thus two faces of the same coin.

**Conflict with Religion**

Darwinism and religion have often clashed with each other over issues that are not properly analyzed by either party. Barring the extremists among religious groups who take every word in their sacred books literally, there is a growing awareness of the principle of evolution and a possible role for God in the evolutionary process. Pope John Paul II,[14] for example, questions evolutionary theories of the mind which claims to have emerged from the forces of living matter as they are incompatible with the concept of the dignity of man. He argues that there is a direct divine intervention in the transition from the animal to the human state, a discontinuity in the otherwise continuous process of evolution. Eventhough he doesn't explicitly mention the word soul, he means it's creation by God. He says: "...the experience of metaphysical knowledge of self awareness and self reflection, of moral conscience, freedom or again, of aesthetic and religious experience, falls within the competence of philosophical analysis and, while theology brings out its ultimate meaning according to the Creator's plan..." The Darwinists' claim that there is nothing in man that is not a product of evolution, as there are animals possessing similar faculties. As far back as 1967, the zoologist Desmond Morris[15] made the interesting observation that our activities such as feeding, grooming, sleeping, fighting, mating, and care of the young have counterparts in other species. An important problem with the religious view is to decide whether Homo sapiens are the only humans endowed with a soul, while other human/humanoid species continue to be soulless. There is some evidence suggesting that the Neanderthals who lived in various parts of the globe till about 30,000 years ago, may have had some crude form of religious belief as indicated by the way in which they buried their dead. They might have worshipped the forces of nature as gods. This conjecture is not without controversy. Religion, art, music, and language are cultural universals of humanity. Some experts hold the view that all these developed simultaneously about 50,000 years ago.[16]

Progress has been reported recently in understanding the genetic basis of self awareness in the bacterium *Proteus mirabilis.*[17] These bacteria form colonies while moving on solid surfaces, the process being called swarming. Boundaries form between swarming colonies of the same strain, but not between colonies of a single strain. The ability to discriminate between self and non-self (other) is an essential prerequisite for boundary formation. Some mutant bacteria of this species were seen to be isolating themselves from their parent colony in a bid to start a new one. Apparently, there is no comparison between the human self and the 'bacterial self' but the difference is only in the scale of complexity. The human body may be regarded as a colony of single celled organisms bound by proteins fibre - call them bacteria, if it suits - just like a swarm of Proteus mirabilis. If the bacterial swarm can be treated as an exemplar of self-assembly, why not use the same paradigm to describe the human body. Self-assembly,[18] which involves bottom-up architecture, is the physical mechanism employed in the building of a termite mound or an ant's nest as well as in the development of an embryo. In all these processes there is no top down guidance or control. So may be, some day the details of articulation of the self and the mind will be exposed.

The principle of natural selection is simple but powerful, as revealed by the structures, order and chimera of purpose it can give rise to. The emergence of Homo sapiens is a landmark event in the history of evolution. There is no need to involve the direct intervention of the Almighty at that stage because evolution has not stopped and the species keeps on improving in terms of health, life expectancy and creativity. Who knows if some super species will not appear replacing the sapiens! One cannot also dismiss the possibility of an unprecedented case of degradation of flora and fauna due to global warming. Millions of species may be casualties of this disaster in the coming decades. Arguments based on order in the universe are meaningless in the sense of thermodynamics since entropy, a measure of disorder, is increasing. The biosphere is a micro-island of order in a vast ocean of disorder that is the universe. Even if extraterrestrial life is discovered, the total contribution of all life forms to negative entropy or order, would be marginal. Attributing motive on the part of God in causing the emergence of Homo sapiens is an instance of anthropomorphic thinking, and this lacks credibility because there is hardly any merit this species can boast of vis-à-vis others. Some animals are known to be superior to humans in their capacity for compassion, love and loyalty.

**Convergence**

It is abundantly clear that evolution is the mechanism behind the appearance or disappearance of species on the earth. The environment selects the suitable species by mercilessly eliminating the unsuitable ones. Nature is not a static background; it is dynamic and location-dependent. Global warming, if left uncontrolled, will destroy forever tens of thousands of species - a proof of the dynamic character of nature. Evolution is not without its bag of woes. It is not successful in explaining the origin of life, for which there are only tentative theories at present, but as Dawkins has admitted a year or so ago, there is currently no convincing theory about this. The situation is reminiscent of Big Bang to which both theory and observation point, but the detailed physical mechanism remains a mystery, as physics breaks down at this point. In his article Moritz[19] quotes the science writer Richard Robinson: "Give biologists a cell and they will give you the world. But beyond assuming that the first cell somehow came into existence, how do biologists explain its emergence from the pre-biotic world four billion years ago?" The simplest bacterium *Mycoplasma genitalium* has about 387 protein-coding genes but a theoretical study by Gil et al, cited in Ref 18, puts the minimum number of genes for sustained metabolism at 216. The big question is how come an extremely complex network of so many proteins has arisen by itself. Stanley Miller's famous experiment[20] showed that amino acids could have formed by sparking in a mixture of methane, hydrogen, ammonia, and water in the reducing atmosphere of the early earth. Nevertheless, the passage from amino acids to the living cell is a dark alley. There is a theory claiming that RNA was a precursor to both protein and DNA in the sense that it can function both as a catalyst and as carrier of genetic information. DNA and RNA have the same ingredients except for one: instead of thymine (T), RNA has uracil (U). Though DNA is usually made in the lab from RNA, its precursor role is yet to be proved. More speculative scenarios also have been discussed without any definitive conclusion.

Teilhard de Chardin, a philosopher and paleontologist, makes the following remarks about the advent of life:[21] "No amount of historical research is likely to reveal the details of this story. Unless the science of tomorrow is able to reconstruct the process in the laboratory, we shall probably never find any material evidence of this emergence of the microscopic from the molecular, of the organic from the chemical, of the living from the pre-living. One thing is certain, however - a metamorphosis of this sort could not have been the result of a simple continuous process." Though Chardin's postulate of the existence of a Within and Without in all things is likely to invite criticism, his characterization of the transition from the pre-biotic to the biotic as a discontinuous process is significant. Were it a smooth process, it would have been more common in the universe. The currently available evidence for extraterrestrial life, let alone extraterrestrial intelligent life, is shaky. So the beginning of life on earth must have been one of the rarest of rare events in cosmic history. In Ref. 2 the present writer proposed a scientific description of God in terms of energy and information or probability. Even diehard atheists can agree with this definition. The physicist tells us that energy is the capacity for doing work. Work implies change and therefore, the advent of life, portrayed by the believers as a miracle, represents a manifestation of Energy/God with a high degree of information or low level of probability. The rest of the story is as told by the evolutionists.

## Concluding Remarks

Evolution is a physical process in which living things negotiate equilibrium or peace with the surroundings. Since this is not a stable state, species win or fail in making adaptations and the losers face the threat of extinction. So long as there is no reliable explanation of the onset of life on the earth, it can be considered to be an act of creation which is nothing but an energy transaction with low probability. In this scenario, the physical and the spiritual are unified. Established religions with their elaborate ritual framework are rather cultural constructs than philosophical or spiritual inventions. Which strengthens the case for secularism.

### *Notes and References*


1. Dr. K. Babu Joseph is a former Vice-Chancellor of Cochin University of Science and Technology, where he is currently Professor Emeritus in the Department of Physics.
2. Richard Dawkins, *The Greatest Show on Earth* (London: Bantam Press, London, 2009), pp. 150-151.
3. K. Babu Joseph, "The Concept of God According To Quantum Theology," *Omega*, Vol.1 (2002), pp. 58-72.
4. K. Babu Joseph, *"Towards a Theory of God," in Together Towards Tomorrow: Interfacing Science and Religion in India, Essays in Honor of Professor Job Kozhamthadam, S. J.*, Kuruvila Pandikattu S. J , editor, (Pune: Association of Science Society and Religion, 2006), pp. 261-267.
5. K. Babu Joseph, "Studies in Quantum Theology," report of research under a project sponsored by IISR, Pune, during 2003-2004, unpublished, 2005.
6. For history of evolution especially pre-Darwinian theories see, for example, Monroe W. Strickberger, *Evolution* (Third Edition) (Boston: Jones and Bartlett, 2000), pp. 3-9.
7. Charles Darwin, *The Origin of Species*, Sixth Edition of *On the Origin of Species*, 1872, Indian Reprint (Delhi: Goyal Saab), pp. 18-19.
8. Ernst Mayr, *What Evolution Is* (New York: Basic Books, 2001), p. 25.
9. Charles Pasternak, Quest: *The Essence of Humanity* (Chichester: Wiley, 2004), pp. 5-6.

10. See, for example, Dawkins, Op. Cit, pp. 184-207.

11. *Science Week This Week*, December 18, 2009, 326 (5960) (*alerts@info-aas.org*)

12. See, for example, Matt Ridley, *Genome: The Autobiography of a Species in 23 Chapters* (New York: Harper Collins, 1999), Perennial Edition 2000, pp. 4-10.

13. Sean B. Carroll, The *Making of the Fittest: DNA and the Ultimate Record of Evolution* (London: Quercus, 2009), pp. 60-62.

14. Pope John Paul II, "Message to the Pontifical Academy of Sciences," English translation reprint in *Evolutionary and Molecular Biology: Scientific Perceptives in Divine Action*, Robert John Russell, William Stoeger, S.J, Francis Ayala, eds., jointly published by Vatican Observatory and Centre for Theology and Natural Sciences, 1996, pp. 6, 8.

15. Desmond Morris, *The Naked Ape* (London: Vintage, 1967), p. 7.

16. See, for example, *http://www.garwandwane.com religion/religion I. html.*

17. Karime A. Gibbs, Mark L. Urbanonski, and E. Peter Greenberg, *Science*, Vol. 321, (2008), pp. 256-259.

18. Dawikns, *Op. Cit,* pp. 216-220

19. For a recent review of various models, see Albrecht Moritz, "The Origin of Life," *http://www.talkorigins.org/atroprob/origin of life. html*

20. Stanley Miller, Science, Vol. 117 (1953), pp. 528-529.

21. Pierre Teilhard de Chardin, *The Phenomenon of Man* (London: Collins, 1955), p. 79. *religion/religion I. html.*

# Eschatology as Cosmic Transcendence: An Evolutionary Perspective

3

Augustine Pamplany[1]

The Evolutionary Theory has come a long way since its original appearance. More than a theory that is concerned with the origination of species and the associated environmental factors, the subsequent developments have been able to situate this theory in a wider scientific and natural framework, pregnant with several philosophical and theological underpinnings. Metaphysical evolutionists extend the idea of evolution to include the mind, the soul and the entire universe. Evolution is no more limited to the scientific realms but it becomes essential in the context of religion to which the universe seems as the drama of progressively unfolding consciousness. Evolution becomes, in their hands, a cosmic phenomenon shaped either by divine forces or by mysterious emergent tendencies that operate from within the forces themselves.

On a general philosophical plain, one could say that the Theory of Evolution has brought out an inherently creative, dynamic and evolutionary worldview, a view of the world that is ever in the making. The older assumptions of immediate creation with its static and fixated account of origination reserved no place for a dynamic worldview. The evolutionary, changing and historical nature of the world as has been discovered today owes much to the Theory of Evolution. This worldview is so profound that drawing out the implicit anthropology and cosmology of it would be reformative of our self-understanding and our understanding of any reality at large. The poetic observation of Darwin himself is a legitimate appreciation of the Theory of Evolution. "There is grandeur in this view of life, with its several powers, having been originally breathed into a few forms or into one; and that whilst this planet has gone cycling on according to the fixed law of gravity, from so simple a beginning endless forms most beautiful and most wonderful have been and are being, evolved."[2]

## The Sacramentality of the Cosmos

As a mode of divine revelation and an expression of the divine nature, the world has been considered to be a symbolic reality in Christian theology, though this perspective is yet to be developed in its full details. The world is the expression of an opaque depth and a testimony to the supernatural beauty and glory of the divine. "Ever since the creation of the world, the invisible existence of God and his everlasting power have been clearly seen by the mind's understanding of created things" (Rom.1:20). "The heavens declare the glory of God, the vault of heaven proclaims his handiwork (Ps.19:1)"

The world is the primary locus of the divine manifestation. The Trinitarian mystery is presented in terms of the activities of the triune God in creation. A symbol is that which evokes the presence of the reality. The presence of the reality of the divine in the symbol of the world transcends every imagination as the divine being placed itself in the very stuff of the universe in the incarnation in Jesus Christ. The sacramentality of the cosmos declares its fullest potentialities in actualising the divine incarnation. As He who was to become the centre of every sacrament placed Himself in the matrix of the world, the world has the prerogative of being part of the constitutive core of the sacraments. As the world is being continuously transformed by the Christic reality, the sacramental dynamic of the world is ever towards the fullness of its sacramentality, towards the fullest outbreaking of the contained or the symbolized.

Therefore the history of the world is in a way the first literature on sacramental theology. The natural processes and the cosmic phenomena are the "cultic" events that impact the sacramental efficacy and evoke the experience of the core for the cosmic community. The inquiries into the nature and processes of the world and activities directed towards the world are sacramental in nature by the very sacramental matrix of their operation. Rather than promoting a naive optimism or an unrealistic justification for all the happenings in the world, this view envisages a more ontologically beautiful and graceful world. The liberation theologian Leonardo Boff has developed the sacramental view of creation in his sacramental theology. The whole universe, according to Boff, is shot through with the reality of God.[3] Through the notion of the transparence of the world, Boff envisages a new sacramental structure and sacramental thinking. The world is not divided between transcendence and immanence, but the intermediary category, transparence, embraces the other two and participates in both the transcendent world and immanent world. Thus the transcendent is rendered present in the immanent and the immanent is transfigured by the transcendent.[4] These categories are summed up in Eph.4:6: "There is one Lord, one faith, one baptism and one God and father of all, over all (transcendence), through all (transparence) and within all (immanence)." What the Psalmist has poetically expressed or what Paul has stated of the created things seem to imply that there is a definite surplus of meaning, surplus of reality and surplus of mystery that is present with our cosmos. This intention has been resembled in the conclusive observation of Davies in the scientific field: "No one who has studied the forces of nature can doubt that the world about us is a manifestation of something very very clever indeed."[5] It is this graceful inward realm of the mystery of the world as articulated in revelation and implied by the sciences that enables us to regard the entire cosmos as a sacramental reality that makes God present to us and provides meaning to our existence by participating us into it. This sacramental understanding of the world has much in common with what Vatican II calls the symbolism model of sacraments.[6] In this symbolism model world is the locus of God's presence. The Christian mission is the explicitation of the grace which is already at work. God is present in Christ who is in a world which is already redeemed.

### The Evolutionary Newwardness of Creation

At a more fundamental level the most substantial unit of this new worldview is to be identified as the grand discovery of the inherent and inbuilt potentialities of matter. The evolutionary perspective has enormously enhanced our understanding of matter. The ability of matter to organise itself into self-organising systems and its inbuilt urge towards greater complexity are the vital dynamisms of the evolutionary process. One will be caught by surprise to learn the miraculous paths that matter has trodden and the revolutionary choices that it has made to obtain such behaviours to which we attribute consciousness and all the more, self-consciousness in a complex mechanism like human brain. "Each level of the development of the cosmos can, it appears, legitimately be regarded as a manifestation of the potentialities of matter which have been implicit in it from the beginning in its simplest forms and have only gradually unfolded."[7] The intrinsic and self-contained mechanism of this transition requiring apparently not any, what is traditionally termed as, direct intervention or occasional visits of the divine may carry with it many unknown blueprints of divine action and divine providence.

The continuity between the living and the non-living worlds as implicated by the matter mechanisms implicit in Evolutionary Theory warrants the cosmic and totalistic applicability of the theory itself. The neo-Darwinian synthesis of the Evolutionary Theory discovers a wider cosmic process implicit in the evolutionary emergence of matter. "Today we can place biological evolution in a cosmic context that involves a continuous development of the forms of matter from the original `hot big bang', through atoms and molecules, to those complex structures that could self-produce their pattern of organisation and can be properly designated as `living'... The potentiality of matter to develop new forms of organisation... stretches back beyond the beginning of living forms, and may well stretch on into the future beyond their eventual demise on the surface of the earth."[8]

Evolutionary theory, analogically put, can challenge the wide-spread popular conception that science has nothing to do with personal qualities like love, freedom, humour, beauty, irritation, etc. From a contemporary point of view, although no claim for the full analysability of these are made in science, exploring the holistic depths and the cosmic roots of such phenomena would rule out the misconceptions associated with the absoluteness of such allegations. As there are no phenomena which are not cosmically evolved, the personal properties experienced at the human realm, also testify to the remote personalistic character of the universe. The "extra-physical" mechanisms operative in the evolutionary world can generate unimaginable products of evolution. This factor alone can give us an allusive glimpse into the possibility of a personal mechanism - the fullness of the personal qualities, operative within the cosmic process.

The stuff and structure of the universe is such that it is the fundamental matrix of the development of personality and personal quality. The inherent vitality of the cosmic process can attain new properties to being, can decorate it with new dimensions of existence and convert the unknown possibilities into ever new actualities. This extraordinary stuff must have extraordinary properties so as to actualize the divergent possibilities combining the most complex and the most simple, unifying the opposites and integrating the contradictories. The sciences shed light on such mysterious horizons of reality.

The nuanced epithets of holistic, open-ended, non-reductionistic, emergent, evolutionary, dynamic, non-local, trans-material, superluminal, continuous, self-organizing, self-transcending, etc., are substantially essential for the description of reality from an evolutionary new perspective. The strangeness and diversity of expressions correspond to the strangeness of the enigma underneath. The new perspective on matter which implies the potentials for several other perspectives is at the chore of this new worldview. "There is less and less support for any form of matter-spirit dualism, except for the radical dualism of God and not God .... Matter and spirit must be different aspects of the same reality - spirit arises out of matter and is based somehow in matter."[9] "I would say that if `dead' matter has reared up this curious landscape of fiddling crickets, song sparrows and wondering men, it must be plain even to the most developed materialist that the matter of which he speaks contains amazing, if not dreadful powers, and may not impossibly be ...`but one mask of many worn by the Great Face behind."[10]

If the inner being of matter is essentially dynamic and evolutionary, the becoming of matter into grater complexities opens up further transcendental possibilities to it. As Rahner has observed: "take into consideration the known history of the cosmos as it has been investigated and described by modern natural sciences: this history is seen more and more as one homogeneous history of matter, life and man. This one history does not exclude differences of nature but on the contrary includes them in this concept, since history is precisely not the permanence of the same but rather the becoming of something entirely new and not merely of something other."[11]

The essential newwardness and upwardness of the evolutionary matter and its consequent natural potentialities and supernatural possibilities for the world at large give us a vantage point from which to conceive the naturalistic dimensions of a cosmic transcendence. Thus the evolutionary theory has given us a new theological framework for cosmological reflections. This framework can substantially enhance the biblical view of eschatology in cosmic categories.

Evolution always implies the emergence of the new. This emergence is not merely the appearance of complex structures but the actualization of new dimensions of existence, new modes of being and radically new properties of becoming. The entire orientation of this open-ended process is towards harmony and interrelationship. As the prime cosmic directiveness is towards harmony, the subsequent biological, psychic, social and moral domains cannot deviate themselves from harmony. From the Christian point of view, Christ as the principle of unity and fullness (Col.1:19; 1Cor.8) must retain the creation in its unity and fullness.

### Eschatology: The Cosmic Transcendence

For Christians, Christ and the Resurrection affirm the eschatological fulfillment in terms of its axiological, temporal and ontological dimensions. Christian Eschatology primarily deals with the axiological Eschatology, of a God who "will wipe away tears from all faces" (Is.25:8). The axiological, personal and social dimensions are stressed in the eschatological descriptions in Mt.25 and in the book of Revelation. By Eschatology, however, science would refer only to the future of the cosmos. Hence the intersection of scientific and theological Eschatology necessitates that we affirm and respect the autonomy of both.[12] The statement of Pannenberg acquires significance in this context: "The biblical eschatology which portrays an imminent end of the world - even if no specific timetable is set (Mk.13:22) - is not congruent with scientific extrapolations which point toward the remote future in regard to a possible end of the world. It cannot, therefore, be easily contended that both have to do with the same event."[13]

What the biblical Eschatology affirms fundamentally is that God is the ultimate destiny and goal of human beings as well as of the whole cosmos. This will be true both in a universe which exists forever or in a universe that ends in a big crunch. Hence, scientific Eschatology, though it leads to positive appraisal of the cosmic destiny does not diminish the import of the biblical Eschatology. Even in a universe infinitely existing, we can still meaningfully talk of individual and social eschatologies. However, this does not allow us to carry on the distinction between personal, social and cosmic eschatologies beyond certain limits. These are deeply intertwined notions.

In the context of the vision of the human and the world provided by the modern scientific and theological scenario, the personal is intrinsically merged with the horizon of the cosmos. Hence to speak of the personal Eschatology is also to speak of the cosmic Eschatology. At a more fundamental level, the personal Eschatology cannot be considered apart from the cosmic Eschatology. There can be no axiological fulfillment apart from personal and social fulfillment. To imagine that love will ultimately triumph without the existence of the person or the cosmos would be hardly possible. Hence scientific Eschatology can indirectly enhance the biblical Eschatology in several ways. Each can contribute to each other by offering insights, criticism and background for reinterpretation.

**The Unrest of the Cosmic Heart**

The extra-ordinary features of matter and the world as we have evolutionarily read into the world and the innate potentialities of it compel us to think of the final destiny of the cosmos. Can the future of the cosmos even if infinite and eternal be as dry and dull as have been portrayed by the open and closed universe eschatologies? The dynamisms of the inner structure of the world, the intra-cosmic upwardness, the effluence of the divine into the cosmos, the cosmic actualisations in the emergence of the humans - all serve as a compelling framework which becomes a conducive interpretative horizon of the new heaven and the new earth. The ultimacy of the heat death or cold death of the divinised and enchanted cosmos will be an unjust sabotage of the essential nature of reality entailed by our modern scientific and religious experiences. The inward and onward dynamisms of the evolutionary world is the urge for a restful comfort: "everything that *is*, is restless and on the search for a place ... for a `resting place'. It is not merely the human heart which is `restless' until it finds rest in Thee', as Augustine said. The whole creation is filled with this same unrest, and transcends itself in the search for the rest in which it can abide."[14]

The movement of a world that draws its being from the divine fullness, a world that continues to be filled with the divine fullness in ongoing creation, a world that exhibits clear qualitative transcendence in its emergent evolutionary stages can be depicted as a pilgrim movement towards the heavenly Jerusalem; towards a new heaven that will appropriate its urges, a new earth that would be full of actualities. "A world (without heaven)... would be a closed system, resting and revolving within itself. A world without transcendence is a world in which nothing new can ever happen. It is the world of the eternal return of the same thing."[15]

Where the ontological gap between God and the creation is reduced, it also cuts short the distance between heaven and the earth. The ethereal earth of ours is in a way a natural heaven. Heaven need not be anything that we find only at the end of a long journey, but a proximate possibility that always accompanies the world that is embedded in the spirituality of the universe. According to Moltmann, the divine openness of the cosmic system enables us to call the determined side of this system 'earth' and the undetermined side 'heaven'.[16] According to Moltmann, the *eschaton* of the Bible is neither the future of time or eternity but it is God's coming. God's arrival means the establishment of his eternal kingdom and his indwelling in the cosmos, in his creation. All particular promises in history points forward to this universal appearance of God. When he comes in glory, he will fill the universe with his glory and radiance.[17] Because, basically our Christian belief consists of faith and hope. It is a faith in a loving God who created the world and sustains it. And it is a hope in God that He will not allow his beloved creation to come to nothing. The redeemer God of Christianity would not be the loving God if He does not redeem what He has created.[18] The human in the Bible is intrinsically part of the cosmos. Therefore, it is reasonable to think that there is no redemption of human nature apart from nature. "*Thereforc, to conceive the human salvation, there is a need for a redeemed creation, a new creation and new earth.* Can there be an eternal life for human beings without the change in cosmic condition? The new world is God's home, God's eschatological *shekinah.*"[19]

**The Universal Eschatological Feast**

The biblical Eschatology could be broadly seen in a cosmic context. The biblical literature is rich with eschatological references not only of the individual and the social, but of the world as well. An integral eschatological perspective is available from the setting of creation in the book of Genesis itself.

> Because Genesis 1 is a portrait of what God intends, it is also an eschatological statement. This serene, beautiful world, in which all is ordered to humans, and humans are ordered to God, is how it will be at the end. The stories of human sin, which follow Genesis 1, cannot permanently disfigure the original divine intent. God's world will triumph. Rev 21-22 is the description of God's new world, appropriately drawn on this chapter.[20]

The idea of cosmic redemption comes to light quite powerfully in the Pauline theology. In the Pauline thought all reality has a touch of God who inserted himself into his creation especially in his incarnation. The world has been given to us as a manifestation of God's love. Material reality has an intrinsic value. With the spread of the Church in the gentile world, it was Paul's eschatological vision that was more firmly established. However, Church's fight against the gnostic ideas sought to exclude material body from salvation and gradually Pauline cosmic emphasis was sidelined.

Paul speaks of the eschatological aspects especially in the light of creation to redemption and the eschatological happenings at the end of time (Rom.5:12-21; 1Cor.15:21ff, 21& 45ff; 1Cor.8:6; Rom.11:36; Eph.4:5-6; Col.1:16; Eph.1:3-14; Phil.2:6-11, Eph.1:20-21; Col.1:15-20, 2:8-10; Rom.8:8-39). These texts, especially Rom.8:19-23, present Paul's theology of creation to redemption:

> for the whole creation is waiting with eagerness for the children of God to be revealed. It was not for its own purposes that creation had frustration imposed on it, but for the purposes of him who imposed in - with the intention that the whole creation itself might be the children of God. We are well aware that the whole creation, until this time

> has been groaning in labour pains. And not only that: we too, who have the first fruits of the Spirit, even we are groaning inside ourselves, waiting with eagerness for our bodies to be set free.- Rom.8:19-23.

Here we find Eschatology merged with cosmology and anthropology. The world cursed for sin in Gen.3:7, now shares the destiny of the humanity, to be redeemed and glorified like the human body. The reality of Christians and the reality alongside are bound by the one redemptive purpose at work in both Christians and other creatures. They have the characteristic of hope as the creation is waiting with eager longing for the revealing of the children of God. "The `sons of God' are not selected for their own sake alone, but their redemption means the redemption of a world of being besides themselves."[21]

When the entire creation is referred to, Paul intends to say that there is a relation and fellowship between human beings and the rest of the creation and the rest of the creation is affected by what human beings do.[22] Also, in its very 'creatureliness' the creation is a receiver of God's grace in 'hope'. Paul holds that one cannot speak of creation without speaking of human or validly speak of human without speaking of the world in which he/she lives. Redemption takes place in human and also in the world he/she lives in.[23] The worth of creation does not depend on the presence of human in the universe, but on God's grace. The world is something that is made by God, not something neutral. Thus the eschatological imagery detectable in Rom.8:38-39 suggests a renewed and fulfilled creation. Rom.8:19 and the following is one of the many instances of the universal character of a kind of the "cosmic liturgy."[24] Paul assures that the hope of the creation is hope assured by the Resurrection of Christ. The suffering of the creation with Christ will result in glorification with him. It is the glorified Christ who is the ultimate answer to the groaning and unrest of the cosmos. From a different angle, Rahner also has underscored the cosmic significance of the Resurrection. "Jesus's resurrection ... is the beginning of the transfiguration of the world as an ontologically interconnected occurrence. In this beginning the destiny of the world is already in principle decided and has already begun."[25]

### Notes and References


1. Dr. Augustine Pamplany is the founder director of the Institute of Science and Religion at Little Flower Seminary, Aluva, Kerala.
2. Darwin, *The Origin of Species by Means of Natural Selection* (London: John Murray, 1859), p. 460.
3. Leonardo Boff, *Sacraments of Life, Life of the Sacraments* (Washington, D. C: The Pastoral Press, 1987), p. 77. See Marie Conn, "The Sacramental Theology of Leonardo Boff," in *Worship* 64 (1990), p. 525.
4. See Marie Conn, "The Sacramental Theology of Leonardo Boff," in *Worship* 64 (1990), p. 525.
5. Paul Davies, *The Forces of Nature*, 2nd. ed. (Cambridge: Cambridge University Press, 1986), p. 167.
6. *Sacrosanctum Concillium* 7.
7. Arthur Peacocke, God and the New Biology (San Francisco: Harper and Row Publishers, 1986), p. 94.
8. Arthur Peacocke, "Biological Evolution and Christian Theology," in John Durant (ed.), *Darwinism and Divinity* (New York: Basil Blackwell Ltd., 1985), p. 116.
9. William R. Stoeger, "Key Developments in Physics Challenging Philosophy and Theology," in W. Mark Richardson and Wesley J. Wildman (eds.), *Religion and Science - History, Method, Dialogue* (New York: Routledge, 1996), p. 198.
10. Loren Eiseley, *The Immense Journey* (New York: Vintage Books, 1957), p. 20.
11. Karl Rahner,"Christology Within an Evolutionary View," *Theological Investigations*, vol. 5 (London: Darton, Longman and Todd, 1966), p. 166.
12. Kuruvilla Pandikattu, "Eschatology: Interaction between Science and Theology," Manuscript of the Article to *Jeevadhara* (April 1999), p. 6.
13. Pannenberg, *Systematic Theology*. Cited in Worthing, *God, Creation and Contemporary Physics*, p. 177.
14. Juergen Moltmann, *God in Creation: A New Theology of Creation and the Spirit of God* (San Francisco: Harper and Row, 1985), p. 282.

15. Moltmann, *God in Creation*, p. 163.
16. See Moltmann, *God in Creation*, p. 163.
17. See Juergen Moltmann, *The Coming of God* (Minneapolis: Fortress Press, 1996), p. 23.
18. See Moltmann, *The Coming of God*, p. 259.
19. Moltmann, *The Coming of God*, pp. 260-261.
20. Roland E. Murphy and Richard C. J., "Genesis," in *The New Jerome Biblical Commentary* (Bangalore: Theological Publications in India, 1995), p. 11.
21. Sanday and Headlam, *The Epistle to the Romans* (New York: Scribner's Sons, 1896), p. 212.
22. John G. Gibbs, *Creation and Redemption: A Study in Pauline Theology* (Leiden: E. J. Brill, 1971), p. 40.
23. A. N. Wildern, "Eschatological Imagery and Earthly Circumstance," in *New Testament Studies* 5 (1958-59), p. 232.
24. See Gibbs, p. 41.
25. Karl Rahner, "Resurrection," *Sacramentum Mundi*, vol. 5 (New York: Herder and Herder, 1972), p. 39.

# Human Origins and Original Sin in an Evolutionary Context

4

PATRICK McDONALD[1]

## Introduction

If humans have evolved over millions of years from non-human primates, is there a good reason to doubt one of the central teachings of Christian faith? Namely, Jesus Christ came to earth to provide the means for our salvation because without Jesus we are unable to climb out of our sinful lives. I argue that there is good reason to believe humans have so evolved, and that this may raise very serious questions about one account of original sin, it does not impact the central dynamic of the emergence of sin in human history and the need for healing and redemption.

Accepting an evolutionary account of human origins does not undermine belief in God, belief in Christ, belief in the Bible, belief in a soul, belief in the salvation of that soul, nor belief that the means for such salvation have been offered to us. However, holding all of these together consistently and plausibly might require some rethinking of what these beliefs mean and how we understand the sources of such beliefs. Much work has been done, but the fruits might not be readily available to a wider audience. I hope this essay might contribute to that end.

Here I focus on three main tasks. First, I sketch out an outline of the apparent tension between a Biblical narrative and a scientific narrative of human origins and the meaning of our lives and sinfulness. Second, I give a brief outline of the story of human evolution and some of the main lines of fossil evidence supporting belief in that narrative. Thirdly, I address the basic conception of human nature in the doctrines of the Divine Image, Original Righteousness, and Original Sin. I outline the case for what Robin Collins has called the Historical Idealist conception of original sin. In concluding, I say a bit about the broader context of this discussion concerning the meaning of human agency and the nature of the creation-evolution debate.

**Two Competing Narratives?**

Does the story of our origins have a clear connection to the grounds of our fundamental hopes? Consider two possibilities that have the adherence of a number of people around the world. The first is the Biblically based narrative and the second is the reigning scientific narrative. I will look at the Biblical narrative first. It is based not just in Genesis, but clearly laid out there in the first few chapters. God created the heavens and the earth (i.e., the earth, this planet, everything else in the universe, the entire universe itself, and in some way, the rules by which the universe exists). God created all the inhabitants of earth, from Archaea that live in thermal vents deep under the sea, to algae that grow in the oceans, lakes, and swimming pools, to viruses that infect many mammals, to human beings–and all manner of life in between. And with human beings, as Genesis 1 tells us, and we will explore below, God created human beings in God's image. God created us for many specific purposes, but with a unifying underlying purpose - to share in a relationship with God, as the old *Baltimore Catechism* puts it: why did God make you? Answer: God made me to know Him, to love Him, and to serve Him in this world and to be happy with Him forever in heaven." Human beings were made intentionally, purposefully, and distinctively by God to share a special relationship with God. God gave us the means to do so. God also gave us the means to do otherwise. The story of Adam and Eve in the Garden reveals to us this dynamic.

The story of the Garden also reveals that in history human beings abandoned a path of intimate connection to God to a relationship characterized by alienation; more directly by disobedience to God's wishes for us, and not simply disobedience by a kind of ignorant blundering; but rather knowing and willful disobedience. The story from that point forward is one where in various ways God reaches out to address this alienation and human beings variously respond positively, at least some do, and yet manage to renew our mode of disobedience and deeper alienation. In the Bible God takes some very important steps to address this: the expulsion of Adam and Eve, the mark of Cain, the encounter with Noah and his family as well as the flood, the calling of Abraham and the covenant thereby established, the encounter with Moses and liberation of the Jewish people from Egypt, and the story of Israel outlined in the Old Testament. A culmination of this narrative from a Christian perspective is the Incarnation, birth, ministry, passion, death, resurrection, and post-resurrection commission of the disciples to establish the Christian Church. We believe that our existence is intimately bound up with this story. Our origins as a community and as individuals reflects this story. Our daily existence reflects this story. Our hopes for tomorrow, and all possible tomorrows reflect this story. So, what we do today, and expect in the future is bound up intimately in our beliefs about our individual and collective past – our origins.

Part of the meaning of Christian Faith is that God as Creator has a plan for Creation. The specificity of that plan, i.e., whether God has planned out and "ordains" every detail of the history of Creation or whether God's "plan" allows for creatures to contribute with some measure of autonomy – this is a much-debated question within the Christian community. As we look at the world and the acts of human beings we are both inspired to deeper belief, but sometimes horrified. The latter points out a perennial challenge for belief in a God of perfect goodness, power, and knowledge who actually is a Creator in a traditional sense - that is, the "problem of evil." One way of understanding this question rooted in the Scriptures, is that God created the earth good and in particular created human beings in the divine image with a certain charge to have "dominion" within the Creation and to be in a certain state of a realized relationship with God. Humans originally, Adam and Eve specifically, were in a state of justice and righteousness and that being in the image of God knew God, knew themselves as beings in God's image, and honored this relationship in the appropriate way. Despite what appear in Genesis to be God's intentions for Adam and Eve to enjoy a healthy, loving relationship with God, they chose to disobey God's clear and direct command to avoid eating of the tree of knowledge of good and evil. This original "sin" had profound consequences, some of which are enumerated in Genesis 3:14-24, and some of which have been outlined in Christian traditions building upon other Scriptures (e.g. Romans 5), and Christian theological thought.

In contrast to this, the story that science offers to us appears to be radically different from the Biblical story and from the story that has been part of the Christian tradition for most of our history. It seems to some that the science of evolutionary biology in general, and the demonstration in particular that human beings are products of evolution - undermines the crucial foundation stones of the portrait of human being taught historically by the Christian faith. Furthermore, the modern sciences may seem to speak to the process of the universe's formation and the time in which this has occurred in a way that contradicts the Biblical witness concerning God's work of Creation. In short, the Big Bang, the processes of stellar and galactic formation, the process of the formation of the solar system, the earth, the history of life on earth, and evolution as the big story of that process - these contradict the Genesis account of God's manner and timing of Creation.

Now if Genesis is wrong about all that, how could it be that the Bible is trustworthy in its testimony, in Genesis 2:7 for example, that "the Lord God formed the man from the dust of the ground and breathed into his nostrils the breath of life, and the man became a living being"(NIV). As the argument sometimes is put, if we can't trust Genesis 1 about the days of creation (how long, in what order, by what means) then why should we trust it or Genesis 2 about the origins of humans beings. That is, why should we believe that there is meaning to the testimony that we are created by God, in God's image, and that God made us with a sense of a relationship of solidarity with God as expressed in Genesis 3? However, the problems reconciling science in general with Genesis 1 are merely the tip of the iceberg. When we look at the message of the sciences relating to human beings we see a much deeper challenge. From the perspective of biology applied to human beings, it looks more difficult to reconcile things.

First, it does not look like we were created specially by God as suggested by Genesis 2 (and re-affirmed elsewhere in Scripture such as in Romans 5). Rather, it looks like we emerged gradually over millions of years from non-human (i.e., not modern *Homo Sapiens*) primates such as *Ardipithecus ramidus* and/or *Australophithecus afarensis* (and the line of descent therefrom). It looks like there was not an exact "point" in time when there was a non-*Homo Sapiens* population, then through some special act, there was a *Homo Sapiens* population. Evolution of a new species of higher primate is not a single generation phenomenon. Rather the emergence of modern *Homo sapiens* is a gradual, fitful, ambiguous narrative in many ways. Further, this story seems to make it clear that we are thoroughly biological beings, from the animal world, and belonging to it. This seems deeply confirmed by other biological sub-disciplines. The genetic studies exploding in the last few decades, capped by the now famous sequencing of the human genome, and the comparative studies of higher primate genomes (chimp, Neanderthal, etc.) allow for locating our genes in a clearly delineated "family tree" of non-human primates. The exploding field of neuroscience and the grounding of the study of human cognition in the detailed study of the brain and our nervous system is revealing what seems to undergird our deepest processes of thought, feeling, cognition, and consciousness (including self-consciousness). It suggests to many that all those aspects of the Divine Image are thoroughly biological – from our consciousness of God, to our love for God and others, to our choices to act accordingly. How can something explained by "blind" laws of nature be considered a "free choice"? What happens with humans as biological beings appears to proceed by a process whereby given certain conditions, certain outcomes follow either as a mechanical outcome of the conditions plus the guiding laws, or those two plus random-chance – how can some such process be called a "free choice"? Furthermore how could there be a state of original righteousness from which humans could freely choose "obedience" or "disobedience"? And if we are biological beings, could it make any sense that we are made human in part by a spiritual soul?

If it is the case that so go origins, and so goes our daily self-understanding, and so goes our hopes for tomorrow (both in the ordinary colloquial sense of hope, and especially a theological sense), THEN the very different account of origins from science should indicate a very different sense of our daily purpose and hope for ultimate purpose to our lives. Right? Not necessarily.

This is a complicated issue and the purpose of this inquiry is to honor that complexity. But let me simplify for a moment. There are a few basic strategies of response to this conditional statement. One is to affirm it, and then to do two things in response to that affirmation – namely, reject science as part of the affirmation of Christian faith; the other, is to reject Christian faith as part of the acceptance of the scientific narrative. Affirming the conditional means that accepting the scientific narrative about human origins (in short, it's a 13.7 or so billion year story of unbroken natural processes – the evolution of the whole cosmos from Big Bang to Los Alamos, and beyond) does indeed change the meaning of our daily purpose and our hope for ultimate purpose. Now, there are many people who reject science and its narrative because of its consequences for the meaning of being human. The cost of acceptance is too high. We might point to many kinds of horrible examples where people without a grounding in the Biblical narrative, taking it as the inspired Word of God (thus, true) will act as people without a purpose, without a guiding framework of goodness, love, and obedience.

I wish to explore the geography of a negative answer to the question posed by the conditional. That is, no, a different narrative of our origins as far as the conditional states them does not lead to a vision of our purpose and meaning in life. That is, the scientifically current account of origins, and specifically of human history and pre-history in the evolution of great apes in equatorial Africa, does NOT indicate a very different sense of our daily purpose and hope for ultimate purpose to our lives. In short, having evolved doesn't fundamentally alter the meaning of our lives as human beings. It does not any more than cooking dinner in a microwave or on a modern electric stove fundamentally changes the meaning of preparing food for a family meal. Some aspects of these questions may be different. Some are mysterious in ways that they formerly were not. Some are understood to have different connotations. And so on. However, I will argue that the core meaning is the same. Furthermore, the place of the Biblical narrative is the same, at bottom. We may indeed need to understand aspects of the Biblical narrative in new ways. However, this is not new to the project in the Christian tradition nor should we expect that process of ongoing engagement with key questions about the meaning of the Bible to come to a close any time soon. There are many hard questions raised by the prospect that human beings evolved from non-human primates. However, the truth for us of those central teachings of the faith about being human and the meaning of being human are untouched at their core. Now to show this requires that we address a number of things. First, in this text we will take a brief look at the science relevant to human evolution. There are very good reasons to believe, biologically speaking, modern humans are truly the descendents of a long line of distinct species of hominins and then before hominins, non-hominid apes.[2]

### Basic Argument for the Evolved Status of Modern Humans (*Homo Sapiens*)

Why should we take seriously the hypothesis that "humans evolved biologically according to the mechanisms and historical narrative outlined by the biological theory of evolution"? We might begin by noting, recently, a significant trove of fossils of *Ardipithecus Ramidus* was made public by the publication of a series of articles in *Science.*[3] Also within the past year, a nearly complete draft of the Neanderthal genome was published by a group led by Svante Paabo in Leipzig, Germany. These are the latest in a long string of studies since Huxley's 1863 that have engaged the array of science and the question of human evolution in light of Darwin's theory. It is important to note that there will be no "proving" that humans evolved in a common use of the word "prove". The best we may hope for in our lifetime is to provide very strong grounds for belief. I, for example, come at the science of human evolution from a layperson's perspective. So, I will never personally be well-acquainted enough with whatever direct and closely indirect evidence there is to have a clear "proof" of the case. However, I have seen enough evidence and argument to make the case seem quite compelling.

Some of the basic outlines of the argument include the following considerations. 1. The case from multiple sciences for an ancient earth/ universe. 2. The case from multiple sciences that the "basic" evolutionary theory is well-grounded. This is an argument from consilience or convergence of many distinct, independent lines of evidence. This is absolutely crucial when we consider the lines of evidence salient to human evolution. These include:

(a) What we know about dating the hominid and more/ less closely related primate species.

(b) What we know about the classification and understanding of behavior of pre-hominid primates.

(c) What we know about the non-*Homo* fossils and paleo-biogeography.
(d) Fossils from early *Homo* species to *H. Erectus and H. Heidelbergensis (or the like).*
(e) Study of Neanderthals
(f) Study of Homo Sapiens showing to be clearly distinct as a type and how ancient they go.
(g) Mechanisms of Biological evolution applied to hominin evolution.
(h) Genetic studies (e.g. the comparison of human genetics to closely related primates and to the available DNA from Neanderthal remains).

This paper will mostly survey the outlines of the narrative based upon a survey of major fossil finds. In a later version I will also discuss in some detail the techniques of dating, e.g. bio-stratigraphic dating and radio-isotopic dating (as well as other methods) that allow the scientists the confidence they have in the ability to tell this story.

Why do we believe that it's plausible that anatomically modern humans have walked the earth likely for at least 160,000 years and that as a species we have descended through a significant line of ancestor species going back several million years (maybe 6-7 mya; possibly more, say up to 10 mya)[4] to the last common ancestor of us and chimpanzees?[5] There exists a considerable set of fossils, many thousands of individual fossil remains, from probably hundreds or thousands of individual beings that chronicles a very marked trend in time. The trend looks for all the world to fit something like what one would expect on the theory of evolution, especially focusing on the concept of descent with modification. On a number of different features going back in time there are trends that track the emergence of distinctive human characteristics over a gradual process of change. Some of these include the following: the development of bi-pedal capacities, the increase of average cranial size (and so brain size), the decrease in canines, the decrease in ratio of arm length to leg length (so legs get longer compared to arm length), the flattening of the face (so less "prognathic"), the increasing sophistication of tools, the development of cultural knowledge and its transmission (e.g. cooking, language, tools, ritual practices, etc.).[6]

Let's begin this narrative at the branching point. Some time, likely between 6 and 10 million years ago there is thought to have existed a population of primates who are considered the last common ancestor of humans (*Homo sapiens*) and chimpanzees. Very interesting, for example, there is a table of many anatomical features that Tim White et al[7] infer to belong to this population. From that population there branched at least one distinct group though we do not know how exactly.[8] There are various ways it seems that primate groups may become *de facto* reproductively isolated and that this isolation can lead to *de jure* reproductive isolation. Geographic isolation is just one example (e.g. the isolation of bonobos from chimps by the Congo river?). Down one line emerged the population of hominins that left the fossils now called *Ardipithecus ramidus*. The first of these were discovered in 1992 at Aramis in Ethiopia. They continued to dig more in 1993 and published their initial findings in 1994.

However, there was a virtual treasure trove of fossils there and the whole set has been very carefully prepared and the preliminary studies done. All was published in a special issue of *Science* in 2009. What are the key findings of this? A number of them, but two are key. First, that Ardi et al were "facultative bi-peds" but also retained significant tree-climbing capabilities; and this occurred not in an edge/savannah ecology but in a woodland habitat (though not apparently deep jungle - see Appendix for link to images).

Next in time (and in the "family tree - see Appendix, Smithsonian Hominin Family Tree) are the *Australopithecines*. The oldest fossils of the genus *Australopithecus* – i.e., southern ape are classified *Australopithecus anamensis*, and Kanapoi in Kenya is the site of the main fossils belonging to this species. Kamoyan Kimeu discovered a tibia in 1994, dated to be 4.1 mya. Until the remains of Ardi were published this was the oldest known evidence for bipedalism.[9] "Lucy" is probably the most well-known Australopithecine fossil and was unearthed in Ethiopia in 1974. Her remains document about 40% of the skeleton and cranium and is to this date, one of the most complete hominin fossils to date. The subject of much discussion and a recent national exhibition, Lucy is one among numerous finds of the species A. afarensis that document their place as dedicated bi-pedal hominins with a combination of ape-like facial features and small crania coupled with more Homo like locomotion. There are as well a group of "robust" Austalopithecines. But, some interesting features of these "fossils" and of the creatures they represent is what they tell us about certain adaptations, about the nature of hominid evolution (the kind of diversity); that there were numerous species living at once in the 2 mya to 1mya era - that is, Australopith species lived at the same time (not necessarily alongside of exactly) as what looks to be at least 2, maybe several species of the genus "Homo" - e.g. Rudolfensis/ Habilis/Ergaster/Erectus.

The first members of the genus HOMO are *Homo rudolfensis* and *Homo habilis*. They mark the first chapter in history of the existence of creatures belonging (according to the taxonomy) to the same genus to which we belong. This first seems to have occurred about 2.2 mya. Some of the key features include an increased cranial capacity, (reduced canines - even further - changes in bipedal structure, less prognathic faces, etc.). There are debates continuing about whether Habilis specimens truly fit the Homo genus or would better fit Austalopith. But, it seems clear - and in a broad sense is important - that by the time we get to *Ergaster/Erectus*, that we have a range of specimens that clearly seem quite distinct from Australopiths, from living apes, e.g. chimps, bonobos, gorillas, etc., and yet also are quite distinct from *Homo sapiens*. This is the key set of fossils, it seems to me, that presses so strongly the issue of human evolution for those who are skeptical.

For the time period from, about 1.8 mya to as recently as 27 kya, we have fossils from Africa, Asia, the Middle East, and Europe (but NOT from the Americas), that seem quite clearly much bigger brained than living great apes, dedicated and highly capable bi-pedal beings, developing over time distinct tool-making traditions, and yet also seemingly, *distinct* in many important ways from modern humans. Following this set of fossils and related cultural artifacts (and their dates; surrounding geological and paleo-ecological evidences) suggests very important questions about the gradual emergence of what we call unique features of humans. As Michael Roe pointed out in his lecture last Fall at SPU, and many others have noted as well, it's a real question whether there are truly unique human features that we possess and all animals lack. For example, chimps, bonobos, and gorillas have shown capacities to learn language - at least fairly extensive symbol manipulation (see cases of Koko the gorilla and Kanzi the famous bonobo); numerous animals show various interesting and complex capacities to communicate; animals show capacities to behave in seemingly altruistic ways; various animals use tools and some seem capable of passing on the capacity of tool use (pass on tool "cultures" where one group in one region of same species will show evidence of a "cultural tradition" while another lacks it); some show intelligent attachment and grief; some show some ability for recognition of self (see experiments on "red dot" in the mirror). One would expect that if such capacities are possible with animals that show relatively less sophistication than our *Homo* ancestors, with much smaller brains, and likely less sophistication in community structures, then our Homo ancestors would be likely to have quite interesting and impressive capacities. Thought this raises questions about modern humans bearing uniquely the image of God, I don't think the problems are terribly special.

The *Ergaster/Erectus* fossils are the first that very clearly belong to the genus *Homo* (there is ongoing debate about *Habilis*). There is a great deal of lore associated with fossils classified as *Homo Erectus* (and some now called H. Ergaster).[10] The finding of Java Man (later *H. Erectus*) and associated fossils were some of the first hominin fossils found after the Neanderthal discovery in 1856. The digs in East Asia (first in Indonesia then in China) raised questions about where the first human ancestors appeared. The old story that *H. Erectus* stood up in Africa, stayed there for nearly a million years, and then migrated East to Asia is now more complicated.[11]

It is not completely clear where the fossils classified as *Ergaster/Erectus* first emerged. There are specimens dated back to 1.8 mya in Africa, in Georgia (i.e., near Russia), and in Indonesia (Java).

Still, the vast preponderance of pre- Ergaster/Erectus ancestor candidates have been unearthed in Africa (e.g. *H. Habilis and H. Rudolfensis*).[12] One of the oldest specimens was unearthed in Koobi Fora (Kenya). Fossil KNM-ER-3733 is a nearly complete cranium and is dated radiometrically to about 1.7 - 1.8 mya. Another very important early African Ergaster/ Erectus is the famous Turkana or Nariokotome Boy, KNM WT 15000. This is possibly the most complete pre-*Homo Sapiens* hominin fossil and dates to about 1.6 mya (see Appendix).

Among the earliest in Erectus/Ergaster fossils in Eurasia are the findings from Dmanisi, Georgia. First uncovered in 1992 by an international team, the fossils from this site date to about 1.6 to 1.8 mya. Partly because the fossils found in East Asia earlier this century were uncovered before the maturation of radiometric dating techniques, partly from lack of available volcanic "tuffs", they have proved difficult to date exactly. However, in 1994 Swisher and Curtis surprised many by announcing new dates (using single crystal laser fusion techniques) for specimens from Modjokerto (1.8 mya) and Sangiran (1.6 mya) sites in Java.

One gets the picture of H. Ergaster/Erectus emerging in Africa and then "sprinting" across the continents to land finally in Java. Foley and Lewin observe;

> If they [Swisher and Curtis] are right, the new work changes the question anthropologists must answer about Homo erectus: there is now no delay to be explained, but the pattern of the species' origin is less clear. Although KNM-ER 3733 and the Modjokerto skull are of equivalent age, a sufficient margin of error exists in the dates to permit a gap in age of at least 100,000 years. A quick calculation shows that, even at the glacial pace of population expansion of 16 km per generation, *Homo erectus* could move from east Africa to east Asia in a mere 25,000 years.[13]

So, an African origin for *Erectus* and then a subsequent migration through Asia is consistent with currently accepted dates. This keeps in view that the time frames with which we are talking here are vast. What is startling (to me anyway) is the dating of some fossils classified as *Erectus* as recently as approx. 27 to 53 kya (e.g. Ngandong 6 from Java). This would make the H. Ergaster/Erectus (*sensu lato*) type a survivor on earth from 1.8 mya to possibly as recent as 27 kya - a run of about 1.77 mya. Furthermore, looking at the other types in various phylogenies, *H. Erectus* in the east appears to have survived and even thrived while *H. Heidelbergnsis* persisted in Africa and in Europe and then while Neanderthals thrived in Europe and the Middle east, and then while anatomically modern *H. Sapiens* emerged in Africa and then possibly exited Africa between 40 and 70 kya or so. Quite possibly as modern *H. Sapiens* took over the prior range of *H. Neanderthals*, did they take over the range of H. Erectus in the east. (This of course raises the question of the Out of Africa v. Multi-regional Evolution Model, the latter defended for years by M. Wolpoff of U. Michigan).

One of the important questions for responding to some of the deepest skeptics are whether the dates are at all reliable (something I will only hit briefly) and whether the anatomical differences between the range of H. Erectus and those of modern humans.[14] Erectus had a typical cranial range of 850 to 1100 cc. Their body size averaged about 1.8 m and 63 kg for males while 1.55m and 52 kg for females. This summarizes fossils from Africa, Western Asia, E. Asia and S.E. Asia. Of note are the significant findings of *H. erectus* from Zhoukoudian, including many of the casts made of the lost fossils by Weidenreich, including 14 partial crania, 11 lower jaws, many teeth, some post-crania (i.e., non-head bones), and many stone tools.[15]

So, *Homo Erectus/Ergaster* had a long run. While there are specimens dated to have lived in Africa and Europe (possibly) in the years between 1 mya and 500 kya, there are other species that seemed to have ranged in Africa and Europe (mid East too?). *Homo Heidelbergensis* is a species name given fossils found thought to have ranged in time from approximately 800 kya to about 200 kya. According to the Smithsonian website[16] the Mauer mandible, a jaw and teeth found near Heidelberg Germany in 1907 is the basis for the species name. Another specimen is the Kabwe cranium. Specimens with certain traits somewhere intermediate between H. Erectus and modern H. Sapiens were previously lumped into the category *Archaic H. Sapiens*. Now, it is becoming more common to call them *H. Heidelbergensis*.

The Kabwe cranium was found in Zambia in 1921 in Kabwe, Zambia. It is dated to approximately 125 kya to 300 kya first classified as *Homo rhodesiensis* in v. 108 of *Nature* in the article by Arthur Smith Woodward.[17] The date is based in part on associated animal fossils from the same site. There is some debate as to whether this specimen belongs to the African population from which it is thought all modern humans evolved (see Herto hominids, Appendix). Braincase in profile is low and slopes back from a large supraorbital torus in strong affinity with H. Erectus. The sagittal keel and occipital torus may also resemble *H. Erectus*. However, the face is less prognathic and the brain size is about 1300 cc., much larger than any *H. Erectus*. A more recent find, the Sima de los Huesos site in Spain has yielded a significant cranium (number 5 "Miguelon"). Many fragments (over 5000) and fossils of up to 28 individuals, dated to over 350,000. The tool, a biface called Excalibur, is made of red quartzite. The findings include fragments of other crania, such as Skull 4, nicknamed Agamenón and skull 6, nicknamed Rui (from El Cid, a local hero). There is also a complete pelvis (Pelvis 1), nicknamed Elvis, in remembrance of Elvis Presley as well as mandibles, teeth, and numerous postcranial bones (femurs, hand and foot bones, vertebrae, ribs, etc.) The members of this species seem to have used the Acheulian took it much like *Erectus*. There is some thought that *Heidelbergensis* was ancestral to Neanderthals; one wonders about the relationship of the population producing the Kabwe cranium to the H. Sapiens in Africa. However, the existence of such specimens fills in some of the morphological "space" between *Erectus* and *H. Sapiens* and Neanderthals.

We are now at the part of the story where *H.Sapiens* and Neanderthals emerge. The story of the Neanderthals goes back to 1856 with the discovery by Johann Fuhlrotte in 1856 of a skullcap, thigh bones, part of a pelvis some ribs and some arm and shoulder bones. This was in Feldhofer in the Neander valley (i.e., the "thal"; pronounced like "tall" in English) of Germany. This launched the search taken up very much in earnest after the publication of Darwin's *Origin*, for evidence pertaining to the evolution of humans. The Neanderthals have been documented by numerous rich fossil finds, with nearly complete skeletons from several finds (Spy 1 and 2 from Spy d'Orneau in Belgium; the Old Man fossils from La-Cha;elle-aux -Saints in France (with a brain capacity of 1620 cc); the Krapina site in Croatia, among several others.[18] There has been a long debate about the relationship of Neanderthals to modern humans. It is not completely certain when they first appeared, but are thought to have flourished in Europe and ranged to the Middle East, even to Central Asia from 150 kya to about 35 kya. The Neanderthals are characterized by thick bones that were likely heavily muscled, by on avg. larger crania with larger brains on avg. than *H. sapiens,* and short limbs. Their skulls are relatively longer and low (i.e., to *H. sapiens*) with sloping frontals and often a protuberance in the occipital. Their faces are large and prognathic; the prognathism differs from that of earlier hominins in that it occurs in the mid-facial region. They seem to have had large noses, pulling the face forward. Some think this is a cold adaptation to the extreme cold of Europe in the last glacial period. Finally, according to Foley and Lewin, "during the course of their existence in Europe they do not show a trend toward the modern human condition – rather, if anything they become 'more Neanderthal.'"[19] The debate concerning how the Neanderthals disappeared rages. Some argue that they were integrated into *H. Sapiens* migrating out of Africa; some argue they were part of a mixing of hominins throughout Eurasia and Africa in the grand Multi-regional hypothesis; but the trend these days seems to be that they did not mix with modern H. Sapiens and that between 45 kya and 27 kya the moderns displaced the Neanderthals.

One of the most famous Upper Paleolithic H. Sapiens finds occurred in Cro Magnon, France in 1868. The estimated age of these fossils is 30 kya. The site contained what was determined to be 5 individuals with stone tools, carved reindeer antlers, ivory pendants and shells. The type of *H. Sapiens* called Cro-magnon, now called Early European Homo Sapiens, lived in Europe from possibly as far back as 45 kya to about 10 kya. Some of the most important recent fossils attributed to *H. Sapiens* were uncovered in Herto, in the Middle Awash region of Ethiopia. They were found in 1997 and were radiometrically dated (Ar 40/ Ar 39?) to be about 160 kya. The fossils include a nearly complete adult male cranium (BOU-VP-16/1) and significant remnant of a child's cranium. The authors argue that these fossils predate classic Neanderthals and lack some of their "derived" features; further they[20] argue that the Herto hominins are morphologically and chronologically intermediate between archaic African fossils (such as Kabwe and the like - classified either as *H. Heidelbergensis* or *H. Rhodesiensis*) and anatomically modern Late Pleistocene humans (see Appendix). The authors have lobbied to call them a new subspecies, *H. Sapiens idaltu*, in part to signify that they have some distinct characteristics when compared to modern *H. Sapiens* and seem to be a good candidate for the immediate ancestor of moderns. White et al. argue that this set of fossils strongly confirms the "Out of Africa" replacement hypothesis. Some of the key characteristics of moderns include: a smaller face and more protruding chin than more archaic forms (e.g. H. Heidelbergensis, Neanderthals), a higher skull with pronounced forehead, and a less robust post-cranial skeleton (see comparsion of Neanderthal and modern *H. Sapiens*, Appendix).

## Christian Doctrine of the Human – A Closer Look

Central to Christian belief is the notion that to be human is to bear the image of God in a unique way among God's creatures. As some have noted, we are unique among creatures in that we have the capacity for self-consciousness while being embodied (so, angels and demons may be self-conscious but not embodied; while other embodied creatures, even cognitively advanced mammals, are embodied but not self-conscious in anything like the way we are). One way to put this is that we think, we know we think, we think about our thinking, we discuss it, etc. We also know of God's existence - even those who deny that God exists know that there is such a question. Put differently, humans are unique among embodied creatures in our awareness of God's existence (in the various ways in which we are and have been so aware). Furthermore, we have a sense of what it is to live in a way that honors who God is and in a way that fails to do so. And we have the ability to make meaningful choices about that - i.e., self-consciously to choose to act and form a story to our life that in various ways honors our deeper conscience (yes to God's will) or fails to so honor it (no to God's will, yes to our "selfish" will). From the Biblical narrative and a tradition of Christian theology, the first humans have been thought to have the capacity to make such choices from a basis where they were not encumbered by sinful dispositions. By freely choosing to disobey God, they were responsible for consequences, and also in fact passed on a state of sinfulness (at least a state of disposition to sin) to their descendents. And this "passing on" is not simply a kind of "free imitation" but a passing on by something that has been called propagation suggesting that before we even make free choices we find ourselves within a state of sinful dispositions- literally highly prone to miss the mark.

### *Created in the Divine Image*

It is not at all possible here to develop in detail a history of the concept of humans as created in the Divine Image. I will briefly note some historically affirmed elements of the notion and ask what this could possibly mean given an evolutionary history to our becoming human. First, the first chapter of *Genesis* 1:26-27 states (from NRSV):

> Then God said, 'Let us make humankind (*adam*) in our image, according to our likeness and let them have dominion over the fish of the sea and over the birds of the air, and over the cattle, and over all the wild animals of the earth, and over

> every creeping thing that creeps upon the earth.' So God create humankind in his image, in the image of God he created them, male and female he created them.

This notion of being created in the image of God has been understood to mean created with a rational soul, combined with a human body (that was created out of the ground). This seems suggested by *Genesis* 2:7-8.

> . . . then the Lord God formed man (*adam*) from the dust of the ground and breathed into his nostrils the breath of life; and the man became a living being. And the Lord God planted a garden in Eden, in the east; and there he put the man whom he had formed.

It has been understood to mean standing for God here on earth, i.e., being the stewards of the earth as God's servants and that this is taught in the first passage above. In addition, has been added the capacity to reason, the capacity to love, and the capacity for both the awareness of God and self-awareness. It may go one step further as an awareness of both God and ourselves (and each other) as in a set of mutual relationships.

Some of these features are noted by Thomas Aquinas in the *Summa Theologiae*. There he follows Augustine in citing our intellectual nature as crucial for setting us apart as embodied creatures on earth who uniquely bear the image of God. To this he adds the following gloss:

> Since man is said to be the image of God by reason of his intellectual nature, he is the most perfectly like God according to that in which he can best imitate God in his intellectual nature. Now the intellectual nature imitates God chiefly in this, that God understands and loves Himself. Wherefore we see that the image of God is in man in three ways. First, inasmuch as man possesses a natural aptitude for understanding and loving God; and this aptitude consists in the very nature of the mind, which is common to all men. Secondly, inasmuch as man actually and habitually knows and loves God, though imperfectly; and this image consists in the conformity of grace. Thirdly, inasmuch as man knows and loves God perfectly; and this image consists in the likeness of glory. Wherefore on the words, 'The light of Thy

> countenance, O Lord, is signed upon us' (Psalm 4:7), the gloss distinguishes a threefold image of 'creation,' of 're-creation,' and of 'likeness.' The first is found in all men, the second only in the just, the third only in the blessed.[21]

So, in the most minimal sense, we may be said to exist in the image of God if we have an aptitude to know and love God, to know ourselves and each other as humans, to act as God's stewards on earth, and in our having a moral worth that accords with those features (what exactly that means is a matter of ongoing debate, but seems crucial to moral obligations to respect others' fundamental interests and for them to respect ours).

### Original Righteousness-Augustine and Irenaeus

A second feature of the notion of being human in Judaeo-Christian heritage is the idea that humans first existed in a state of integrity and justice or righteousness. Abraham Calovius, 17th century Lutheran theologian, described original righteousness as follows:

> It is called a state of integrity, because man in it was upright and uncorrupt (Eccl. 7:29) in intellect, will, the corporeal affections and endowments, and in all things was perfect. They call it also the sate of innocence, because he was innocent and holy, free from sin and pollution.[22]

This takes up a notion of the original state of Adam and Eve in the garden before they ate of the fruit of the tree of knowledge. It goes back at least as far as Augustine and has had a significant influence on the articulation of the concept of the meaning of the Fall in Genesis 3 and its relation to the Incarnation of Christ, his ministry, passion, death, resurrection and judgment. It seems that Adam and Eve were considered perfect as humans in every way; whether this means they had the intellectual ability and moral courage of great heroes and geniuses is not completely clear, but seems a common way of understanding this conception.

A somewhat different gloss on the meaning of the original state of integrity in the garden is associated with the names of Theophilus of Antioch (2nd c.) and Irenaeus of Lyon (2nd c.). In this view, more prevalent in the Eastern Orthodox Church, Adam and Eve were created in a state of relative innocence, both without sin in some sense and also more like children than full-grown adults (i.e., who have in a sense lost "our innocence"). Theophilus describes the rationale for the prohibition against eating of the tree of knowledge this way "Adam, being yet an infant in age, was on this account as yet unable to receive knowledge worthily."[23] Irenaeus adds that, "The man was a young child, not yet having a perfect deliberation" and "It was necessary for him to reach full-development by growing in this way."[24] It seems a key piece of the idea here is that humans were not made in our initial existence as wholly developed. Rather, we were made with the capacity to relate and know in human fashion, but also with much "room to grow". Conceivably, without willing us to sin, God placed us in a situation of abundance, but also with opportunities to do well or ill, the capacity to choose, and a whole set of natural/spiritual consequences that effect a long term "plan of salvation." On this view, the entire history of humanity from the very beginning may be considered a history of salvation with the Biblical narrative telling us a very specific and important piece of the story.

### *Original Sin*

Though the notion of original sin as a cause and consequence of the Fall seems not to have been first articulated by Augustine,[25] it was Augustine's battle with the Pelagians that put a fairly definitive stamp upon the doctrine in the West. Nearly a century after Augustine's death, the Council of Orange met to put an official stamp upon the teaching. The first two canons published in the documents of the council are especially definitive of the key pieces of the doctrine.

> CANON 1. If anyone denies that it is the whole man, that is, both body and soul, that was "changed for the worse" through the offense of Adam's sin, but believes that the freedom of the soul remains unimpaired and that only the body is subject to corruption, he is deceived by the error of Pelagius and contradicts the scripture which says, "The soul

that sins shall die" (Ezek. 18:20); and, "Do you not know that if you yield yourselves to anyone as obedient slaves, you are the slaves of the one whom you obey?" (Rom. 6:16); and, "For whatever overcomes a man, to that he is enslaved" (2 Pet. 2:19).

CANON 2. If anyone asserts that Adam's sin affected him alone and not his descendants also, or at least if he declares that it is only the death of the body which is the punishment for sin, and not also that sin, which is the death of the soul, passed through one man to the whole human race, he does injustice to God and contradicts the Apostle, who says, "Therefore as sin came into the world through one man and death through sin, and so death spread to all men because all men sinned" (Rom. 5:12).[26]

The doctrine of original sin means several things: a. the sin that Adam and Eve committed; b. the consequences of this – i.e., that which we inherit by virtue of having descended from Adam (and Eve); c. this latter includes importantly a loss or privation of sanctifying grace. This has been understood to entail both "mortality" i.e., a loss of access to the tree of life, and spiritual death, i.e., an alienation from God, such that we are no longer connected by grace to God such that we can live lives of holiness, purity, and perfectly love of God and neighbor. Some have understood this in a more radical sense, as in the following from the 1530 *Augsburg Confession*:

Furthermore it is taught among us that since the Fall of Adam, all human beings who are born in the natural way are conceived and born into sin. This means that from birth they are full of evil lust and inclination and cannot by nature possess true fear of God and true faith in God. Moreover, this same innate disease and original sin is truly sin and condemns to God's eternal wrath all who are not in turn born again through baptism and the Holy Spirit.[27]

Roman Catholics have sometimes emphasized that we still possess human nature and the image of God and thus maintain some of the natural capacities to know and love God. However, because of the inherited sin, these capacities are significantly distorted and to become just and holy requires grace for the reparation and our redemption of those capacities. One of the key Scriptural bases for this doctrine is the letter of St. Paul to the Romans. In the following I will consider that briefly in light of a pair of recent interpretations of the doctrine of original sin.

### *The Historical/Ideal View of Original Sin*

In his helpful overview of the issue in the essay "Evolution and Original Sin" (2003, 469 – 501), Robin Collins develops and defends what he calls an "Historical/Ideal (HI)" view of the meaning of original sin. There are several important background assumptions. The first is to understand Genesis 2 as a kind of "golden age" story. However, it is not a "mere" myth as some understand that term. It is a story with a kernel of important literal and historical truth. Secondly, Adam and Eve represent in a way both all people AND the first hominids who had the capacity for free-choice, self-consciousness, minimal awareness of God and God's commands. Thirdly, in some way, the first hominids may have been in some state of original justice and holiness (Collins, like Murphy, seems to favor a modified Eastern/Irenaean sense of relative childlike innocence). But the first humans were still subject to many "sinful" temptations and capable of some meaningful choice re: how to respond.[28]

On the HI view, original sin itself refers to three key pieces: i. sinful choices made from very early on; ii. continuing sinful choices over time of successive generations of "humans" – i.e., what Murphy calls fully theological humans; and, iii.the resulting bondage to sin as such spiritual darkness is passed on. This raises the question regarding the mode of inheritance (not just "imitation" but "propagation"). To capture the historical core of the doctrine, the modes must capture a robust enough sense of being trapped in sin such that a relationship with God (and so Christ) is a necessary condition for liberation, not just one way among many possible remedies

Collins carefully notes that the mode of inheritance is intertwined with genetic and cultural inheritance and is analogous to such inherited attributes of human beings (p. 471). And just as cultural inheritance operates at its own level, the psychological and social, so does the spiritual mode operate at its own level. Like cultural inheritance, spiritual inheritances are communal. What exactly makes an inheritance "spiritual" over and above the psychological, social, and cultural is not wholly clear in his essay. My brief answer is that it has to do with those realities as bound together in relation to God. For example, I have feelings (psychology) about my children (social) in a context of American values and assumptions (social plus cultural) - but these may be understood in a broader metaphysical framework bound up with beliefs and commitments to God and other spiritual beings (e.g. saints).

Why does the HI view increase (in Collins view) the plausibility of the doctrine? Because it shows how the reality of original sin is a natural consequence of humans being spiritually interconnected and having free will; that is, if our ancestors had free will and misused it then such misuse would have significantly negative spiritual (and otherwise) consequences for us, their descendents. Second, he argues (noting his own version of the meaning of original righteousness), the relatively "clear" awareness of God by our first ancestors is what one would expect if we accept that God did not abandon early humans (or the "first" theological humans) to moral and spiritual darkness from the very beginning. So, God is not to be thought of as an abandoning father.[29] For Murphy[30] the important point here is that God is not to be thought of as the author of sin. Humans who first became fully theologically human knew enough about God to know what it meant to obey God or not, had the capacity in some sense to do so, or not, and did in fact choose freely not to do so in important ways. The consequences of such choices have been passed on from generation to generation in likely complex and multi-leveled ways. The transmission reaches to a true spiritual depth that encompasses the genetic, physiological, psychological, social, and cultural, yet is something more, in part because it means those realities *as oriented* to God and the transcendent, i.e., the spiritual world.

Collins considers the strengths of the H.I. view in light of Romans 1:18-32; 5:12-21, and in light of Genesis 1-4. A few of his points are worth mentioning here. In his essay Collins reminds us of key factors guiding how we interpret the Scriptures.[31] We must keep in mind that in working through human authors in specific places and times and revealing content concerning the deepest mystery of reality, it may well be a complex task to discern the meaning. Thus Scriptural interpretation should reflect understanding of historical context, of the rest of Scripture, the history of interpretation and doctrinal development, elements of literary study, science, philosophy, and not least experientially based common sense. Collins argues that Romans 1:18-32 is the key place in the letter where it offers an account of the Fall, i.e., how we came to be and remain in bondage to sin. Paul talks there not primarily about individual actions but about human communities all the way back to the first emergence of humans, "for they knew God, but they did not honor Him as God or give thanks, but they became futile in their thinking and their senseless minds were darkened." And if this occurred through communities acting over time, then if fits the logic of the HI view.

Regarding, Romans 5:12-21, what Collins calls the *locus classicus* of the traditional (esp. Augustinian) doctrine of original sin, he develops his case. The first point is that the content is primarily about the identity of Jesus as the answer to sin and that Paul articulates the point in the context of his own and his hearers presuppositions informed by the Jewish Scriptures and traditions. In this point, he notes the rhetorical structure of the repeated "just as" this, so that, v. 18 providing a crucial example. Two, the texts (e.g. Genesis 3 or Romans 5) do not say clearly that our natures changed through Adam's sin. Even if the first sins were a special conduit for sin's entry into the world (especially as a form of spiritual death), the act of the first human or humans did not obviously, according to the Scriptural text, single-handedly change human nature. Thirdly, Collins argues that Romans suggests ongoing sin brought alienation and condemnation. So he says that Adam provides a theological representation for all humans and for the first theologically human hominins,[33] whenever and wherever they came to be. Adam represents not just the first humans, but also the first disobedience of humans (and he notes, the lack of a mention of Eve may underscore the symbolic nature of Adam). Also, with Murphy, Collins reiterates that Romans 5 suggests that through Adam, and so let's say by the free agency of humans, and not by God's doing, we die. We die not simply as a direct inheritance from two individuals, but by a profound spiritual interconnectedness to the whole history of humans. God intervenes repeatedly (quite possibly *constantly*) in this history, but does not break the chain by force. God respects human dignity, our capacity to make meaningfully free choices, thus also, choices that have consequences and that affect the nature of our interdependence.

Finally, as a brief example of comparison, we might peak at Collins's objections to the view of C.S. Lewis. In what may surprise some of his readers, Lewis argued in the *Problem of Pain* that an the doctrine of original sin is consistent with humans having evolved. In the view of Lewis, when hominins (i.e., ancestors of full humans) reached the "right" stage of development, God gifted them with the capacity for self-consciousness and consciousness of God, and put them in a paradisal state with morally relevant appetites under control. The people lived in harmony and in genuine communion with God. But eventually, selfish choices occurred, and a darkening of hearts, minds, and souls followed that went with alienation from God and each other. Collins argues that at least three significant problems beset the view. One, how the Fall occurred is mysterious (as it is on a traditional Augustinian view) if it was the case that with moral and intellectual perfection there would be no temptation to sin. While this objection could possibly be handled, one might argue that an Eastern view whereby the first humans were relatively "innocent" but not morally and intellectually perfect (as much as humans as creatures could be perfect) better fits any plausible scenario roughly concordant with evolutionary history. Second, Collins argues that God placing the first theologically human people in a state of paradise by a miracle knowing that they would sin seems unmotivated and a relationally fruitless "experiment". Finally, Collins observes that the realization of the kind of consciousness here supposed seems to imply the existence of language. Either the language slowly evolved (contrary to Lewis's model) or it would require a significant miracle on the part of God. Again, none of these objections seem to be knock-down (as I may suggest below). However, one might argue that a view of the doctrine that preserves well its core meaning while being a good fit with science, might be a marginally better way to understand the relevant Scriptures.

### *Gradual or Punctuated?*

Initially, it looks as if humans - on the evolutionary picture - would only have come gradually into the capacities that make possible bearing the image of God, being thus theologically human. For example, it does not seem plausible that merely having large brains, making and using tools, capturing fire, caring for kin, ritual burying of kin, practicing art, engaging in ritual practices of other sorts, cooperating in hunting, and being linguistic would by themselves qualify *H. sapiens* as having the capacities traditionally associated with bearing the divine image. Many of these capacities are indeed instantiated in human communities, going back at least 30,000 years or so, in ways that may be distinctive to *Homo Sapiens* (even if Neanderthals had some impressive capacities and practices). Furthermore, it does not seem likely that those capacities would come together all at once, in one generation, much less in a male and a female at the same time and place. Of course, a miracle could bring this about and might do so in a way that did not leave its exact trace.

We are left with two broad options. One, conceive of this doctrinal set as emerging gradually or as coming to be in something much more "puncutated" say in a relatively very short period of time. And furthermore, each of those scenarios admits of a dualistic or a physicalist flavor. Often, one thinks of dualism as belonging to a punctuational conception only, but if one were say, to follow the view of William Hasker (*Emergent Self*), then it may be possible that the "emergence" of souls occurred gradually in evolutionary history, and that the emergence of theologically humans by virtue of, in part, having theologically human souls may also have occurred gradually. If we were to accept a physicalist conception of the human, it would seem at first that a gradualist picture is obviously the best candidate for thinking about the narrative of becoming theologically human. Why? That's how the theory conceives of speciation – it is not a one generation phenomenon. Furthermore, as we've noted, many of the human distinctives (not just what we can do, but how we do it), appear to have emerged over a very long period of time, and likely in fits and starts (along with the gradual growth and development of relevant physiological characteristics, such as brain size and neural architecture as well as capacities for manual dexterity and the relevant cultural capacities such as language and cooking). However (and this may seem a bit wild), just as we have "a-ha" moments of insight, and these require many pieces of the puzzle to be in place without the puzzle itself being solved, so also might it be the case that the history of evolution set the table for a special mutation (in, say, a key regulatory gene) to take place that made possible the emergence of (even dimly) a God-conscious human (or two) in one generation.

How does this look on a dualistic conception? First, let's define dualism. In general dualists about human nature hold that some part of the human person is non-physical in nature. Substance dualists have held that there is a non-physical substance that either is the person, or combines with body in some way to be a human person. Property dualists hold that some features of humans, such as minds, intentional states (e.g. beliefs about things, or desires for things), or qualitative states (e.g. pains, sensational states) are non-physical. This brings up the question, what is the physical? That's a difficult question and one I would like to forestall. However, we might in a preliminary sense define the physical as follows. The physical includes things that are studied by our fundamental physics, and those entities composed of such things. For example, physics conceives of the "universe" as composed of a veritable zoo of fundamental particles such as quarks, electrons, neutrinos, bosons, hadrons, gravitons, and so on. These might also be composed of vibrating strings (if some version of string theory works out). In addition there is thought to be a space-time continuum which is conceived in various ways. Furthermore, we are surrounded by entities thought to be composed of the things physics studies and existing according to the rules that physics attempts to articulate (e.g. Einstein's Field Equations, the Schroedinger Equation, the Standard Model of physical particles, etc.). This includes all forms of life, and the units of biochemistry of which they are composed and according to which they exist. Now, something, whether an substance or a property, belonging to a human being that in some important sense does not *per se* belong to such physicality (isn't strictly composed of physical things or existing according to the relevant "laws") may be thought of as non-physical.

Now might it have been the case that at some point in our long evolutionary history, God brought it about that a non-physical dimension came to be to change an individual from a run-of-the-mill *H. sapiens* to a theological human? And might this be thought of as conferring a non-physical "soul or mind or spirit" that is distinctly "human" in the relevant sense of bestowing the divine image? And might this be something that did not show itself in any obvious outward change of behavior - such as a sudden emergence of art, or writing, or tilling the soil, or cooking, hunting, or speaking? Some of those things seem quite possible to think of as having been developed by hominins with sufficient brain power to learn the relevant skills and pass them on, but still lacking something that would confer the ability to know God, even dimly, and be able to make some meaningful decision in life to follow God or in some way, choose a path of not doing so. This reminds us of the deep difficulty of finding through the reconstruction of our deep past the clear signs of the first humans in a theological sense.

So, it seems possible that on various conceptions of dualism, humans could have been gifted with non-physical capacities in one generation that made the difference between having and lacking the divine image. Now would this be a situation that would match the conception of original righteousness. Not likely will this fit well an Augustinian conception, but quite possibly may fit a more Irenaean conception in Collins' style of conceiving it.

This sort of model can stand with a dualist or physicalist conception of the human person. I won't go through all of the different possible scenarios now. A key consideration is that we distinguish between *H. Sapiens* as a biological species and "human - in God's image" as a theological reality. Furthermore, if our notion of original righteousness is sufficiently open-ended while still holding to the notion that with the gift of the divine image there was something clearly different and also without the effects of sin, then we can maintain a robust picture of both humans emerging in a narrow band of history, spatially and temporally, having a special state of existence (integrity), then losing it because of free and "sinful" choices, and setting up a state of affairs that is a sinful state that is passed on not just psychosocially but also in some meaningful sense, spiritually. The mode of transmission to all of humanity may be left somewhat open ended, and one that is not a point of doctrine, which it never seems to have been.

**Final Thoughts**

What does it take to inherit eternal life (see Luke 10:25-27; Matt 22:34-40)? When asked this or a similar question, which commandment of the law is the greatest, Jesus responds with the two great commandments. In Matthew Jesus says, "You shall love the Lord your God with your whole heart, with your whole soul, and with all your mind.' This is the greatest and first commandment. The second is like it; 'You shall love your neighbor as yourself.' On these two commandments the whole law is based, and the prophets as well." (Jesus here quotes Deut 6:5 and Lev 19:18). So participating in eternal life with God and keeping the heart of God's commandments seems central to our reason for existing. It is the sort of goal or purpose that makes sense for beings created in God's Image. It is the kind of purpose that is deeply frustrated by sin. It is the purpose that can be fulfilled only with the aid of Grace. And the failure to realize it is most profoundly addressed by the events and actions of the Paschal Mystery. Jesus, the Lamb of God, takes away the sins of the world. These are central issues in the teaching of Christian Faith, in the teaching of Jesus, and in the teaching of the Scriptures.

Just as God did not coerce, program, or force the first humans to disobey, to miss the mark, "to eat of the tree of knowledge of good & evil" neither does God force us to remain with our state of disposition to sin and thus alienation from a more fully realized relationship with God. In the history of God's relationship with Israel from the deliverance of Noah and family from the Flood, to the calling of Abraham, to the covenant with Moses and the Israelites in delivering them from Egypt and the giving of the Mosaic law, to the work of the prophets, we see God reaching out to offer ways to overcome the disposition to sin. In Jesus, God Incarnate, we Christians believe that God has offered a fundamentally new, radical, and universal pathway to the overcoming of the effects of sin – the ultimate answer to the problem of the original sin. And in keeping with the original meaning of the gift of the Divine Image and the ability to share in a life of loving solidarity with the triune God, the offer of a pathway out of sin through a relationship to God through Faith in Christ is not something we believe to be coercive. God grants us the freedom, in thousands of ways that add up to a basic decision, to follow Christ, to be His disciple, or to go another way. This freedom honors God's dignity as creator and ours as created in God's image; furthermore, it plays a role in explaining why God is not the author of sin and a part in explaining why there is horrific wickedness and evil in the world in spite of God's goodness, knowledge, and power. God loves the world, and specifically, loves all creatures who suffer unfathomably, and knows of their (our) suffering, and has the power to end it. Yet, as part of God's love and justice, in some sense God allows free creatures to act in wicked and hurtful ways as part of honoring their dignity, and thus freedom. Some passages of Scripture suggest that God's hope is for all freely to choose a life of discipleship and that God will ultimately be victorious over wickedness and that God indeed does work to a good end even through wickedness and suffering. In all of that, God honors human beings enough not to make us his puppets or "obedience" robots, or the like. In short, God does a tremendous amount, and in the person of Christ has made His presence profoundly evident in the history of Creation - in order to address the ravages of the sin in which live and that we inherit. However, in some way, God has given us meaningful say, some autonomy, in our choice of our day to day response to God's invitation to relationship.

The troubles with evolution are not simple, they are not just questions of reading the Bible as a theological text and not a science text book and by distinguishing Christian theology and church teachings from a literal or "plain-sense" reading of the Bible. They go deeper, maybe much deeper. And the problems, the difficult challenges of seeing an even remotely plausible way through them might suggest the ongoing cultural battle of the creation-evolution controversy. I think it is a bit patronizing for some to suggest that Christians who bear deep reservations about evolutionary theory, especially applied to humans, simply need to learn more about the Bible, and about science. The challenge is just not that simple. A set of things are involved in making such an adjustment and this paper has in no way enumerated all of them. We need a theological portrait of human nature that strongly affirms our embodied nature that is still open to libertarian free will and a sense of our "soul" as an aspect of our being that fits such a notion of free will. We need a portrait of the Scriptures and the teaching of the tradition of Christianity that has authority - i.e., a sense that the central teachings of Christianity are not simply an intersection set of fallible human cultural traditions, practices, and beliefs. And we need a solid understanding of what is well-grounded human knowledge, as opposed to yet another set of passing opinions, well-grounded in the evidence, but nonetheless mistaken. So, the task of charting a tentative model or map of reconciliation will operate at various levels and will be in principle at this time and place - incomplete. I hope that it gives some people the courage to embrace this exciting and amazing dimension of human investigation - the science of human nature and especially the evolutionary perspective on the question. But in doing, I hope even more that the process of reconciliation deepens one's sense of WHO God Is, of God's word, and of one's profoundly important place in God's act of sharing in God's being as Creator.

### Notes and References

1. Patrick McDonald is Assistant Professor in the Department of Philosophy at Seattle Pacific University, 3307 Third Ave. W, Seattle, WA 98119.
2. Definition of Hominin from: *www.hominin.net*
3. Tim D. White, et al. 2009. "Ardipithecus ramidus and the Paleobiology of Early Hominids." Science 2 October: vol 326. No. 5949, pp. 75-86.
4. see T. White, et al. 2009
5. mya = millions of years ago; kya – thousands of years ago
6. Definition of Hominin (from: www.hominin.net) "Because of the genetic closeness of humans to other African great apes (bonobos, chimpanzees, and gorillas), some scientists have argued for a revision of the current classification system to one that is more inclusive of all evolutionary relationships. Thus, the orangutans, gorillas, chimps, bonobos and humans, are classified under the Family Hominidae. But since orangutans diverged sometime around 13 million years ago, they've been re-categorized into the sub-family Ponginae. The African apes, including humans, on the other hand, have been placed into a different sub-family Homininae. Ultimately, the bipedal apes have been assigned a new tribe Hominini or hominin. And ll members of the fossil genera, such as Australopithecus, Ardipithecus, Kenyanthropus, Sahelanthropus, Orrorin and Homo, are members of this tribe."
7. Tim White et al 2009.
8. Throughout this essay regarding Hominin history, I will adopt the narrative stance and just say, "this happened, that happened"– all the while under that assumption that what we have is a set of evidence. Under the available evidence and analysis of competent scientists this narrative may make the "most sense."
9. Robert A. Foley, and Roger Lewin, Principles of Human Evolution. (Oxford: Blackwell, 2004); William H. Kimbel, "The Human Species on the Tree of Life," Proceedings of the BSCS, AIBS Symposium (Colorado Springs: BSCS, 2005).

10. One piece of lore is Franz Weidenreich's story of rushing to get a trove of fossils shipped to New York from China in 1941 only to lose the shipment once the port "fell" to the Japanese on Dec. 7, 1941.
11. see Foley & Lewin 2004.
12. For slight evidence of a pre-Erectus Asian fossil see: Wanpo et. al. Nature 1995, pp. 275-278.
13. Foley/Lewin, 2004, p. 340.
14. for a diagram, see Foley and Lewin 2004, p. 342.
15. Weidenreich 1937.
16. see: *http://humanorigins.si.edu/ha/heid.htm;* Foley and Lewin 2004.
17. see: *http://humanorigins.si.edu/ha/brokenhill.htm.*
18. for a review, see Richard Klein, "Whither the Neanderthals?" in *Science.* 7 March 2003: Vol. 299. no. 5612, pp. 1525-1527.
19. Foley & Lewin, 2004, p. 387
20. White, et al. 2003
21. Thomas Aquinas, *Summa Theologica* 1a.93.a.4, Second and Revised Edition, Literally translated by Fathers of the English Dominican Province, 1920. From: *http://www.newadvent.org/summa/.* Retrieved, January 20, 2010.
22. George Murphy, "Roads to Paradise and Perdition: Christ, Evolution, and Original Sin," *Perspectives on Science and Christian Faith,* Vol. 58, No. 2, 2006, p. 113.
23. "Letter to Autolycus" in Ante-Nicene Fathers; from Murphy 2006, p. 114.
24. On the Apostolic Preaching, 47; from Murphy 2006, p. 114.
25. see Tatha Wiley, *Original Sin: Origins, Developments, Contemporary Meanings* (Mahwah,N.J.: Paulist Press, 2002).
26. Canons of the Council of Orange. 529 CE. From:*http://www.reformed.org/documents/index.html?mainframe=http://www.reformed.org/documents/canons_of_orange.html.* Retrieved, August 25, 2009.
27. Murphy 2006, p. 113.
28. Robin Collins, "Evolution and Original Sin" in Keith Miller, (ed.), *Perspectives on an Evolving Creation* (Grand Rapids, MI: Eerdmans, 2003), pp. 470-471.

29. Collins, 2003, p. 473.
30. Murphy, 2006, pp. 111, 115.
31. Collins, 2003, pp. 473-75.
32. Collins, 2003, p. 481.

## Appendix

### Web-sites with Images (and Video) of various Hominin Fossils

Smithsonian Hominin Family tree:
*http://humanorigins.si.edu/ha/a_tree.html*
Hominin Crania compared:
*http://www.britannica.com/EBchecked/topic/275670/human-evolution*
Ardipithecus Ramidus:
*http://news.nationalgeographic.com/news/2009/10/photogalleries/oldest-human-skeleton-ardi-missing-link-chimps-pictures/#025050_600x450.jpg*
Australopithecus Afarensis: Lucy
*http://www.talkorigins.org/faqs/homs/lucy.html*
Homo Ergaster/Erectus: Turkana Boy
*http://www.talkorigins.org/faqs/homs/15000.html*
Homo Ergaster/Erectus?: Dmanisi Hominids
*http://www.talkorigins.org/faqs/homs/d2700.html*
Herto Hominids: (for picture and brief npr news account:
*http://www.npr.org/templates/story/story.php?storyId=1295624*
*and: http://www.npr.org/templates/story/story.php?storyId=1295460*
Neanderthal – Human Comparison
*http://www.britannica.com/bps/image/547371/73008/Skeleton-of-a-Neanderthal-compared-with-a-skeleton-of-a*
NOVA Becoming Human - originally aired in November 2009
*http://www.pbs.org/wgbh/nova/beta/evolution/becoming-human-part-1.html*

# Between Evolution and Creation: A Forgotten Lesson

5

JACEK TOMCZYK[1] & GRZEGORZ BUGAJAK[2]

## Introduction

Human beings as a species belong to the world of animate nature but we have always been convinced of our unique status in this world. The theory of the stability and invariability of species, accepted until the 19th century, placed humankind at the "top" of the animate world. The biological vision of the stability of species was perfectly compatible with the biblical image of the creation of the world. The Book of Genesis presents people as special creatures, made in the image and likeness of God. The second half of the 19th century saw the rise of Charles Darwin's theory of evolution. It is worth to note that Darwin himself had mixed feelings about publishing his work. In a letter to Charles Lyell he wrote: "I treat you as the lord of natural sciences, therefore I beseech you to revise, after reading the whole text, the titles of the last section wherein I recapitulate. With great anxiety I am waiting for your judgement concerning the balance of arguments for and against my book" [back translation from the Polish edition].[3] Darwin's doubts resulted from his awareness of challenging the former vision of the human. In the light of his theory, human being was but one of the biological species which was subject to the same biological laws as other organisms. His anxiety about the possible conflict was then quite well-founded, but it is very unlikely that in his even most daring thoughts he could foresee the fact that the theory of evolution would be the proverbial bone of contention for the following 150 years. Time and again, natural scientists, theologians and philosophers engage in debates which take up the issues of evolution. Quite often, such discussions facilitate the casting of new light on some old problems. However, there are also many fruitless controversies, which not only fail to provide any new answers, but on the contrary, breed more confusion.

## The Theory of Evolution and the Creation of the Human

Until the second half of the 19th century, the natural sciences accepted without any exceptions the theory of the fixity of species, which assumed the stability and invariability of all species. According to this theory, all living creatures, including human beings, have always existed in the same forms as the ones which were known at the given time. Any findings of extinct animals were instantly explained away as the evidence of great catastrophes and never led to the suspicion that the species could change over time.[4] The concept of the fixity of species allowed Linneus to classify all living organisms; the results of his taxonomic endeavours were published in his monumental work: *Systema naturae*. The scientific theory of the fixity of species co-existed then peacefully with the theological concept, according to which all creatures emerged in the act of divine creation. This creationist thought was founded, on the one hand, on the literal understanding of the first chapters of Genesis and, on the other, on the scholastic principle of causality (*nihil reducitur de potentia ad actum nisi per ens actu*); this principle took for granted such a relation between cause and effect which made it impossible to conceive the rise of a more perfect ("greater") being from a lesser one. Both the scientific and theological view seemed so perfectly complementary that the theory of the fixity of species was for many centuries identified with the theory of creationism.[5,6] This seamless concordance ended in the second half of the 19th century.

The juxtaposition of the scientific theory of evolution with the theological concept of creation was one of the reasons for the heated controversy, raised by Darwin's famous *On the Origin of Species*, which was first published in 1859. The discussions between theologians and scientists, which immediately followed this publication, were all based on the false assumption that if the theory of evolution was true, then the biblical idea of creation had to be rejected. Nobody noticed that Darwin did *not* contest in his work the theological idea of the creation of the human, but only opposed the biological concept of the fixity of species. From what he claimed himself, it clearly follows that he did not intend to reject God as the creator of the humankind. He was only convinced that the scientific concept of the fixity of species was wrong.[7]

The theory of evolution gave an impulse for a revised scientific interpretation of the human fossils which had already been discovered at the beginning of the 19th century. In 1829 Phillipe Charles Schmerling excavated three human skulls at Engis (Belgium). The first was destroyed during exploration, the second one was huge and massive, it was similar to a skull of modern human. The third one, which once belonged to a child, was characterized by archaic features. Schmerling inferred that people had been undergoing a morphological transformation over centuries.[8] Charles Lyell, who visited Belgium in 1833, examined the child's skull, but completely rejected Schmerling's suggestions. In Lyell's opinion, the skull was ordinary. Under criticism, Schmerling then sold the Engis fossil to the University of Liége. Almost twenty years later, in 1848, another human skull was found in obscure circumstances in Forbes' Quarry (Gibraltar). It had a prominent brow ridge and a flat forehead. Unfortunately, the find from Gibraltar was treated only as a natural oddity and handed over to the Royal

Museum of Surgery in London.[9] Potentially important findings were neglected because of the concept of the fixity of species. Biologists were unable to face the idea that the recovered fossils could belong to ancient people who should be assigned to a species different from our own. Rather, they believed that the remains from Belgium and Gibraltar belonged to diseased or mentally handicapped people. By accident, in 1856, the next ancient human remains were found in Neandertal, Germany. Herman Schaaffhausen, an anatomy professor from Bonn, wanted to give the remains a new taxonomic name different from *Homo sapiens*,[10] because they displayed features significantly different from those of our species, and in his opinion they had to have belonged to a primitive pre-human being. His approach, however, was totally alien to the way of thinking of most anthropological authorities of the day. Carter Blake, an amateur-anthropologist, was convinced that the bones belonged to an idiot.[11] In the opinion of a physician, Bernard Davis, the big skull with prominent brow ridges bore traces of pathological changes.[12] Schaaffhausen's proposal to classify the Neandertal fossil as a new species was also criticized by August Franz Mayer, who came to the conclusion that the remains belonged to a Cossack who reached Germany in January 1814 when the Russian army was attacking Napoleons' troops. Also Rudolph Virchov, a famous German pathologist did not accept Schaaffhausen's thesis. In 1873, at the International Anthropological Congress in Wiesbaden, Virchov presented the results of his own research. In his opinion, the Neandertal remains belonged to a human being who had suffered in his/her childhood from rickets and certainly could not be remains of our ancestor! He repeated this opinion in Ulm in 1892. Furthermore, he claimed that the "cripple" from the Neandertal Valley could not have survived without help from his companions, and altruism is characteristic only of modern human beings. If, therefore, Neandertals were altruists, they had to belong to the species of *Homo sapiens*. Virchov was a pathologist so he often examined human bones affected by syphilis or rickets, and he knew the changes effected by these diseases. It is, therefore, surprising that he should have recognized symptoms of rickets in a fossil that did not show any signs of the disease! Virchov continued to defend the old concept of the fixity of species according to which modern man could not have primitive ancestors.[13]

He died in 1902, and until the end believed that the fossil from Neandertal belonged to an individual who certainly could not be classified as a separate species - *Homo neanderthalensis*. Only after Darwin's publication could all these findings be finally recognised as the remains of some earlier forms of *Homo*. Darwin provided many examples which proved the fixity of species concept invalid. His thesis was that all forms of life were related by ancestry. This meant that all species, extinct and living, descended from a single ancient ancestor. Excavations carried out in Asia and Europe at the turn of the 19th and 20th centuries were in line with the theory of evolution and not that of the fixity of species. Paradoxically however, the fact that the re-interpretation of old discoveries corroborated Darwin's controversial hypothesis raised even more fear among theologians.

Many theologians saw Darwin's theory as a dangerous threat to the idea of divine creation. They maintained that evolutionism inevitably led to atheism, therefore they could not accept it. For example, Joseph Pohle insisted in his textbook on dogmatics that the description of creation in Genesis was a realistic and literally true story, and therefore he claimed that Darwinism offended God who created the body of the first human being.[14] Similar views were expressed by Cardinal Ernesto Ruffini, a very influential person in the Catholic Church of the time.[15] On the 30th June -1909, the Papal Biblical Council issued a special document which reminded Catholics that the basic truths of faith included the following concepts: 1. God is the direct creator of the first human; 2. Woman originates from man's body; 3. Humankind has one beginning.[16]

Scientists in turn, who were frequently accused of forging their evidence, tried to reinforce their claims by arguing that biblical statements contradicted scientific discoveries and inferring that the theological concept of the creation of human being was simply false.

However, it was already at the time of this bitter confrontation between theology and the sciences that the first attempts to formulate different views on the process of hominization appeared. For example, L. Janssens in his "Summa Theologica" stated that God was directly involved in the creation of human being, but he also argued that from the theological point of view it was not important how the human body was first made.[17] Likewise, Bernhard Bartmann did not reject the possibility of the evolutionary origin of human being, when he maintained that God created human soul from nothing and human body from existing matter.[18]

These lines of reasoning were pursued further by other theologians who, in the light of new discoveries (further evidence of the gradual development of human being were found in the meantime: *Pithecanthropus erectus* near Bejing in 1890/1891, *Neanderthal* in La Quina in 1908 and Saccopastore in 1929, *Australopithecus africanus* in Taung in 1924), could no longer reject the idea of evolution. It seems that the first theologian who tried to reconcile creationism with the natural sciences was Hubert Junker, according to whom the story of the creation of the First Parents was a narrative designed to illustrate the truth about human nature and dignity, rather than a historical report on the consecutive phases of the creation of humankind.[19]

In this way, Junker followed the directions included in Pope Leon XIII's encyclical *Providentissiumus Deus* (published in 1893). The pope declared that the Bible was the source of infallible knowledge about salvation and no conclusions other than theological could be derived from the biblical stories. In this document we can read: "Now, the authority of the Fathers, by whom after the apostles, the growing Church was disseminated, watered, built, protected, and nurtured, is the highest authority, as often as they all in one and the same way interpret a Biblical text, as pertaining to the doctrine of faith and morals."[20]

Another attempt at reconciling the theory of evolution with the Christian vision of the origin of human being was undertaken in the 20th century by a French Jesuit, Pierre

Teilhard de Chardin. As a theologian and a scientist he always supported the idea of evolution. In his opinion, the natural sciences did not have to conflict with theology because the former employed a different, that is *biological*, concept of causality, which simply defined a chain of subsequent events. Theology, on the other hand, deals with *ontological* causality, that is with the dependence of a lower being on a higher one. The creative act of God, which takes place beyond time, cannot be identified with temporal and immanent causes. One can therefore both accept the theory of evolution and believe in the idea of creation.[21]

The works of such thinkers as Junker and Teilhard de Chardin initiated the process of separating theology from natural anthropology. A possibility of solving the conflict between the idea of creation and the theory of evolution appeared when theologians and the Church authorities accepted that scientific theories should not be evaluated according to the biblical texts or theological knowledge. In other words, the solution was found in the peaceful area of separation. It is quite another matter, however, if such a solution, although methodologically sound and correct, can also be genuinely satisfactory.[22]

Doctrine-wise, the conflict between the theory of evolution and creationism ended in the 1950s. In 1948 Cardinal Achille Lienart pronounced the view that God created the human when human body was connected with an immaterial soul. Theologians agreed that the Scriptures and theological knowledge cannot be used to question a scientific concept such as the theory of evolution.[23] In 1950, Pius XII, in his encyclical "Humani generis", wrote: "For these reasons the Teaching Authority of the Church does not forbid that, in conformity with the present state of human sciences and sacred theology, research and discussions, on the part of men experienced in both fields, take place with regard to the doctrine of evolution...."[24] These statements closed the debate on the agreement between the Revealed Truth and the theory of evolution, which eventually ceased to be perceived as a threat to faith.

The Church and theologians should remain interested in this theory, as it is advised in pope John Paul II's address to The Pontifical Academy of Science: "Today, more than a half-century after the appearance of that encyclical [*Humani Generis*], some new findings lead us toward the recognition of evolution as more than an hypothesis. The magisterium of the Church takes direct interest in the question of evolution because it refers to man who, according to the Revelation, is created in the image and likeness of God."[25] It appears, however, that the importance of 'the question of evolution' for theological thinking has yet to be discovered by many theologians, who either neglect this issue completely, or, when challenged, chose to reply the old and outdated tune of evolution being a 'mere hypothesis', or even go back in their thinking to the time when Darwinism was being perceived as the most hostile enemy of the true faith. One would wish that the history of the late 19th and early 20th century disputes had been learnt better.

Evolution or Fixity of species
*Scientific ground*
— — — — — — — — — — —
Creation or Anti-creation
*Theological ground*

**Figure 1:** *Scientific vs. theological approach to the problem of the origin of human being*

## Monogenism and Original Sin

The Book of Genesis presents in a very vivid way the sin of the First Parents. The consequences of their fall affect all humankind. This biblical image served as a basis for the assumption that all people have a single pair of ancestors: Adam and Eve.[26] The literal understanding of the Scripture resulted in linking the doctrine of Original Sin with the concept of monogenism. Up to the 1940s, nobody paid attention to the fact that the theological truth about Original Sin should not follow from any biological hypothesis. Many theological texts from the beginning of the 20th century still referred to the single ancestry of humankind, that is to a concept proper to natural sciences. For instance, Franz Diek-amp described monogenism as a necessary condition for accepting the doctrine of Original Sin.[27] Theology accepted then the following syllogism: if all people are burdened with the stigma of Original Sin, then all people must have one ancestor, i.e., an individual called Adam, whose story is narrated in the Book of Genesis.[28]

In 1941, Pope Pius XII issued an encyclical "*Divino afflante Spiritu*", wherein he rejected the literal understanding of the narrative about the creation of human being, and recommended its re-interpretation.[29] One of the issues undertaken in the studies that followed the papal advice was the problem of Original Sin. It was pointed out that Original Sin was universal, i.e., every human being was subject to it. This conclusion bears special significance in theology because it accounts for the necessity of salvation. At the time when it was formulated, however, it also appeared that the belief in the existence of a unique Adam and Eve, the very first and only pair of parents of all humans, was indispensable for sustaining this teaching. Looking for evidence to support this hypothesis, some theologians turned to the anthropological notion of monogenism as an opportune concept to suit their aims. They interpreted this notion in the way which answered their needs: it was assumed that at the very beginning of humankind there must have existed a single and unique pair of people who were "everybody's parents." This raised an obvious objection among scientists because paleoanthropology speaks about the beginnings of humankind only with regard to population, and therefore cannot accept a view that the entire species evolved from a single couple. What is a real scientific issue is the problem of mono- or polycentrism, i.e., the question if humankind could have evolved from one or many different populations. But even if this issue could be decided in favour of monocentrism, it still would not be the solution required by theologians. A population of people could not have committed a sin which, according to the traditional teaching, was committed by a single Adam and then was 'inherited' by his descendants.

Various attempts in the 1950s to reconcile the theological teaching on Original Sin with scientific findings prove this issue to be a difficult one. Vittorio Marcozzi, for instance, claims that biology cannot deal with the problem of monogenism.[30] M. Schmaus, in his textbook of "Dogmatics," does not see the possibility of proving monogenism on the ground of natural sciences, either. At the same time, Schmaus proposes three theses: 1. The evolutionary process which resulted in the origin of human being was intended by God; 2. Evolution affected only the soul, not the body; 3. All humankind derives from one couple.[31] Similarly, Karl Rahner supported the explanation of the universality of Original Sin on the grounds of the monogenic origin of humankind, although he tried to prove it by means of metaphysical, not scientific concepts.[32] In his exegetical exposition of the Book of Genesis, Stanis³aw Styœ writes that the biblical text cannot imply either the creation of one human couple or many couples, since the biblical word *Adam* simply denotes "a human being" in general.[33]

The problem became even more serious when not only anthropologists but also some theologians, like for instance P. Teilhard de Chardin, criticised the demand raised by the theologians that science should support the idea of monogenism. Teilhard stressed the fact that the 'hypothesis of monogenism' was not scientific, and pointed out that whenever anthropology speaks about 'the first man' the concept should always be understood as referring to a population and not a single individual. As a scientist, Teilhard was well aware of the fact that all species originated in the process of speciation, which is always a group phenomenon, and this is why all mankind could not descend from one couple. In his opinion, monogeneity and poligeneity were purely theological concepts and, as such, they remained scientifically unverifiable.[34]

An encyclical, "Humani generis", issued by Pius XII in 1950, did not help much in this matter. The pope explicitly rejected the view that after Adam there could have existed some humans who did not descend from him as a common ancestor, nor did he accept the idea that the word *Adam* may refer to many 'fathers'. The encyclical says: "When, however, there is a question of another conjectural opinion, namely polygenism, the children of the Church by no means enjoy the liberty [of opinion]. For the faithful cannot embrace that opinion which maintains that either after Adam there existed on this earth true men who did not take their origin through natural generation from him as from the first parent of all, or that Adam represents a certain number of first parents. We do not know how such an opinion can be reconciled with that which the sources of revealed truth and the documents of the Teaching Authority of the Church propose with regard to Original Sin, which proceeds from a sin actually committed by an individual Adam and which, through generations, is passed on to all and is in everyone as his own."[35]

The issuing of the encyclical caused divergence of opinion among theologians who disagreed on the weight of the Pope's pronouncement. Some, like Charles Boyer, were convinced that the encyclical contained a papal doctrinal statement which definitively solved the problem of the single origin of the human.[36] Others argued that the encyclical contained no definitive or irrevocable decision. A Jesuit priest, Leon Renwart, wrote that the form used by Pius XII did not imply a promulgated doctrinal definition. Moreover, he pointed to the lack of consistency in the interpretation of the biblical book of Genesis. On the one hand, theologians rejected the literal understanding of the text and unanimously accepted the possibility that the human body could undergo evolution as postulated by the natural sciences. On the other hand, however, they still literally interpreted the same passages with regard to the existence of the single couple of the First Parents.[37] A similar objection was raised by A. Galin who asked if monogenism was really implied by faith.

However, both theologians and scientists who were involved in this debate on *Humani generis* failed to pay due attention to the fact that the Pope referred to monogenism in the context of a sin of a 'real human being' ("there existed on earth a true man"). Pius XII was then concerned with describing human being from the perspective of Christian anthropology, not that of the natural sciences, for the latter do not have any comprehensive or scientifically verifiable definition of human being, and therefore cannot identify the spatio-temporal point where the first "true man" appeared. We should remember that the picture of the past, drawn in contemporary paleoanthropology, is a joined effect of three different research methods: the morphological, the archaeological and the genetic. Each of these has produced its own definition of a 'human'. Different preliminaries of knowledge about contemporary human thus result in different scenarios of the *Homo sapien's* history. For the proponents of the morphological method such criteria of belonging to the species of *Homo sapiens* as: the growth of the braincase accompanied by the evolution of its shape, the reduction of the facial part of the skull and the ever more gracile skeleton, remain crucial. Those who prefer this approach will seek the origins of our species in the past reaching the Middle Pleistocene.[38,39]

A different picture of our past emerges from the accounts proposed by the proponents of the archaeological approach who argue that the history of *Homo sapiens* is only about forty thousand years long. In this period, known as Upper Paleolithic, we come across such evident traces of human existence as cave paintings, decorations and quite sophisticated tools.[40] All such evidence clearly point to the development of abstract and symbolic thinking, which is of course unique for *Homo sapiens*. Last but not least, the genetic method places the origin of man in the past dating back to 200 Ka.[41] So the way in which the history of human evolution is presented clearly depends on the choice of a particular research method. Each of the above mentioned methods results in a different description of the beginnings of man.[42]

The controversy lasted until late 1950s because theology could not free itself from biological lines of reasoning. For quite a long time theologians remained anxious about the fact that a resignation from a biological support for monogenism would diminish the reality of Original Sin. It was believed that the biblical interpretation of Original Sin called for a complete rejection of scientific arguments which denied monogenistic origins of our species.

What eventually helped to reach a solution was the growing awareness of vital differences between scientific and theological discourse. The interpreting of the biblical texts largely depends on recognising their unique literary and narrative character. As Erich Auerbach once stressed, Hebrew prose is distinguished by the following features: first, clear emphasis falls on some parts of the narrative while others are left in the background; second, there are sudden interruptions or unexpected beginnings of new plots and, last but not least, one must take into account an exceptionally wide range of meanings and semantic nuances of terms used in biblical texts. This is why the exegetes' task consists mainly in retrieving those senses which the author of the text outlined or implied in a manner proper to him. Also, when biblical authors spoke about the universe and human being, they did not articulate a scientist's or a philosopher's point of view, but they spoke from the perspective of believers who wished to glorify the good and powerful hand of God, the Maker of all, by praising the beauty of the visible world.[43]

The aforementioned discussion, concerning the relation between monogenism and the truth about Original Sin, seems to have come to an end with majority of theologians recognizing and admitting that whenever natural sciences speak about "the first man" they always mean by this term a representative of an entire population.[44] In 1968, Pope Paul VI in his *Credimus*, defined monogenism as a theological truth without which the teaching about Original Sin would be hardly defendable, although at the same time he admitted that one should not demand from the natural sciences any evidence in favour of the theological concept, whose main task was to illustrate the claim of the universality of Original Sin.[45] In other words, monogenism is a theological thesis concerned with the origin of sin, and as such it cannot be referred to on the same grounds as monocentrism, which is a scientific thesis concerned with the origins of *Homo sapiens*. The teaching about Original Sin does not explain how it first came into the world and how it is transmitted - this will always be a part of *misterium iniquitatis* - but rather concentrates on the fact of human disobedience and, implied by it, the necessity of Redemption.[46,47]

Similarly, the teaching about the creation of the world should not be identified with a temporal moment of coming into existence. The main sense of the dogma is that the world *has been* created by God. In other words: whatever exists, is continually sustained by the Creator and owes to him its existence. What is at stake then, is not the temporal beginning of the world, but its continuous dependence on God with regard to its existence.

| Monocentrism or Policentrism |
|---|
| *Scientific ground* |
| Monogenism or Poligenism |
| *Theological ground* |

**Figure 2:** *Scientific vs. theological approach to the problem of human roots*

## Final Remarks

In the course of the last 150 years, discussions between proponents of the theory of evolution and advocates of the creationist view of the origin of human being have been frequently fraught with mutual hostility and accusations. Many theologians, who felt threatened by the scientific interpretation of human prehistory, rejected the theory of evolution, considering it a view which contradicted the biblical narrative and the principle of causality, and therefore was offensive both towards God and humankind. Natural scientists, on the other hand, frequently accused by theologians of forging the evidence, tried to turn the tables on their adversaries and were thus determined to prove that certain biblical statements contradicted the results of their research, and concluded therefore that the vision of the origins of human propagated by theologians was contrary to scientific truth. In brief: in their eyes it was false. Thus both theologians and scientists confused the spheres of their competence. Theologians formulated verdicts in matters of biology whereas natural scientists deemed themselves competent to interpret the Book of Genesis. Viewing this period with hindsight, it becomes clear, however, that the theory of evolution prompted both scientists and theologians to address anew the phenomenon of the human. This challenge seems to remain actual still. Today, although an official statement of the Church voiced by John Paul II has finally put an end to some misunderstandings, it cannot be granted that all problems have been definitively solved.

## Notes and References

1. Jacek Tomczyk lectures at the Institute of Ecology and Bioethics, Department of Anthropology, Cardinal Stefan Wyszynski Universit, Polland.
2. Grzegorz Bugajak lectures at the Institute of Philosophy, Department of the Philosophy of Nature, Cardinal Stefan Wyszynski Universit, Polland.
3. Michael White, John Gribbin, *Darwin* (Warszawa: Prószyñski i S-ka, 1998), p. 210.
4. Charles Darwin, *The Origin of Species* (Kent: Mackays of Chatham, 1998), p. 7.
5. Bernard Ha³aczek, "Man Between Biological and Theological Thinking," in *Œl¹skie Studia Historyczno-Teologiczne,* 33 (2000), p. 165.
6. Jacek Tomczyk, "Paradigm of Anthropology as Causes of Taxonomic Controversies," in *Przegl¹d Antropologiczny-Anthropological Review,* 65 (2002), p. 83.
7. Charles Darwin, *The Origin of Species* (Kent: Mackays of Chatham, 1998), p. 369.
8. Erik Trinkaus, Pat Shipman, *The Neandertals of Skeleton, Scientists and Scandal* (New York: Vintage, 1994), p. 39.
9. Louis Leakey, Vanne Goodall, *Unveiling Man's Origins* (London: Methuen & Co., 1969), p. 81.
10. Herman Schaaffhausen, "On the Crania of the Most Ancient Races of Man," in *Natural History Review,* 2 (1961), p.151.
11. Carter Blake, On the Cranium of the Most Ancient Races of Man, in *Geologist,* 6 (1862), p. 206.
12. Gustav Schwalbe, *Der Neanderthalschädel* (Bonn: Univeritatäts Buchdruckerei von C. Georgi, 1901), p. 56.

13. Rudolf Virchov, "Untersuchung des Neadertalschädels," in *Verhandle Berliner Ges Anthropologie Ethnologische*, 4 (1872), p. 163.
14. Joseph Pohle, *Lehrbuch der Dogmatik, t.I* (Padeborn: Schöningh, 1908), p. 424.
15. Ernesto Ruffini, *La teoria dell'evoluzione secondo la scienza e la fede* (Rome: Libreria Editrice Vaticana, 1948), p. 150.
16. Pontifical Biblical Commission, "De charactere historico trium priorum capitum Geneseos, Sul carattere storico dei tre primi capitoli della Genesi," in *Acta Apostolicae Sedis*, 1(1909), p. 568.
17. Laurentius Jansens, *Summa Theologica, t.I* (Freiburg: Herder, 1912), p. 673.
18. Berhnard Bartman, *Lehrbuch der Dogmatic, t.I* (Freiburg: Herder, 1911), p. 251.
19. Hubert Junker, *Die biblische Urgeschichte in ihrer Bedeutung als Grundlage der alttestamentlichen Offenbarung* (Bonn: Hanstein, 1932), p. 40.
20. Ed Schomelzer, Heinrich Denzinger, *Enchiridion Symbolorium* (New York: Crossroad Pub Co., 1998), sec. 1943-1953.
21. Pierre Teilhard de Chardin, *The Phenomenon of Man* (New York: Harper Perennial, 1955), p. 154.
22. Johannes Hessen, *Das Kausalprinzip* (Augsburg: Filser, 1958), p. 16.
23. Achille Lienart, "Der Christ und die Entwicklungslehre," in *Stimmen der Zeit*, 142 (1948), p. 84.
24. Ed Schomelzer, Heinrich Denzinger, *Enchiridion Symbolorium* (New York: Crossroad Pub Co., 1998), sec. 2327.
25. John Paul II, "Message to the Pontifical Academy of Science: On Evolution," in *L'Osservatore Romano* 1 (1997), p.18.
26. Michael Ruse, *The Evolution-Creation Struggle* (London: Harvard Univ. Press, 2005), p. 9.
27. Franz Diekamp, *Katolische Dogmatik nach der Grundsätzen des heiligen Thomas, t.I* (Münster: von Dr. Klaudius Jüssen, 1918), p. 105.
28. Peter Morant, *Die Anfänge der Menschheit. Eine Auslegugng der ersten elf Genesis-Kapitel* (Luzern: Röber, 1960), p. 135.
29. Ed Schomelzer, Heinrich Denzinger, *Enchiridion Symbolorium* (New York: Crossroad Pub Co., 1998), sec. 2293-3830.

30. Vittorio Marcozzi, "Poligenesi ed evoluzione nell origini dell' uomo," in *Gregorianum*, 29(1948), p. 343.
31. Michael Schmaus, *Katolische Dogmatik* (Münster: von Dr. Klaudius Jüssen, 1954), p. 408.
32. Karl Rahner, "Theologisches zum Monogenismus," in *Schriften zur Theologie*, 1(1954), p. 318.
33. Stanis³aw Styœ, "Biblijne ujêcie stworzenia œwiata wobec nauki," in *Studia Biblijne*, 19(1959), p. 29.
34. Pierre Teilhard de Chardin, *The Phenomenon of Man* (New York: Harper Perennial, 1955), p. 206.
35. Ed Schomelzer, Heinrich Denzinger, *Enchiridion Symbolorium* (New York: Crossroad Pub Co., 1998), sec. 2327-2328.
36. Charles Boyer, "Les Leçons del'Encyclique Humani generic, in *Gregorianum*, 31(1950), p. 256.
37. George Vandebroek, Leon Renwart, "L'Encyclique 'Humani Generis' et les sciences naturelles," in *Nouvelle Revue Théologique*, 73(1951), p. 349.
38. Leslie C. Aiello, "The Fossil Evidence for Modern Human Origins in Africa: a Revised View," in *American Anthropologist*, 95 (1995), p. 73-96.
39. Christopher B. Stringer, Jean J. Hublin, Bernard Vandermeersch, "The Origins of Anatomically Modern Humans in Western Europe," in Fred Smith, Frank Spencer (eds.), *The Origins of Modern Humans. A World Survey of the Fossil Evidence* (New York: Alan R. Liss, 1984), p. 51-135.
40. Richard Leakey, *The Origin of Humankind* (London: Phoenix, 1995), p. 100.
41. Rebeca L. Cann, Mark Stoneking, Alan C. Wilson, "Mitochondrial DANN and Human Evolution," in *Nature*, 325(1987), p. 31-36.
42. Jacek Tomczyk, "The Origins of *Homo sapiens* In the Light of Different Research methods," in *Human Evolution*, 21 (2006), p. 230-213.
43. Erich Auerbach, "Odysseus' Scar," in *Mimesis: The Representation of Reality in Western Literature*, (Princeton: Princeton Univ. Press, 1968), sec.1.1.
44. E.g. Rene Lavocat, "Reflexions d'un paleontologiste sur l'état originel de l'humanité et le péché original," in *Nouvelle Revue Théologique*, 89 (1967), p. 584.

45. Ed Schomelzer, Heinrich Denzinger, *Enchiridion Symbolorium* (New York: Crossroad Pub Co., 1998), sec. 1968.
46. Henryk Pietras, *Grzech pierworodny* (Kraków: WAM, 1999), p. 50.
47. Raymund Schwager, *Erbsünde und Heilsdrama. Im Kontext von Evolution, Gentechnologie und Apokalyptik* (Münster: Lit-Verlag, 1997), p. 116.

# Can a Christian Believe in Darwin's Evolutionary Theory?

6

SAROJINI HENRY[1]

When Charles Darwin died in April 1882, the British authorities decided to bury him in Westminster Abbey, London. This was certainly an affirmation that Darwin belonged to the nation and to the history of the British Isles. Darwin had indeed made a significant contribution with his theory of evolution producing a wealth of evidence and suggesting a plausible mechanism for the evolution of all biological beings. However, for some of the mourners, there were doubts about the place of burial. Darwin, after all, had demolished the concept of the uniqueness of the human person and also undermined one of the eloquent arguments for the existence of a designer God. The journal *Guardian,* then, reassured its readers that they should not have any "misgivings, lest the sacred pavement of the Abbey should cover a secret enemy of faith." Rather, the honour of the burial should be seen as "a happy trophy of the reconciliation between faith and science."[2]

Charles Darwin was buried in the Westminster Abbey near Isaac Newton and a few yards from the great Evangelist David Livingston. Did Darwin share the orthodox faith of these two leaders? Perhaps he did, as a student at Cambridge, pursuing theological studies. At the time he joined the HMS *Beagle* trip, he held onto his inherited Anglican beliefs. If he were not called as a naturalist on the ship *Beagle,* Darwin might well have become one of the numerous Anglican parson-naturalists who studied God's creation in the English countryside. His experience during the *Beagle* journey not only prevented his entry into the parsonage, but also provided him plenty of opportunities for reflection, radical questioning and deep thinking about life and all its complexities.

Darwin was a changed person when he emerged from the trip on *Beagle.* With his new frame of mind, Darwin began to question many of the historical details in both the Old and New Testaments, questions that are raised by several theologians and philosophers now in the twenty-first century. Darwin added nothing new on that score. Like many contemporary scholars, Darwin also struggled over what constitutes legitimate and sufficient evidence for religious beliefs.

Darwin was not the first naturalist to realize that evolution might have occurred; scholars since the time of the Greek civilization, including his own grandfather Erasmus Darwin, had toyed with the idea of evolution. For a long time, such beliefs remained speculative and confused without evidence and support. Based on a lifetime of careful scientific study and observation, Darwin not only presented a vast amount of evidence for evolution, but also proposed the mechanism of natural selection, which operating on random variation across enormous time spans could result in a tremendous variety of life-forms. Darwin defines natural selection: "The preservation of favourable variations and the rejection of injurious variations I call natural selection. Variations neither useful nor injurious would not be affected by natural selection and would be left a fluctuating element."[3]

Darwin's theory of evolution is often taken as a very close approximation of the way life has evolved on Earth over billions of years. Darwin had indeed provided a scientific explanation, essentially correct, but incomplete with some notable gaps of how evolution actually occurs. Throughout the years he worked on his idea, Darwin was inwardly afraid of alienating his people, his family and the whole British church and society. He did not publish his findings until he was nearly fifty years old. How he worked through these years and why he eventually published his theory make a fascinating story. This is the story of one man's struggle to comprehend a world explained both by religion and by the evolutionary science that bears his name.

Darwin had indeed revolutionized humanity's perception of itself, challenging Christian orthodox thinking which was already fraying at the edges. It is here that Darwin's own religious journey fits in. A short history of Darwin's religious odyssey is given below. It is followed by some pertinent Christian responses to Darwin's theory of evolution over the years. Finally there is the discussion of how some theologians seek to affirm that Darwin's theory is compatible with the Christian idea of God and God's action.

## Darwin's Faith Journey

Charles Darwin was born in a Christian family deeply embedded within an aristocratic Christian culture. His father Robert and grandfather Erasmus Darwin were Anglican and fairly free thinking, while his mother's relatives were strong Unitarians, believing in God but rejecting the doctrines of the Trinity, Incarnation, Fall, Atonement and Revelation. Charles himself was tutored by a Unitarian minister at his mother's wishes. Charles's mother died when he was eight and his sister took over the responsibility of raising him up. Watched over by his elder sisters and maidservants, Charles grew up amidst wealth, comfort and country sports.

In 1825, Charles left for Edinburgh to study medicine with a view to becoming a physician like his father. Edinburgh was the best choice for medical studies at that time, but Charles showed little academic interest in medicine and was a bit shocked by the brutality of medical surgery. After two years,

Charles dropped out of medical studies, although Edinburgh developed in him a passion for science and nature. At this juncture, his father suggested to him the calling of an Anglican clergyman.

On October 15, 1827, Charles was admitted a member of Christ's college in Cambridge. During his three years of theological studies, Charles became more interested in collecting biological specimens; he became a passionate amateur naturalist on the natural theology of William Paley who had argued that the complex structures of living things and the remarkable adaptations of plants and animals required an intelligent designer. At Cambridge, Charles also studied geology with Adam Sedgewick, finding about the ancient age of the Earth and then went with him on a geological excursion in Wales. When he returned, he found to his amazement an invitation to join Captain Fitzgerald as a naturalist on the ship HMS *Beagle*.

On 27th December 1831, Charles Darwin boarded HMS *Beagle* in Plymouth and set out on a journey that lasted nearly five years. Before the trip, Charles was 'a sort of Christian,' namely orthodox in a conventional, rational Anglican kind of way. He was probably not exactly as orthodox as he portrays himself before the *Beagl*e voyage. For Darwin, personal experience of Jesus or the Holy Spirit had been always peripheral. Scripture played a significant part but mainly as a source material for arguments that proved Christian truths. Darwin's Christianity was based more on rational defence of the creeds accepted in the church. The *Beagle* effected a profound change in his way of seeing and understanding reality - both of nature and of God. About Darwin's voyage on the *Beagle*, Nick Spencer wrote: "Just as the *Beagle* gave Darwin material for his theory of evolution but did not witness the formulation of that theory, so the voyage gave him material for the loss of his Christian faith without witnessing that loss."[4]

The years 1837-39 were crucial to Darwin's attitude to Christian scriptures and its doctrines. In his autobiography, he has a short chapter on "Religious beliefs" positioned after a chapter entitled "From my return to England Oct. 2, 1836 to my marriage Jan. 29, 1839." Here, Darwin begins by saying how orthodox he was on the Beagle trip and then described the ways by which he came to doubt Christian faith during this period. It is possible that disbelief was an acceptable trait within the Darwin family, as his father and grandfather were both free-thinking.

Charles Darwin began to doubt "the Old Testament with its manifestly false history of the world, with the tower of Babel, the rainbow as a sign, etc." Darwin also recognized that the Old Testament writers "attribute to God the feelings of a revengeful tyrant," and concluded that it "was no more to be trusted than the sacred books of the Hindus, or the beliefs of any barbarian."[5] As for the New Testament, he wondered if the gospels had been written about the same time because they differ in many important details, and do not possess the accuracies of eye-witnesses. On the miracles in the New Testament, Darwin opined that the more we know of the fixed laws of nature, the more incredible miracles become.

All these ruminations on life gradually led him to doubt the very scriptural details in the Bible. Are the Gospels from eye witnesses? How can the miracles in the New Testament be taken as true in this scientific age? How true is the creation story given in Genesis? In his Autobiography, Darwin had summarized all these observations, "I gradually came to disbelieve in Christianity as a divine revelation."[6]

Spencer also refers to the problem of suffering which was tormenting Darwin ever since he formulated the idea of natural selection. Spencer writes:

> The years of intense speculation after he arrived back from the *Beagle* voyage destabilized the comfortable, Paleyian Christianity of Darwin's youth. And the theory of evolution by natural selection that he formulated during and after this period certainly highlighted the problem of suffering for him in a new and problematic way.[7]

Spencer further points out, "It was no surprise, therefore, that when he first recognized that the natural world was not as ordered, purposive or benign as had been thought, the Christian structure that had towered about these foundations toppled."[8] The final blow for Darwin, however, came when he lost his beloved daughter Annie aged ten, at Easter in 1851. He realized that religion or belief in a loving God offers no real comfort or consolation in times of sorrow; the sense of injustice and the feeling of loss only become overwhelming. Spencer concludes, "Once he had lived through Annie's wretched death, he could not reconcile the reality of suffering ... with his understanding of God."[9]

Darwin had unparalleled powers of observation, and speculation; his method was supremely thoughtful and tactful. It is possible that he understood that his theory at least redeemed his fellow Christians from the religious fastidiousness over the creation story in Genesis and has allowed them to see the creation of the universe in a scientific way. Yet, Darwin could sense a tension in relating Christian faith with his theory of evolution. Nick Spencer reports about Darwin: "He was sure that it was possible to accommodate religious faith with his theory, a view he held right up to the end of his life, telling one correspondent, John Fordyce, in 1879 that, 'it seems to me absurd to doubt that a man may be an ardent Theist & an evolutionist.'"[10]

**Some Responses to Darwin's Theory of Evolution**

The publication of *The Origin of Species* ushered in a new era in the intellectual history of humanity. It produced considerable public excitement and many scholars discussed the book defending or deriding Darwin's ideas. Among those favourable to evolutionary theory in contemporary times are Richard Dawkins and Daniel Dennett. They are both in the ultra-Darwinist camp; by adding a materialistic metaphysics to the science of evolutionary biology, they replace divine purpose and providence with blind and uncaring natural law. By attempting to reduce life to chemistry and evolutionary theory to a purely mechanical process, they tend to make Darwinism fundamentally equivalent to atheism.

For the creationists, there could be no compromise with Darwin's evolutionary theory and they believe that the theory contradicted the biblical view of a six-day creation as divinely dictated in the book of Genesis. Writing on creationists, John Haught argues, "These are predominantly Christian theists who agree with skeptics that Darwinian evolution, if true, would logically rule out the idea of God and a purposeful Universe."[11] It was this opposition to Darwin's theory that set the stage for the creationists to preserve biblical inerrancy and literalism and to eventually claim scientific credibility for the Genesis creation story, thereby placing biblical creation stories alongside evolutionary theory as a competing set of scientific ideas.

Among believing Christians, even those who accept the main trend of Darwinian explanation for the origin of species by natural selection, argue that God's intervention is necessary for the creation of the human soul. According to the Bible, humans were created separately from the rest of creation. Christians tend to assume that humans are different from, indeed higher than animals. Thus humans are unique and not the accidental by-products of blind natural forces. They also bemoan that human existence, hitherto considered sacrosanct, has been brought within the natural law of the natural sciences. To be suddenly removed as a very special child of the Creator and placed in the zoo with all the other animals turned out to be a traumatic experience.

Before Darwin, the best explanation for the ordered and adaptive features of living organisms was that they were designed purposefully by a creator God. Ever since William Paley gave a classic rendition of the argument from design, Christians have been under the assumption that within a static universe, the complex functioning of various parts of the organisms and their harmonious adaptations to their surroundings provide a strong evidence for an intelligent designer. Darwinism, therefore, became a challenge to the idea of intelligent design, because it had offered an automatic, mindless mechanism as an alternative to purposeful design, in order to explain the uncanny good fit between organisms and their environments and each other. Thus the earlier design argument lost much of its appeal when Charles Darwin proposed that the blind process of natural selection acting on random variation could account for the origin of new forms of life.

By the nineteenth century, Christians had understood some of the passages in the Bible as cultural accretions. Thus the controversy was not so much on conformity to the biblical version; rather the issue was that the variations which compose the raw material for evolution are completely accidental and not directed by any divine intelligence. Darwin's views centered on what seemed to be the randomness of natural selection and the appearance of new organisms by chance, meant the exclusion of divine purpose or design in nature. This disinterested manner of natural selection suggests that we live in an impersonal, uncaring world.

Another nagging question for Christian thinkers has to do with theodicy. It is known that evolution by natural selection, with its ruthless struggle for existence involved much agony, aimless wandering, and waste of life. It is believed that since life began on earth, there had been at least five major extinctions events. The most recent, the Cretaceous–Tertiary extinction event, occurred 65 million years ago, marking the elimination of nearly all dinosaur species, which were the dominant animal class of the period. It looks as though a number of species over billions of years have been used only as a means to an end and finally underwent extinction. The question is how to defend a loving, benevolent God, considering the immense suffering caused to creatures of different kinds over millions of years.

Reflecting on this problem of having to justify God in the face of all the pain and suffering that creatures of all kinds had to undergo over the years, John Haught writes:

> How could a powerful and compassionate creator permit all the suffering, aimless wandering, and obscene waste that we behold in surveying the millions of evolution? How could a loving concerned God tolerate the struggle, pain, cruelty brutality, and death that lie beneath the relatively stable and serene surface of nature's present order?[12]

## Theory of Evolution and Christian Theology

Darwinian science is experiencing such a vigorous renewal in the contemporary intellectual world that theologians are wondering if theology ought to think about God in a manner consistent with evolution. Many Christians do not openly reject Darwinian ideas. They often tend to ignore evolutionary theory or remain content by taking the easy way of accepting that evolution is God's way of creating. Some theologians take the trouble to think deeply about evolution, as for example, John Polkinghorne who considers the possibility that specific divine action is hidden in what is called chance in science. Willem B. Drees also refers to D. J. Bartholomew for whom, "chance might really be chance, also from God's perspective; this would not preclude the possibility that God achieves God's purposes through chance processes."[13]

It has already been noted that it is the random way of evolution that is the point of dissent for many people. Theologians are now questioning the above assertion that Darwin's natural selection suggests that we live in an impersonal world. They argue that even if Darwin is right, he has not told the whole story. In this connection, John Haught points out, "There have been considerable refinements in the scientific understanding of evolution since his day, especially in the area of genetics and molecular biology."[14] These two areas have filled in the details about how change occurs, details that Darwin did not know. According to theologians, these two refinements in the Darwinian exposition of evolution are sure proof that Darwin's biology has not done away with all the mysteries of life.

Such an observation has given impetus to many theologians to re-articulate, reformulate and understand theological truths in a more satisfactory way by looking at the relevant knowledge available in the theory of evolution. Theologians are now seeking to find a balanced discussion of the impact of evolution on Christian beliefs in order to understand and appreciate the values at stake. They also seek to transform our theological sensibilities in a way that takes the theory of evolution seriously.

Many theologians are pointing to the concurrence of evolutionary theory with the Christian belief in continuing creation. Christians believe that God not only created the universe in the beginning but also continues to sustain the universe and they point to many biblical verses to prove God's preservation and providence. It looks as though evolutionary theory allows theology to endorse continuing creation more appropriately. In an evolving cosmos, creation is still happening no less in the present than in the beginning. The Big Bang universe continues to unfold and every day is still the dawn of creation.

The process theologians are pointing out the resemblance between process theology and evolutionary biology. Ian Barbour convincingly writes. "Process thought shares with evolutionary biology the assumption of historical continuity, including the continuity of nonhuman and human life."[15] John Haught points to another characteristic namely novelty. He writes, "According to process theology, evolution occurs because God is more interested in adventure than in preserving the status quo."[16]

Apart from these general observations, there are some well-known theologians who have taken up the question seriously and worked out plausible explanations why Christians ought to believe in Darwin's theory. Many theologians have struggled with the problems involved in accommodating evolution to Christian faith and here the expositions of three scholars, namely, Pierre Teilhard de Chardin, Wentzel van Huyssteen and John F. Haught are considered in detail.

### *Teilhardian Perspective*

Pierre Teilhard de Chardin (1881-1955), a paleontologist, philosopher and scholar of extraordinary breadth and originality, tried to reconcile the theory of evolution with Christian faith. Teilhard's scientific studies had already convinced him of the validity of evolution as a suitable paradigm fundamental to the understanding of human existence. In his view, the plausibility as well as the renewal of Christian faith depend upon a sustained encounter with Darwinian ideas. He, therefore, sought to transform theological sensibilities in a way that takes evolution seriously.

While scientists normally consider nature as providing only the raw material for their research, Teilhard affirmed the natural world itself as a source of mystical illumination, and saw God's presence emanating from within the world. The theme of his book, *The Divine Milieu,* is that the natural world is the setting for a vision of the ultimate. In fact, Teilhard's experience of God was always mediated through nature. The evolutionary paradigm greatly modified his understanding of the whole universe, its sacredness and God's involvement with the world.

Teilhard was acutely aware that the materialistic metaphysics, on which is constructed the scientific ideas of many biologists, was not sufficient to incorporate the important features of evolution, particularly that of bringing about a new being or novelty. Rejecting the materialist philosophy with its belief that lifeless, mindless matter alone is real, Teilhard devised a theological metaphysics which allows all of the data of evolution, and especially the fact of emergent novelty to stand out.

Teilhard was influenced by Henri Bergson, who propounded a non-mechanistic portrait of evolution propelled by an inner vital impulse. Using this as a theoretical tool, Teilhard wanted to reconcile evolution with Christian theology, and this led him to envision evolution as directional, meaning that it is oriented towards the human person, and will move toward the Omega Point. In his view, changes in the universe over millions of years has been directional; direction is still going on, no longer in the geosphere, the nonliving layer of the earth, or in the biosphere or life-layer, but in the sphere of human consciousness and thought, namely, the noosphere, and will move toward the Omega Point where all consciousness will converge.

The Omega Point is both the goal toward which we are striving and a supreme consciousness existing independently of time and the laws of matter. Here, Teilhard identifies the Christ of revelation with the omega of evolution. It is with the Cosmic Christ, that the divine purpose to unite all reality will come to fruition. And Teilhard would affirm, "All endeavor cooperates to complete the world in Christ Jesus."[17]

What Teilhard seemed to be looking for is what can be called a metaphysics of the future. According to Chardin, evolution requires that we think of God not as driving or determining events from the past , but as drawing the world toward the future. Teilhard goes on to say that "only a God who is functionally and totally 'Omega' can satisfy us." He asks, "where shall we find such a God? ... And who will at last give evolution its own God.?[18]

Haught refers to Teilhard who "called his proposed alternative a 'metaphysics of *unire*,' that is, a conception of reality to which all things are drawn perpetually to deeper coherence by an ultimate force of attraction, abstractly identified as omega, and conceived of as an essentially future reality."[19] Not surprisingly Teilhard conceives of the world's sacred Alpha as also an Omega beckoning all things towards a transcendent future up ahead.

**Wentzel van Huyssteen' Views**

In his book, *Duet or Duel?: Theology and Science in a Postmodern World*, Wentzel van Huyssteen, professor of Theology and Science at Princeton Theological Seminary, points out, "In fact, the idea of evolution itself has now become a theory with tremendous explanatory force, a theory that explains many otherwise puzzling features of our world in a very elegant way."[20] He concludes that while the process of evolution has shaped our world and our own species, it has also definitely shaped the way we know about the world. His argument is that philosophers, "have long argued that human intelligence can be seen as naturally arising through evolutionary processes," and continues to write:

> The basic assumption of evolutionary epistemology is, therefore, that we humans, like all other living beings, result from evolutionary processes and that, consequently, our mental capacities (our superior intelligence, our ability to construct metaphysical beliefs) are constrained and shaped by the mechanisms of biological evolution.[21]

This means that all our knowledge is grounded in biological evolution. Huyssteen, therefore, argues, "not only are all our different forms of human knowledge, especially scientific knowledge, firmly grounded in biological evolution, but also our claims to religious knowledge."[22]

The conclusion is that our scientific and theological knowledge are not only affected by their social and historical roots but also by their biological origin. This view that evolution, rightly understood, can actually enrich our religious faith considerably, leaves ample scope for humans to develop religious meaning, values and purpose. Thus, evolutionary theory, far from attacking religion, is seen to be positively contributing to our claims to have a meaningful knowledge of God. Therefore, as theologian Aubrey Moore rightly quipped, "Darwinism appeared, and, under the guise of a foe, did the work of a friend."[23]

### John F. Haught's Integration

In his book *God After Darwin,* John F. Haught, professor of Theology at Georgetown University, first examines the question whether theology can make sense of the suffering, wastage, pain and struggle that the story of evolution has placed before us. He appeals to the old notion of divine *kenosis* that is the concept of the self-emptying of the logos implied in Philippians 2:7. In Patristic Christianity, *kenosis* has been successfully employed in Christology. It was the Lutheran theologians in the sixteenth century who realized that the solution to the Christological difficulties lies in the concept of Christ's self-emptying.

Haught himself understood *kenosis* to mean God's withdrawal of his divine power from the world, thereby allowing natural processes in the world to be contingent and free. Haught remarks:

> By ignoring the image of divine humility, it is easy for us to forget that intrinsic to the divine *kenosis* is its authorization of creation's striving for genuine independence, vis-a-vis its creator. Love by its very nature cannot compel, and so any God whose very essence is love should not be expected to overwhelm the world either with a coercively directive 'power' or an annihilating 'presence.' [24]

Haught further claims that divine withdrawal does not necessarily dismiss God's involvement with the world. According to St John 3:16, God indeed loves the world. By divine withdrawal, Haught emphasizes absence and not God's presence. He continues:

> Indeed an infinite love must in some sense 'absent' or 'refrain itself' precisely in order to give the world the "space" in which to become something distinct from the creative love that constitutes it as "other." We should anticipate, therefore, that any universe rooted in an unbounded love would have some features that appear to us as random or undirected.[25]

Haught argues further that it is this humble retreat on the part of God, letting the world to be the world that allows the cosmos to evolve in a relatively autonomous way. Haught concludes:

> So if ultimate reality is essentially self-giving love, and if love in turn entails 'letting the other be,' then, theologically speaking, both the world's original coming into being and its indeterminate Darwinian transformation through time would be completely consonant with the Christian experience of God.[26]

At this stage, Haught introduces the concept of evolutionary theology as an important form of theological engagement with Darwinism. He points out that evolutionary theology discerns in evolution a most illuminating context for theology. In his view, evolutionary theology seeks to show how our new awareness of cosmic and biological evolution can enhance and enrich traditional teaching about God and God's way of acting in the world.

Haught describes the God of evolution as the God of the future. Here Haught along with Teilhard, opts for a metaphysics of the future. He remarks that when we take nature as static, then it has no future of its own. Here he emphasizes the dynamic nature of the universe and, like Teilhard, refers to the notion of novelty emerging. Haught writes, "As It happens, the evolutionary picture of nature passing from 'matter' through life to mind readily allows us to discern in its various past phases a perpetual potency for new being."[27] In the metaphysics of the future, God is experienced as the source of new possibilities and of impingement of the future on the present. Haught claims confidently, "The power of the future is the ultimate metaphysical explanation of evolution."[28]

This is because such a conclusion best accounts for contingency, chaos and novelty. By contingency Haught means a feature that allows for random, accidental or chance occurrences. Haught claims that the prophetic biblical tradition brings the horizon of the futurity into view and provides resonance with evolutionary biology, wherein new life-forms appear over time. He writes:

> Rather than attributing to God a rigid 'plan' for the universe, evolutionary biology prefers to think of God's 'vision' for it. Nature after Darwin is not a design but a promise. God's 'plan,' if we continue to use the term, is not a blueprint but an envisagement of what the cosmos might become.[29]

Haught points out that biblical faith is concerned with what we humans hope for as our ultimate fulfillment. Thus in evolutionary theology, Haught proposes an eschatological understanding of creation, a metaphysics of the future, which better explains both the theology of creation and the science of Darwin's evolutionary theory. Haught concludes that the God of evolution does not design things in advance but shares with all creatures an openness to an indeterminate future in an unfinished universe.

### Notes and References

1. Dr. Sarojini Henry was a former professor of Theology at Tamil Nadu Theological Seminary, Chennai.
2. Kitty Ferguson, *The Fire in the Equations: Science, Religion and Search for God* (London: Bantam Press, 1994), p. 2.
3. Cited in Christopher Southgate, ed., *God, Humanity and the* Cosmos (Harrisburg P. A: Trinity, 1999), p. 140.
4. Nick Spencer, *Darwin and God* (London: SPCK, 2009), p. 23.
5. *Ibid.*, pp. 40-41.
6. *Ibid.*
7. *Ibid.*, p. 118.
8. *Ibid.*, p. 115.
9. *Ibid.*, p. 119.

10. *Ibid.*, p. 83.
11. John Haught, *God after Darwin* (Colorado: Westview Press, 2000), p. 26.
12. *Ibid.*, p. 20.
13. Willem B. Drees, *Religion, Science and Naturalism* (Cambridge: Cambridge University Press, 1996), p. 198. See also D. J. Bartholomew, *God of Chance* (London: SCM Press, 1984).
14. John Haught, *God after Darwin*, p. 82.
15. Ian. G. Barbour, *Religion in an Age of Science* (London: SCM Press, 1990), p. 228.
16. Haught, *God after Darwin*, p. 42.
17. Pierre Teilhard de Chardin, *The Divine Milieu*, trans. Bernard Wall (New York: Harper & Row Publishers, 1960), p. 56.
18. Pierre Teilhard de Chardin, *Christianity and Revolution*, trans. Rene Hague (New York: Harcourt Brace &Co., 1969), p. 240.
19. Haught, *God after Darwin*, p. 84.
20. Wentzel van Huyssteen, *Duet or Duel?: Theology and Science in a Postmodern World* (Harrisburg PA: Trinity, 1998), p. 82.
21. Wentzel van Huyssteen, "Evolution: A Key to Knowledge of God?," in *God for the Twentieth Century*, ed. Russell Stannard (Philadelphia: Templeton Foundation Press), pp. 47-48.
22. *Ibid.*
23. Cited in Arthur Peacock, "The Disguised Friend: Darwinism and Divinity," in *God for the Twentieth Century*, p. 43.
24. John Haught, *God after Darwin*, pp. 111-112.
25. *Ibid.*, p. 112.
26. *Ibid.*
27. *Ibid.*, p. 188.
28. *Ibid.*, p. 90.
29. *Ibid.*, p. 190.

# Science, Religion and Darwin: A Contemporary Appraisal

7

Kuruvilla Pandikattu[1]

## Introduction

Tuesday, November 24, 2009 marked the 150th anniversary of the publication of Charles Darwin's *On the Origin of Species*. All 1,250 copies of the initial print of the book were scooped up by readers eager to see the British naturalist going rogue with his radical new theory of evolution, "By Means of Natural Selection, or the Preservation of Favoured Races in the Struggle for Life,"[2] in the book's full title.

Charles Darwin's *On the Origin of Species* has been called the most important book ever written. How important really is this book? Thomas Henry Huxley ("Darwin's bulldog") proclaimed that "On the *Origin* of Species" was "the most potent instrument for the extension of the realm of knowledge which has come into man's hands since Newton's *Principia*, and lamented to himself: "How extremely stupid not to have thought of that."[3]

The Harvard biologist Ernst Mayr, arguably the greatest evolutionary theorist since Darwin, holds:

"It would be difficult to refute the claim that the Darwinian revolution was the greatest of all intellectual revolutions in the history of mankind." Similarly the Harvard paleontologist and historian of science Stephen Jay Gould called the theory of evolution one of the half dozen most important ideas in the entire history of Western thought.[4]

Introducing the theory of evolution by natural selection, Darwin's book fundamentally altered how scientists look at the natural world, and continues to frame biological research today. Since the day it appeared, the book has been controversial, but today more than ever. That's because by 1859, there had been several books on evolution published in Britain along with the revolutionary scientific work *On the Origin of Species*. "The most famous example being a book that came out in Victorian Britain in 1844 – an anonymous best-seller," says Jim Endersby. It was called *The Vestiges of the Natural History of Creation*.[5]

According to Endersby, professor of the history of science at the University of Sussex and the author of an introduction to a commemorative edition of *On the Origins of Species*,[6] *The Vestiges of the Natural History of Creation* may have captured the popular imagination, but it was lambasted by scientists for its multiple factual errors, and by the clergy for its affront to religious dogma. Darwin's book got a much more positive reception. Further, Endersby affirms: "What really impressed people with Darwin's work was not so much the idea itself, but the book. It was the fact that there was so much detail, so much evidence."[7]

In fact, as soon as the book was published, it was not just scientists who liked the new theory, but also many theologians also. Popular history holds that the church's condemnation of Darwin was immediate and universal. Endersby holds how different the situation actually was. In fact at least some in the Church even tried to collaborate with the work of Darwin. For example, Endersby says Darwin sent a copy of his book to one of the leading members of the Church of England, the Rev. Charles Kingsley. Kingsley wrote back to Darwin: "It's just as noble a conception of God to think that he created animals and plants that then evolved, that were capable of self-development, as it is to think that God has to constantly create new forms and fill in the gaps that he's left in his own creation." Clearly pleased with this comment, Darwin included it in future editions of *On the Origins of Species*.

On Nov. 24, 1859, when the book was published, the historical relationship between religion and science was already changing. As scientists started debating Darwin's ideas about evolution, they were keen to hold the debate in a secular context. "You start seeing people say, 'Well, let's think about this as a scientific question,'" says Jim Secord, the director of the Darwin Correspondence Project at Cambridge University. "That's really what it is. Leave the theology. That will work itself out in some sort of way."

At many instances, the theology does not always work itself out, as evidenced by the strong anti-evolution sentiment in certain religions in the world today. Jim Secord really holds that *On Origin of Species* did not create the rift between science and religion, which appeared right when the rift was opening 150 years ago.

"These debates about science and religion, if anything, have actually increased in the last 10 to 20 years," holds Secord. "And so Darwin is really a big talking point for these kinds of questions. And I think people read Darwin and look to Darwin in some senses as a kind of fault line for these continuing controversies."

In the decades after the 1859 publication, support for Darwin's theory got support from many scientists and grew in all quarters. But Endersby believes that at least some of that support was based on a misunderstanding of Darwin's ideas. He holds that there is no "predetermined endpoint" in the theory of evolution by natural selection.[8]

In this article I hope to focuss on the impact Darwin's theory had on contemporary society, including religion. After exposing the grand idea and the response it has generated in terms of admiration and awe, I look at the relation between science and religion specially among American scientists to study the impact of the theory of evolution on religion. Finally the plea is made for a reasoned and creative response by believers and scientists alike.

### The Grand Idea

In this section we indicate first that the grand idea of evolution is not in fact Darwin's original one. Then we show the grandeur of the human being in Darwin's *Origin*.

### Not Really that New

He wasn't, after all, the first person to suggest that evolution happens, as noted by Olivia Judson, a *The New York Times* columnist.[9] For example, his grandfather, Erasmus Darwin, speculated about the theory of evolution towards the end of the 18th century. Again at the beginning of the 19th, the great French naturalist Jean-Baptiste Lamarck made a strong case for it. Lamarck, however, failed to be generally persuasive because he didn't have a plausible mechanism – he could see that evolution takes place, but he didn't know how, which was provided by the theory of natural selection.

Natural selection is what we normally think of as Darwin's big idea. Yet he wasn't the first to discover that, either. At least two others – a doctor called William Wells, and a writer called Patrick Matthew – discovered it years before Darwin did. Wells described it (admittedly briefly) in 1818, when Darwin was just 9; Matthew did so in 1831, the year that Darwin set off on board HMS Beagle for what became a five-year voyage around the world.[10]

As a matter of fact, it was a few months after returning from this voyage that Darwin first began to consider seriously the possibility of evolution, or the "transmutation of species." At this time he knew nothing of Wells's and Matthew's accounts of natural selection; indeed, both accounts languished in obscurity until after the *Origin* was published.[11]

By 1858, Darwin had spent more than 20 years studying plants and animals and thinking about evolution. He had filled notebook after notebook with his thoughts on how evolution works; he had, in 1844, written a short manuscript on the subject that was to be published in the event of his untimely death; and he had discussed evolution with a few close friends. But he had published nothing on evolution as such. Then, in June of that year, Darwin received a package from a young man named Alfred Russel Wallace containing a brief manuscript in which he outlined the principle of evolution by natural selection.

What happened next is famous in the history of biology. On July 1, 1858, Wallace's manuscript, as well as a couple of short statements on natural selection by Darwin (a segment of the 1844 manuscript, and part of a letter he'd written in 1857), were read at a meeting of the Linnean Society in London. The meeting had been organized by some of Darwin's scientific friends to establish his priority in the discovery.

Of the material presented that night, the manuscript by Wallace is, in some respects, the more impressive: it is clearer and more accessible. Yet it is Darwin who won; it is Darwin who, like a god in a temple, sits in white marble and presides over the main hall at the Natural History Museum in London. The reason is the *Origin*. Without the publication of the *Origin* the following year, the meeting at the Linnean Society could well have passed unnoticed, the Darwin-Wallace statements going the same way as those by Matthew and Wells. Indeed, the meeting had so little impact at the time that, at the end of the year, the president of the Linnean Society said, "The year which has passed has not, indeed, been marked by any of those striking discoveries which at once revolutionize, so to speak, the department of science on which they bear."

And the *Origin* changed everything, notes Judson. Before the *Origin*, the diversity of life could only be catalogued and described; afterwards, it could be explained and understood. Before the *Origin*, species were generally seen as fixed entities, the special creations of a deity; afterwards, they became connected together on a great family tree that stretches back, across billions of years, to the dawn of life. Perhaps most importantly, the *Origin* changed our view of ourselves. It made us as much a part of nature as hummingbirds and bumblebees (or humble-bees, as Darwin called them); we, too, acquired a family tree with a host of remarkable and distinguished ancestors.

The reason the *Origin* was so powerful, compelling and persuasive, the reason Darwin succeeded while his predecessors failed, is that in it he does not just describe how evolution by natural selection works. He presents an enormous body of evidence culled from every field of biology then known.[12]

At the same time, he uses every form of evidence at his disposal: he observes, argues, compares, infers and describes the results of experiments he has read about, or in many cases, personally conducted. For example, one of Darwin's observations is that the inhabitants of islands resemble – but differ subtly from – those of the nearest continents. So: birds and bushes on islands off the coast of South America resemble South American birds and bushes; islands near Africa are populated by recognizably African forms.

He argues that the reason for this is that new islands become colonized by beings from the nearest continents, and that the new inhabitants then begin evolving independently. He then asks: Can animals and plants from the continents get to new islands, especially those that are far out at sea? To investigate this, he conducts experiments to see how long seeds from different plants can remain immersed in saltwater and still begin to grow. In short, he tests his reasoning over and over again.

Again in some respects, he is surprisingly far-seeing. The *Origin* does not just expound natural selection. It contains a wealth of additional ideas and hypotheses, some of which Darwin went on to elaborate in other books. Among them: sexual selection. This is the idea – and it remained controversial until recently – that males in many species are burdened with showy ornaments like enormous tails because the females of their species have, by repeatedly picking the showiest males as their mates, caused them to evolve them that way.

This is not to say that the *Origin* is flawless, or that Darwin was right in every respect. It is not, and he was not. Nor is the book a definitive account of how evolution works. It wasn't even definitive in his lifetime: he published six editions, revising, sometimes heavily, from one to the next.[13] Yet his knowledge of the natural world is so immense, and the scrutiny to which he subjects his ideas is so thorough and scrupulous, that the *Origin* presents a grand new vision of the world. A vision that, as far as possible given the knowledge available at the time, he worked out in every detail. A vision that changed the world forever. [14]

## The Grandeur in this View of Life: The Entangled Bank

An abridged conclusion of *Origin* gives us the grand vision proposed by Darwin.[15]

> During early periods of the earth's history, when the forms of life were probably fewer and simpler, the rate of change was probably slower; and at the first dawn of life, when very few forms of the simplest structure existed, the rate of change may have been slow in an extreme degree. The whole history of the world, as at present known, although of a length quite incomprehensible by us, will hereafter be recognized as a mere fragment of time, compared with the ages which have elapsed since the first creature, the progenitor of innumerable extinct and living descendants, was created.
>
> In the distant future I see open fields for far more important researches. Psychology will be based on a new foundation, that of the necessary acquirement of each mental power and capacity by gradation. Light will be thrown on the origin of man and his history...
>
> It is interesting to contemplate an entangled bank, clothed with many plants of many kinds, with birds singing on the bushes, with various insects flitting about, and with worms crawling through the damp earth, and to reflect that these elaborately constructed forms, so different from each other, and dependent on each other in so complex a manner, have all been produced by laws acting around us.
>
> These laws, taken in the largest sense, being Growth with Reproduction; Inheritance which is almost implied by reproduction; Variability from the indirect and direct action of the external conditions of life, and from use and disuse; a Ratio of Increase so high as to lead to a Struggle for Life, and as a consequence to Natural Selection, entailing

> Divergence of Character and the Extinction of less-improved forms.
>
> Thus, from the war of nature, from famine and death, the most exalted object which we are capable of conceiving, namely, the production of the higher animals, directly follows.
>
> There is grandeur in this view of life, with its several powers, having been originally breathed into a few forms or into one; and that, whilst this planet has gone cycling on according to the fixed law of gravity, from so simple a beginning endless forms most beautiful and most wonderful have been, and are being, evolved.

## Unique Role of Humans

Darwin holds that human beings are, without doubt, descended from less highly organized form and still unique. A brief summary will be sufficient to recall to the reader's mind the more salient points in this work.[16] Many of the views which have been advanced are highly speculative, and some no doubt will prove erroneous; but I have in every case given the reasons which have led me to one view rather than to another.

> It seemed worthwhile to try how far the principle of evolution would throw light on some of the more complex problems in the natural history of man. False facts are highly injurious to the progress of science, for they often endure long; but false views, if supported by some evidence, do little harm, for everyone takes a salutary pleasure in proving their falseness: and when this is done, one path towards error is closed and the road to truth is often at the same time opened.
>
> The main conclusion here arrived at, and now held by many naturalists who are well competent to form a sound judgment, is that man is descended from some less highly organized form. The grounds upon which this conclusion rests will never be shaken, for the close similarity between man and the lower animals in embryonic development, as well as in innumerable points of structure and constitution, both of high and of the most trifling importance, —the rudiments which he retains, and the abnormal reversions to which he is occasionally liable,—are facts which cannot be disputed.

They have long been known, but until recently they told us nothing with respect to the origin of man. Now when viewed by the light of our knowledge of the whole organic world, their meaning is unmistakable. The great principle of evolution stands up clear and firm, when these groups of facts are considered in connection with others... [they] all point in the plainest manner to the conclusion that man is the co-descendant with other mammals of a common progenitor.

We have seen that man incessantly presents individual differences in all parts of his body and in his mental faculties. These differences or variations seem to be induced by the same general causes, and to obey the same laws as with the lower animals. In both cases similar laws of inheritance prevail. Man tends to increase at a greater rate than his means of subsistence; consequently he is occasionally subjected to a severe struggle for existence, and natural selection will have effected whatever lies within its scope...

I am aware that the conclusions arrived at in this work will be denounced by some as highly irreligious; but he who denounces them is bound to shew why it is more irreligious to explain the origin of man as a distinct species by descent from some lower form, through the laws of variation and natural selection, than to explain the birth of the individual through the laws of ordinary reproduction...

The main conclusion arrived at in this work, namely that man is descended from some lowly organized form, will, I regret to think, be highly distasteful to many. But there can hardly be a doubt that we are descended from barbarians. The astonishment which I felt on first seeing a party of Fuegians on a wild and broken shore will never be forgotten by me, for the reflection at once rushed into my mind — such were our ancestors. These men were absolutely naked and bedaubed with paint, their long hair was tangled, their mouths frothed with excitement, and their expression was wild, startled, and distrustful. They possessed hardly any arts, and like wild animals lived on what they could catch; they had no government, and were merciless to every one not of their own small tribe.

He who has seen a savage in his native land will not feel much shame, if forced to acknowledge that the blood of some

> more humble creature flows in his veins. For my own part I would as soon be descended from that heroic little monkey, who braved his dreaded enemy in order to save the life of his keeper, or from that old baboon, who descending from the mountains, carried away in triumph his young comrade from a crowd of astonished dogs— as from a savage who delights to torture his enemies, offers up bloody sacrifices, practices infanticide without remorse, treats his wives like slaves, knows no decency, and is haunted by the grossest superstitions.
>
> Man may be excused for feeling some pride at having risen, though not through his own exertions, to the very summit of the organic scale; and the fact of his having thus risen, instead of having been aboriginally placed there, may give him hope for a still higher destiny in the distant future. But we are not here concerned with hopes or fears, only with the truth as far as our reason permits us to discover it; and I have given the evidence to the best of my ability. We must, however, acknowledge, as it seems to me, that man with all his noble qualities, with sympathy which feels for the most debased, with benevolence which extends not only to other men but to the humblest living creature, with his godlike intellect which has penetrated into the movements and constitution of the solar system—with all these exalted powers—Man still bears in his bodily frame the indelible stamp of his lowly origin.

## 150 Years Later: Awe and Protest

Given the grandeur of the idea, it is not surprising that there is both admiration and panic to the ideas proposed by Darwin even after 150 years.

### Awe and Admiration

Darwin's is the first face we see as we enter National Museum of Natural History at the Smithsonian Institution, from Constitution Avenue, New York: young and pink and beardless; curious, ambitious, and still unaware, when this portrait was painted, of the decisive, divisive role he would play in solving the great mystery of nature and rewriting the biography of humans and even God.[17]

Nearby is a letter in his own hand on fine blue paper. Here are his brown silk scarf, his notebooks, his famous Galapagos mockingbirds, and specimens of tropical plants, plucked and pressed by the seasick young voyager 10,000 miles from home. In another display case, the handwritten tag on the leg of a Hudsonian godwit is dated Jan. 4, 1837. It is signed by the man who collected the shorebird in the Falkland Islands: C. Darwin, Esq.

Charles Darwin's careful, methodical, brilliant little volume was released to a God-anchored London on Nov. 24, 1859. Since then, the work of tens of thousands of lesser investigators has done little to diminish Darwin's achievement, and much to enhance and embellish it. Still, about half of the adults surveyed in Britain and America continue not to accept that humanity arose as a result of billions of years of random, favourable mutations, and thus - as a Tree of Life on the wall of the National Museum of Natural History depicts - we all are cousins to salmonella, Stegosaurus, lemons, leeches and yeast. [18]

Meet One of Your Oldest Relatives, beckons a sign in the Hall of Mammals above a showcase containing a model of Morganucodon oehleri, a shrew-like thing about 10 centimetres long and 210 million years old. "Its DNA was passed on to billions of descendants," the Smithsonian tells us. "Including you." No wonder Darwin wrote to a friend in 1844, early in his meticulous researches, when he realized how his theory would be received, that admitting that species are not immutable "is like confessing a murder." No wonder the great man vomited nearly every day for more than 20 years, expecting to be crushed at any moment by the hammer of what he called "the blindness of preconceived opinions."

No wonder scientists continue to hold him in awe, and museums line their corridors with his portrait, his words, and his wonders. Born on the same day of the same year as Abraham Lincoln, but in much more elegant circumstances, Darwin governed no nation and mustered no army. His 73 years spanned the 19th century from Napoleon to Einstein, and, despite his denigration as the enemy of English religion, he was buried in Westminster Abbey.

"What did Darwin get wrong, 150 years ago?" Allen Abel asked one of his latter-day disciples, a Smithsonian botanist named W. John Kress, who studies the interwoven lives of flowers and hummingbirds on the islands of the Caribbean. The reply was succinct: "Not much at all!"

**Protest and Panic**

Against this wondrous truth, comes a fusillade of confusion in an e-mail headlined "Making a Monkey out of Darwin." It is from Pat Buchanan, the former U. S. Republican presidential candidate, and it would be comical if it were not for the millions of other recipients who might take such spam as truth:

> "For 150 years," Buchanan writes to mark the anniversary, "the fossil record has failed to validate Darwin. Darwin's examples of natural selection . . . have been debunked. That Darwinism has proved `disastrous theory' is indisputable."

But Buchanan has not finished. He goes on: "'Darwin suits my purpose,' Marx wrote. Darwin suited Adolf Hitler's purposes, too. Darwinism is not science. It is faith. Always was."[19]

**American Scientists and Religion**

In the background of Darwinian model of evolution, we study in this section the relation between science and religion. Members of the scientific community are often seen as doubting Thomases, but the reality is more complex. Even Charles Darwin may have made room for God. Today, the overwhelming majority of scientists in the United States accept Darwinian evolution as the basis for understanding how life on Earth developed. But although evolutionary theory is often portrayed as antithetical to religion, it has not destroyed the religious faith of the scientific community.[20]

According to a survey of members of the American Assn. for the Advancement of Science, conducted by the Pew Research Center in May and June 2009, a majority of scientists (51%) say they believe in God or a higher power, while 41% say they do not.

Furthermore, scientists today are no less likely to believe in God than they were almost 100 years ago, when the scientific community was first polled on this issue. In 1914, 11 years before the Scopes "monkey" trial and four decades before the discovery of the structure of DNA, psychologist James Leuba asked 1,000 U.S. scientists about their views on God. He found the scientific community evenly divided, with 42% saying that they believed in a personal God and the same number saying they did not. Scientists have unearthed many important fossils since then, but they are, if anything, more likely to believe in God today.

The scientific community is, however, much less religious than the general public. In Pew surveys, 95% of American adults say they believe in some form of deity or higher power. In fact, the public does not share scientists' certainty about evolution. While 87% of scientists say that life evolved over time due to natural processes, only 32% of the public believes this to be true, according to a different Pew poll earlier this year.

Given that scientists are much less likely than the general public to believe in God, it's not surprising that the percentage who are affiliated with a particular religion is also lower. Nearly half of U.S. scientists say they have no religious affiliation – describing themselves as atheist, agnostic or nothing in particular – compared with 17% of all Americans.

Among scientists there are far fewer Protestants (21%) and Catholics (10%) than in the general public, which is 51% Protestant and 24% Catholic. And while evangelical Protestants make up more than a fourth of the general population (28%), they are only a tiny slice (4%) of the scientific community. One notable exception is Jews, who make up a larger proportion of the scientific community (8%) than the general population (2%).

But the Pew poll found that levels of religious faith among scientists vary depending on their specialty and age. Chemists, for instance, are more likely to believe in God (41%) than those who work in biology and medicine (32%). And younger scientists (ages 18 to 34) are more likely than older ones to believe in God or a higher power.

As for Darwin, his letters indicate that he was probably an agnostic who lost his faith not because his groundbreaking theory was incompatible with religion, but because of his grief after the 1851 death of his favorite child, his 10-year-old daughter, Annie. And even then, he may not have completely rejected the idea of a higher power. The concluding sentence of *Origin of Species* speaks of a "Creator" breathing life "into a few forms or into one." The passage raises at least a little doubt as to how the father of modern evolutionary theory might have responded to the question on belief in Pew's recent survey of scientists.[21]

**Six Reasons for Aversion**

Why, then, do so many Americans not accept the theory of evolution? A 2001 Gallup Poll found that 45 per cent of Americans agree with the statement "God created human beings pretty much in their present form at one time within the last 10,000 years or so," while 37 per cent preferred a blended belief that "Human beings have developed over millions of years from less advanced forms of life, but God guided this process," and a paltry 12 per cent accepted the standard scientific theory that "Human beings have developed over millions of years from less advanced forms of life, but God had no part in this process."

These percentages have remained largely unchanged in subsequent surveys, although most scientists would prefer that the questions were asked without reference to God since the science of evolutionary biology stands or falls on its own whether God directed the process or not, or even if there is a God or not.

As proposed by Michael Shermer, there are at least six reasons that make people resistant to accepting evolution.[22]

1. The Warfare Model of Science and Religion. The belief that there is a war between science and religion where one is right and the other wrong, and that one must choose one over the other.
2. Belief that evolution is a threat to specific religious tenets. Many people attempt to use science to prove certain religious tenets, but when they do not appear to fit, the science is rejected. For example, the attempt

to prove that the Genesis creation story is accurately reflected in the geological fossil record has led many creationists to conclude that the Earth was created within the past 10,000 years, which is in sharp contrast to the geological evidence for a 4.6 billion-year-old Earth.

3. Misunderstanding of evolutionary theory. A significant problem is that most people know so little about the theory. In the 2001 Gallup Poll, for example, a quarter of the people surveyed said they didn't know enough to say whether they accepted evolution or not, and only 34 per cent considered themselves to be "very informed" about the theory. Because evolution is so controversial, public school science teachers typically drop the subject entirely rather than face the discomfort aroused among students and parents.
4. The fear that evolution degrades our humanity. After Copernicus toppled the pedestal of our cosmic centrality, Darwin delivered the coup de grâce by revealing us to be "mere" animals, subject to the same natural laws and historical forces as all other animals.
5. The equation of evolution with ethical nihilism. This sentiment was expressed by the neoconservative social commentator Irving Kristol in 1991: "If there is one indisputable fact about the human condition it is that no community can survive if it is persuaded - or even if it suspects - that its members are leading meaningless lives in a meaningless universe."
6. The fear that evolutionary theory implies we have a fixed human nature. The first five reasons for the resistance to evolutionary theory come almost exclusively from political conservatives. This last reason originates from liberals who fear that the application of evolutionary theory to human thought and action implies that political policy and economic doctrines will fail because the constitution of humanity is stronger than the constitutions of states.

**Plea for Reasoned Response**

All of these fears are baseless, according to Shermer. If one is a theist, it should not matter when God made the universe – 10,000 years ago or 10 billion years ago. The difference of six zeros is meaningless to an omniscient and omnipotent being, and the glory of divine creation cries out for praise regardless of when it happened.

Likewise, it should not matter how God created life, whether it was through a miraculous spoken word or through the natural forces of the universe that He created. The grandeur of God's works commands awe regardless of what processes He used.

As for meanings and morals, it is here where our humanity arises from our biology. We evolved as a social primate species with the tendency of being cooperative and altruistic within our own groups, but competitive and *bellicose* between groups. The purpose of civilization is to help us rise above our hearts of darkness and to accentuate the better angels of our nature.

So Shermer, himself an atheist, urges the believers to embrace science, especially evolutionary theory, for what it has done to reveal the magnificence of the divinity in a depth never dreamed by our ancient ancestors. We have learned a lot in 4,000 years, and that knowledge should never be dreaded or denied. Instead, science should be welcomed by all who cherish human understanding and wisdom.[23]

**Conclusion: You are Here**

Much like Darwin himself aboard the Beagle, Smithsonian botanist named W. John Kress plucks and presses plants on scattered islands and brings them home. He seeks to understand how birds and plants evolved together as they expanded from one island to the next. Every couple of years, he says, he reads *The Origin* over again and marvels at the author anew.

"Darwin was a biological genius," Kress says. "We all yearn to make our own contribution, whether it's the evolution of the birds of the Caribbean, or adding another branch to the Tree of Life."[24] We can very well agree that *The Origin* is not the final word on how living things came to be. The science of genetics had not yet been elaborated to explain how what Darwin called "characters" are passed from parent to child. But even though he scrupulously and nauseously avoided directly referencing human evolution in Origin, the implication was clear. As Gilbert and Sullivan would put it later: "Darwinian man, though well-behaved, at best is only a monkey shaved." Kress adds: "Darwin showed that there is something that connects everything to Homo sapiens. And that is hard for some people to accept."

On the Tree of Life on the wall that begins with animate, primordial slime and ends in a marker that says YOU ARE HERE. "I don't have a problem with that," the botanist smiles.

But with the anniversary of *Origin*, and the new Hall of Human Origins opening in 2010, the Smithsonian has formed a Broader Social Impacts Committee to try to find a way to bridge the crevasse between the two extremes. "Science matters," one of the committee's members, Dr. Connie Bertka, holds. "What science has learned about the world matters, and if someone's religious beliefs are preventing him from engaging the science, that's sad." Bertka is a geologist who studies the nature of carbon deep inside the Earth, and a Unitarian Universalist who lectures at a theological seminary, making her well qualified to lunge at evolution from both the secular and sacred side.

"Everybody wants to try to figure out what Darwin himself believed," Bertka says. "There is a myth that he recanted on his deathbed and declared his belief in God and Christianity. Atheists say he kept quiet about it but he really was an atheist. I think he lost far more sleep agonizing over what the scientific reaction would be than what the religious authorities would think."

"What do you believe?" a reporter asked her. "I think we're unique, but within a framework that relates us to all life on Earth," she replies. "What does it mean to be created 'in God's image?' It means we are co-creators with God. We have capacities that other mammals don't. But whatever this uniqueness is, it is something that evolved."

At the Smithsonian Institution, there's a quotation from Shakespeare's Antony and Cleopatra, the protest of a soothsayer urged to chart the future of the queen. "In nature's infinite book of secrecy," he demurs, "a little I can read."

A century and a half ago, Charles Darwin might have seized the same disclaimer. His hope, he wrote near the end of *The Origin*, was that educated people might "no longer look at an organic being as a savage looks at a ship." And his conclusion was that living things have come to be "not by miraculous acts of creation" and that life had been "originally breathed into a few forms or into one."

Who, if anyone or anything, did the breathing, remains a matter of ferocious dispute, but if there is a middle ground, it is staked out by Connie Bertka "If it's God's stuff to begin with," she says, "it's still God's stuff at the end."[25]

**The Heretic Imperative**

The theory of Evolution has radically altered the way we look at ourselves and the society. But a believer is not obliged to believe or disbelieve in the theory of evolution based on his faith, but depending on her science. Science may come up with better or different theories to replace the current theory of evolution, which is best left to the scientists.

At the same time the challenge confronting modern believers is to be informed by Darwin's theory of evolution critically and creatively and to apply it to other dimensions of religious life: the growth of the idea of god, the origin and development of dogmas, the life experiences of the believing community.[26] Similarly the challenge confronting scientists is to apply the radical evolutionary ideas to science as a discipline. They can utilize Darwinian insights to relativise science, respectfully and reverentially, and be open to religion that too had an evolutionary function.

Can we not have an image of human being that is truly evolving and grand? A self-understanding that is open to the more and still unique? That is the imperative believers and scientists are today confronted with. To choose reasonably and creatively from different possibilities!

## Notes and References

1. Kuruvilla Pandikattu lectures in Philosophy of Science at Jnana Deepa Vidyapeeth, Pune.
2. Charles Darwin, *On the Origin of Species by Means of Natural Selection*, or the *Preservation of Favoured Races in the Struggle for Life* (1st ed.) (London: John Murray, 1859), *http://darwin-online.org.uk/content/frameset?itemID=F373&viewtype=text&pageseq=1, retrieved 2009-01-09.*
3. Thomas Huxley, *Six Lectures to Working Men* "On Our Knowledge of the Causes of the Phenomena of Organic Nature" (Republished in Volume II of his Collected Essays, arwiniana), 1863, *http://aleph0.clarku.edu/huxley/CE2/Phen.html, retrieved 2006-12-15*
4. Michael Shermer. "Religion, evolution can live side by side," Nov 23, 2009, CNN Opinion, *http://www.cnn.com/2009/OPINION/11/23/shermer.why.darwin.matters/.*
5. Joe Palca, "At 150, Darwin's 'Origin' Stirs Even More Debate" National Public Radio, www.npr.org/ templates/ story/ story.php?storyId=120692695, Nov 24, 2009. Retrieved on 12 ecember 2009.
6. Jim Endersby, *On the Origins of Species* (commemorative edition) (Cambridge: Cambridge University Press, 2009).
7. Joe Palca, "At 150, Darwin's 'Origin' Stirs Even More Debate" National Public Radio, *www.npr.org/ templates/ story/story.php?storyId=120692695, Nov 24, 2009. Retrieved on 12 ecember 2009.*
8. Joe Palca, "At 150, Darwin's 'Origin' Stirs Even More Debate," National Public Radio, *http://www.npr.org/templates/story/story.php?storyId=120692695.*
9. Olivia Judson, "Darwinmania!", *The New York Times*, Nov. 25, 2009. *http://opinionator.blogs.nytimes.com/2008/06/17/darwinmania/.*
10. Olivia Judson, "Darwinmania!", *The New York Times*, Nov. 25, 2009. *http://opinionator.blogs.nytimes.com/2008/06/17/darwinmania/.*
11. Judson notes that after the *Origin* appeared, Matthew wrote to a magazine to draw attention to his statements on the subject; he then proceeded to put "Discoverer of the Principle of Natural Selection" on the title pages of his books which annoyed Darwin.
12. He discusses subjects as diverse as pigeon breeding in Ancient Egypt, the rudimentary eyes of cave fish, the nest-building instincts of honeybees, the evolving size of gooseberries (they've

been getting bigger), wingless beetles on the island of Madeira and algae in New Zealand. One moment, he's considering fossil animals like brachiopods (which had hinged shells like clams, but with a different axis of symmetry); the next, he's discussing the accessibility of nectar in clover flowers to different species of bee.

13. In the third edition, which appeared in 1861, he introduced a historical sketch in which he discusses his precursors, including Matthew and Wells.
14. Olivia Judson, "Darwinmania!," *The New York Times*, Nov 25, 2009. *http://opinionator.blogs.nytimes.com/2008/06/17/darwinmania/.* This section is abridged from Judson's article.
15. Charles Darwin, *On the Origin of Species* (Cambridge: Harvard University Press, 1946). (abridged).
16. Charles Darwin, The Descent of Man Vol. II (London: John Murray, 1891) (abridged).
17. Allen Abel, "Charles Darwin still Evokes Awe, Howls of Protest," Canwest News Service, November 21, 2009.
18. Allen Abel, "Charles Darwin still Evokes Awe, Howls of Protest," Canwest News Service, November 21, 2009.
19. Allen Abel, "Charles Darwin still Evokes Awe, Howls of Protest," Canwest News Service, November 21, 2009. Due to lack of space I am not elaborating other instances of panic and protest against Darwinin evolution present today.
20. David Masci "What do scientists think about religion?" *Los Angeles Times*, Nov. 24, 2009 *http://www.latimes.com/news/opinion/la-oe-masci24-2009nov24,0,7022683.story.*
21. David Masci "What do Scientists Think about Religion?" *Los Angeles Times*, Nov. 24, 2009 *http://www.latimes.com/news/*opinion/la-oe-masci24-2009, Nov. 24,0,7022683 story. This section is adapted from this article. David Masci is a senior researcher at the Pew Forum.
22. Michael Shermer, "Religion, Evolution can Live Side by Side," Nov. 23, 2009, CNN Opinion, *http://www.cnn.com/2009/OPINION/11/23/shermer.why.darwin.matters/.*
23. Michael Shermer, "Religion, Evolution can Live Side by Side," Nov. 23, 2009, CNN Opinion, *http://www.cnn.com/2009/OPINION/11/23/shermer.why.darwin.matters/.*

24. Allen Abel, "Charles Darwin still Evckes Awe, Howls of Protest," Canwest News Service, November 21, 2009.
25. Allen Abel, "Charles Darwin still Evokes Awe, Howls of Protest," Canwest News Service, November 21, 2009.
26. Kuruvilla Pandikattu, *The Bliss of Being Human: Science and Religion for Self-Realization* (Pune: Jnanam, 2004), pp. 1-29.

# Christian Responses to Evolution: Evolving Historical Dynamics

# 8

S. JOHN BRITTO[1]

## Introduction

The creation–evolution controversy (also termed the creation vs. evolution debate or the origins debate) is a recurring cultural, political, and theological dispute about the origins of the Earth, humanity, life, and the universe.[2] It is a dispute between those who profess religious belief and thus support a creationist view, as opposed to those who accept evolution, as supported by biological sciences. The dispute in fact involves not only the field of evolutionary biology, but also those of geology, paleontology, thermodynamics, nuclear physics and cosmology.[3] Within the scientific community and academia the level of support for evolution is essentially universal,[4] while support for biblically-literal accounts or other creationist alternatives is very small among scientists, and virtually nonexistent among those in the relevant fields.[5] The debate is sometimes portrayed as being between science and religion.

However, today, for many religious denominations, biological evolution has produced the diversity of living things over billions of years. Many have issued statements observing that theory of evolution and the tenets of their faiths are compatible. Scientists and theologians have written eloquently about their awe and wonder at the history of the universe and of life on this planet, explaining that they see no conflict between their faith in God and the evidence for evolution. Religious denominations that do not accept the occurrence of evolution tend to be those that believe in strictly literal interpretations of religious texts.

**History of the Controversy in Brief**

The creation-evolution controversy originated from Europe and North America in the late 18th century when discoveries in geology led to various theories of an ancient earth, and fossils showing past extinctions prompted early ideas of evolution, notably Lamarckism. In England these ideas of continuing change were seen as a threat to the fixed social order, and were harshly repressed.[6] Conditions eased, and in 1844 the controversial *Vestiges* popularised transmutation of species. The scientific establishment dismissed it with derision and the Church of England reacted with fury, but many Unitarians, Quakers and Baptists opposed to the privileges of the Established church and supported its ideas of God acting through laws.[7]

Publication of Charles Darwin's *On the Origin of Species by Means of Natural Selection* in 1859 brought scientific credibility to evolution, thus making it a respectable field of study.[8] There was deep interest in the study of religious implications of Darwin's book, but the Church of England's attention was largely diverted by theological controversy over higher criticism set out in *Essays and Reviews* by liberal Christian authors, some of whom expressed support for Darwin, as did many nonconformists. However, many Christians were opposed to the idea and even some of Darwin's close friends and supporters including Charles Lyell and Asa Gray could not accept some of his ideas.[9] Thomas Huxley, who strongly promoted Darwin's ideas while campaigning to end the dominance of science by the clergy, coined the term agnostic to describe his position that God's existence is unknowable, and Darwin also concurred with this position.[10] Though evolution was never condemned by the church, initially the seemingly conservative Catholic leadership in Rome held back but gradually adopted a similar position.[11]

**Theistic Evolution**

Theistic evolution is the general view that, instead of faith being in opposition to biological evolution, some or all classical religious teachings about God and creation are compatible with some or all of modern scientific theory, including, specifically, evolution. It generally views evolution as a tool used by a creator God, who is both the first cause and immanent sustainer/upholder of the universe; it is therefore well accepted by people of strong theistic (as opposed to deistic) convictions. Theistic evolution can synthesize with the day-age interpretation of the Genesis creation myth; however most adherents consider that the first chapters of Genesis should not be interpreted as a "literal" description, but rather as a literary framework or allegory. Theistic evolutionists have frequently been prominent in opposing creationism (including intelligent design).

**Deism**

Deism is belief in a God or first cause based on reason, rather than on faith or revelation. Most deists believe that God does not interfere with the world or create miracles. Some deists believe that a Divine Creator initiated a universe in which evolution occurred, by designing the system and the natural laws, although many deists believe that God also created life itself, before allowing it to be subject to evolution. They find it to be undignified and unwieldy for a deity to make constant adjustments rather than letting evolution elegantly adapt organisms to changing environments. Other deists take the stronger position that God ceased to exist after setting in motion the laws of the universe.

## Naturalistic evolution

Naturalistic evolution is the position of acceptance of biological evolution and of metaphysical naturalism (and thus rejection of theism and theistic evolution). A prominent proponent of this viewpoint is British evolutionary biologist Richard Dawkins.[12]

## Progressive Creationism

Progressive Creationists agree with the great majority of scientists that the astronomical and geological data convincingly show the earth to be several billion years old. While they find in the biblical creation story records several supernatural creative acts by God, most progressive creationists believe the "day/age interpretation" to be the best.

## Evolutionary Creationism

Evolutionary creationism (also referred to by its advocates as evolutionary creation[13] states that the Creator God uses evolution to bring about his plan. Eugenie Scott states in *Evolution Vs. Creationism* that it is a type of evolution rather than creationism, despite its name, and that it is "hardly distinguishable from Theistic Evolution."[14] Scott, citing personal communication with prominent evolutionary creationist Denis Lamoureux, states that "the differences between EC [Evolutionary Creationism] and theistic evolution lie not in science but in theology, with EC being held by more conservative (Evangelical) Christians, who view God as being more actively involved in evolution than do most theistic evolutionists."[15]

## Evolutionary Biologists who were also Theists

Although evolutionary biologists have often been agnostics (most notably Thomas Huxley and Charles Darwin) or atheists (most notably Richard Dawkins), from the outset many have had a belief in some form of theism. These have included Alfred Russel Wallace (1823–1913), who in a joint paper with Charles Darwin in 1858, proposed the theory of evolution by natural selection. Wallace, in his later years, was effectively a deist who believed that "the unseen universe of Spirit" had interceded to create life as well as consciousness in animals and (separately) in humans. Darwin had a longstanding close friendship with the American botanist Asa Gray who was a leading supporter of Darwin's theory, and a devout Presbyterian.[16] Gray wrote a series of essays on the relationship of natural selection to religious belief and natural theology, and supported the views of theologians who said that design through evolution was inherent in all forms of life.[17] Darwin had Gray and Charles Kingsley in mind when he wrote that "It seems to me absurd to doubt that a man may be an ardent theist & an evolutionist."[18]

An early example of this kind of approach came from computing pioneer Charles Babbage who published his unofficial Ninth Bridgewater Treatise in 1837, putting forward the thesis that God had the omnipotence and foresight to create as a divine legislator, making laws (or programs) which then produced species at the appropriate times, rather than continually interfering with ad hoc miracles each time a new species was required.

Pierre Teilhard de Chardin (1881–1955) was a noted geologist and paleontologist as well as a Jesuit Priest who wrote extensively on the subject of incorporating evolution into a new understanding of Christianity.[19] Initially suppressed by the Roman Catholic Church, his theological work has had considerable influence and is widely taught in Catholic and most mainline Protestant seminaries.

Both Ronald Fisher (1890–1962) and Theodosius Dobzhansky (1900–1975), were Christians and architects of the modern evolutionary synthesis. Dobzhansky,[20] a Russian Orthodox, wrote a famous 1973 essay, titled, "Nothing in Biology Makes Sense Except in the Light of Evolution," espousing evolutionary creationism.

### The Evolving Christian Response

Evolution contradicts a literalistic interpretation of Genesis; however, according to Roman Catholicism and most contemporary Protestant Churches, biblical literalism in the creation account is not mandatory. Christians have considered allegorical interpretations of Genesis since long before the development of Darwin's theory of evolution, or Hutton's principle of uniformitarianism. A notable example is St. Augustine (4th century), who, on theological grounds, argued that everything in the universe was created by God in the same instant, and not in six days as a plain reading of Genesis would require.[21] Modern theologians such as Meredith G. Kline and Henri Blocher have advocated what has become known as the literary framework interpretation of the days of Genesis.

**Contemporary Christian Denominations**

Many Christian denominations support or accept theistic evolution. For example, on 12 February 2006, the 197th anniversary of Charles Darwin's birth was commemorated by "Evolution Sunday" where the message that followers of Christ do not have to choose between biblical stories of creation and evolution was taught in classes and sermons at many Methodist, Lutheran, Episcopalian, Presbyterian, Unitarian, Congregationalist, United Church of Christ, Baptist and Community Churches.[22]

**Anglicanism**

Anglicans believe that the Bible "contains all things necessary to salvation," nonetheless "science and Christian theology can complement one another in the quest for truth and understanding." Anglicans view "Big Bang cosmology" as being "in tune with both the concepts of creation out of nothing and continuous creation." The United Methodist Church affirms a Creator God and supports the scientific study of creation.

**Catholic Church and Evolution**

Since the publication of Charles Darwin's *On the Origin of Species* in 1859, the attitude of the Catholic Church on the theory of evolution has slowly been refined. For about 100 years, there was no authoritative pronouncement on the subject. By 1950, Pope Pius XII agreed to the academic freedom to study the scientific implications of evolution, so long as Catholic dogma is not violated;[23] since the mid 20th century, its attitude has been one of great acceptance, with Jesuit scientists, Catholic scholars and many high-ranking clerics rejecting both literal biblical creationism and intelligent design.

Today, the Church's unofficial position is a fairly non-specific example of theistic evolution, stating that faith and scientific findings regarding human evolution are not in conflict, though humans are regarded as a special creation, and that the existence of God is required to explain both monogenism and the spiritual component of human origins. No infallible declarations by the Pope or an Ecumenical Council have been made.

Catholic concern about evolution has always been very largely concerned with the implications of evolutionary theory for the origin of the human species; even by 1859, the Church did not insist on a literal reading of the Book of Genesis which had long been undermined by developments in geology and other fields. No high-level Church pronouncement has ever attacked head-on the theory of evolution as applied to non-human species.[24] The early Church Fathers taught creationism—the debate being over if God created the world in six days, as Clement of Alexandria taught,[25] or if God created the world in a single moment as Augustine taught,[26] and a literal interpretation of Genesis was normally taken for granted in the Middle Ages and later, until questioned by science. However modern literal Creationism has had little support among the higher levels of the Church.

The Catholic Church delayed official pronouncements on Darwin's Origin of Species for many decades. While many hostile comments were made by local clergy, *Origin of Species* was never placed on the Index *Librorum Prohibitorum;*[27] in contrast, Henri Bergson's non-Darwinian *Creative Evolution* (1907), was on the Index from 1948 until it was abolished in 1966.[28]

The first notable statement after Darwin published his theory appeared in 1860 from a council of the German bishops, who pronounced: Our first parents were formed immediately by God. Therefore we declare that the opinion of those who do not fear to assert that this human being, man as regards his body, emerged finally from the spontaneous continuous change of imperfect nature to the more perfect, is clearly opposed to Sacred Scripture and to the Faith.[29]

No Vatican response was made to this, which implied agreement.[35] In the following decades, a consistently and aggressively anti-evolution position was taken by the influential Jesuit periodical *La Civiltà Cattolica* which, though unofficial, was generally believed to have accurate information about the views and actions of the Vatican authorities.[30]

In 1868, the Blessed John Henry Newman corresponded with a fellow priest regarding Darwin's theory and made the following comments:

> As to the Divine Design, is it not an instance of incomprehensibly and infinitely marvelous Wisdom and Design to have given certain laws to matter millions of ages ago, which have surely and precisely worked out, in the long course of those ages, those effects which He from the first proposed. Mr. Darwin's theory need not then to be atheistical, be it true or not; it may simply be suggesting a larger idea of Divine Prescience and Skill. Perhaps your friend has got a surer clue to guide him than I have, who have never studied the question, and I do not [see] that 'the accidental evolution of organic beings is inconsistent with divine design – It is accidental to us, not to God.[37]

In 1894 a letter was received by the Holy Office, asking for confirmation of the Church's position on a theological book of generally Darwinist cast by a French Dominican theologian, Fr. Lèroy's *L'évolution restreinte aux espèces organiques.*, par le père Léroy dominicain.

To reconcile general evolutionary theory with the origin of the human species, with a soul, the concept of "special transformism" was developed, according to which the first humans had evolved by Darwinist processes, up to the point where a soul was added by God to "pre-existent and living matter" (in the words of Pius XII's *Humani Generis*) to form the first fully human individuals; this would normally be considered to be at the point of conception.[31] Léroy's book endorsed this concept; what led to its rejection by the Congregation appears to have been his view that the human species was able to evolve without divine intervention to a fully human state, but lacking only a soul. The following year, 1896, John Augustine Zahm, a well-known American Holy Cross priest published Evolution and Dogma, arguing that Church teaching, the Bible, and evolution did not conflict.[32] By 1898 it had been placed on the Index and Zahm forced to recant his views.

## Pope Pius IX

*The Origin of Species* was published in 1859, during the papacy of Pope Pius IX, during the First Vatican Council in 1869-70. The council has a section on "Faith and Reason" that includes the following on science and faith:

> Hence all faithful Christians are forbidden to defend as the legitimate conclusions of science those opinions which are known to be contrary to the doctrine of faith, particularly if they have been condemned by the Church; and furthermore they are absolutely bound to hold them to be errors which wear the deceptive appearance of truth. Not only can faith and reason never be at odds with one another but they mutually support each other, for on the one hand right reason established the foundations of the faith and, illuminated by its light, develops the science of divine things; on the other hand, faith delivers reason from errors and protects it and furnishes it with knowledge of many kinds. (Vatican Council I)

## Popes Leo XIII and Pius X

*Providentissimus Deus* (On the Study of Holy Scripture) was an encyclical issued by Pope Leo XIII on 18 November 1893 on the interpretation of Scripture. Leo stressed the unstable and changing nature of scientific theory, and criticized the "thirst for novelty and the unrestrained freedom of thought" of the age, but accepted that the apparent literal sense of the Bible might not always be correct. The Pontifical Biblical Commission issued a decree ratified by Pope Pius X on June 30, 1909 that stated that the literal historical meaning of the first chapters of Genesis could not be doubted in regard to "the creation of all things by God at the beginning of time; the special creation of man; the formation of the first woman from the first man; the unity of the human race...." As in 1860, "special creation" was only referred to in respect of the human species.[33]

### Pope Pius XII

Pope Pius XII's encyclical of 1950, *Humani Generis*, was the first encyclical to specifically refer to evolution, and took up a neutral position, again concentrating on human evolution:

*Pope Pius XII's teaching can be summarized as follows:*

- The question of the origin of man's body from pre-existing and living matter is a legitimate matter of inquiry for natural science. Catholics are free to form their own opinions, but they should do so cautiously; they should not confuse fact with conjecture, and they should respect the Church's right to define matters touching on Revelation.
- Catholics must believe, however, that the human soul was created immediately by God. Since the soul is a spiritual substance it is not brought into being through transformation of matter, but directly by God, whence the special uniqueness of each person.
- All men have descended from an individual, Adam, who has transmitted original sin to all mankind. Catholics may not, therefore, believe in "polygenism," the scientific hypothesis that mankind descended from a group of original humans (that there were many Adams and Eves).

### Pope John Paul II

In 1996, Pope John Paul II,[34] said "...new findings lead us toward the recognition of evolution as more than a hypothesis." On October 22, 1996, in his address to the Pontifical Academy of Sciences, Pope John Paul II updated the Church's position to accept evolution of the human body:

"In his encyclical *Humani Generis* (1950), my predecessor Pius XII has already affirmed that there is no conflict between evolution and the doctrine of the faith regarding man and his vocation, provided that we do not lose sight of certain fixed points.... Today, more than a half-century after the appearance of that encyclical, some new findings lead us toward the recognition of evolution as more than a hypothesis. In fact it is remarkable that this theory has had progressively greater influence on the spirit of researchers, following a series of discoveries in different scholarly disciplines. The convergence in the results of these independent studies - which was neither planned nor sought - constitutes in itself a significant argument in favor of the theory."[35] In the same address, Pope John Paul II rejected any theory of evolution that provides a materialistic explanation for the human soul.

**Pope Benedict XVI and Today**

A five-day conference held in March 2009 by the Pontifical University in Rome, marking the 150th anniversary of the publication of the *Origin of Species*, generally confirmed the lack of conflict between evolutionary theory and Catholic theology, and the rejection of Intelligent Design by Catholic scholars.[36] The Church has deferred to scientists on matters such as the age of the earth and the authenticity of the fossil record. Papal pronouncements, along with commentaries by cardinals, have accepted the findings of scientists on the gradual appearance of life. In fact, the International Theological Commission in a July 2004 statement endorsed by Cardinal Ratzinger, then president of the Commission and head of the Congregation for the Doctrine of the Faith, now Pope Benedict XVI, includes this: According to the widely accepted scientific account, the universe erupted 15 billion years ago in an explosion called the 'Big Bang' and has been expanding and cooling ever since. Later there gradually emerged the conditions necessary for the formation of atoms, still later the condensation of galaxies and stars, and about 10 billion years later the formation of planets. In our own solar system and on earth (formed about 4.5 billion years ago), the conditions have been favorable to the emergence of life. While there is little consensus among scientists about how the origin of this first microscopic life is to be explained, there is general agreement among them that the first organism dwelt on this planet about 3.5 - 4 billion years ago. Since it has been demonstrated that all living organisms on earth are genetically related, it is virtually certain that all living organisms have descended from this first organism. Converging evidence from many studies in the physical and biological sciences furnishes mounting support for some theory of evolution to account for the development and diversification of life on earth, while controversy continues over the pace and mechanisms of evolution.[37]

In a commentary on Genesis authored by Cardinal Ratzinger, titled, "In the Beginning..." Benedict XVI spoke of "the inner unity of creation and evolution and of faith and reason" and that these two realms of knowledge are complementary, not contradictory. .... The story of the dust of the earth and the breath of God, which we just heard, does not in fact explain how human persons come to be but rather what they are. It explains their inmost origin and casts light on the project that they are. And, vice versa, the theory of evolution seeks to understand and describe biological developments. But in so doing it cannot explain where the 'project' of human persons comes from, nor their inner origin, nor their particular nature. To that extent we are faced here with two complementary – rather than mutually exclusive – realities."

On September 2–3, 2006 at Castel Gandolfo, Pope Benedict XVI conducted a seminar examining the theory of evolution and its impact on Catholicism's teaching of Creation. The essays presented by his former students, including natural scientists and theologians, were published in 2007 under the title *Creation and Evolution* (in German, *Schöpfung und Evolution*). In Pope Benedict's own contribution, he states that "the question is not to either make a decision for a creationism that fundamentally excludes science, or for an evolutionary theory that covers over its own gaps and does not want to see the questions that reach beyond the methodological possibilities of natural science," and that "I find it important to underline that the theory of evolution implies questions that must be assigned to philosophy and which themselves lead beyond the realms of science."

## Conclusion

A Christian's view of science is highly dependent on whether one believes that this universe created by God is for the growth of the human spirit through experience and discoveries, or for the random amusement of God at the expense of human suffering and imperfections. We should believe that God is love, human suffering has purpose, and knowledge supports our spiritual growth. Then, Christianity is for science conducted with the inspiration offered by the Holy Spirit and the faith that all knowledge will converge to God's truth when complete. We know that God's will is to help us understand His patterns of creation. Our inability to grasp His ways is a result of our rational arrogance as opposed to the Creator's deceptions. In this context, the Theory of Evolution as formulated by Charles Darwin is good science but incomplete science. To understand why the science is incomplete and why the incompleteness has led to philosophical differences between scientists with faith and without faith, we must carefully separate the scientific evidence from scientific theory. Further, we must question the degree of credibility for different pieces of evidence and examine the different conceptual ways in which God's pattern of creation can be most accurately described. Our goal by this means is to figure out the real issues in the evolution vs. creationism debate and why Christians have been so unable to use the incomplete knowledge acquired through evolution science to further their spiritual understanding about the work of God.

### *Notes and References*

1. Dr. S. John Brito was a former professor of Biotechnology at St. Joseph's College, Trichy.
2. Kent Hovind, *Creation Science Evangelism, http://www.drdino.com/articles.php?spec=67, retrieved on 17.01.2007.*
3. Mark Isaak, *An Index to Creationist Claims,* (Talkorigins Archive, 2006).
4. Myers 2006; NSTA 2007; IAP 2006; AAAS 2006; and Pinholster 2006; Ruling, Kitzmiller v. Dover, pp. 83.

5. Larson 2004, p. 258 "Virtually no secular scientists accepted the doctrines of creation science; but that did not deter creation scientists from advancing scientific arguments for their position." See also Martz & McDaniel 1987, p. 23, a Newsweek article which states "By one count there are some 700 scientists (out of a total of 480,000 U.S. earth and life scientists) who give credence to creation-science, the general theory that complex life forms did not evolve but appeared 'abruptly'."
6. Adrain Desmond and James Moore, *Darwin* (London: Michael Joseph, Penguin Group, 1991), pp. 34–35
7. See John van Wyhe, *Charles Darwin: Gentleman Naturalist: A Biographical Sketch*, 2006. *http://darwin-online.org.uk/darwin.html, retrieved on 24.01.2007.*
8. John van Wyhe, 2006.
9. *Evolution Dialogues: Science, Ethics and Religion Study Guide*, *http://darwin-online.org.uk/darwin.html,* retrieved on 24.01.2007.
10. Larry Witham A., "From Broadway to Biophilia," in Kindle (ed.), *Where Darwin Meets the Bible: Creationists and Evolutionists in America* (Oxford: Oxford University Press, 2002).
11. Ian G. Barbour, *Religion and Science: Historical and Contemporary Issues*, (Harper: SanFrancisco, 1997), pp. 58, 65.
12. Richard Dawkins, *River Out of Eden* (Basic Books: 1995); Richard Dawkins, "Is Science a Religion?", *Humanist, http://www.thehumanist.org/humanist/articles/dawkins.html, retrieved 30.01.2007.*
13. Denis Lamoureux 2008 Evolutionary Creation: A Christian Approach to Evolution
14. Eugenie Scott and Niles Eldredge, *Evolution Vs. Creationism*, Antievolution And Creationism In The United States". *Annual Review of Anthropology* 26 (1): 263–289. doi:10.1146/annurev.anthro.26.1.263.
15. *Ibid.*
16. "Historical Resources". Darwin Correspondence Project. 2009. *http://www.darwinproject.ac.uk/religion-historical-resources.* Retrieved 2009-12-14.
17. "Essays & reviews by Asa Gray". Darwin Correspondence Project. *http://www.darwinproject.ac.uk/* essays-reviews-by-asa-gray. Retrieved on 14.12. 2009. Asa Gray (January 15, 1874).

"Essay: Evolution & theology". *Darwin Correspondence Project*. The Nation. *http://www.darwinproject.ac.uk/*gray-essay-evolution-theology. Retrieved on 14.12.2009.

18. "Letter 12041 – Darwin, C. R. to Fordyce, John, 7 May 1879". Darwin Correspondence Project. *http://www.darwinproject.ac.uk/ entry*-12041. Retrieved on 14.12.2009.
19. Pierre Teilhard de Chardin *Le Milieu Divin (Tome 4: Essai de vie intérieure)*, Seuil (1 January 1998).
20. Theodosius Dobzhansky, "Nothing in Biology Makes Sense Except in the Light of Evolution", *American Biology Teacher* (National Association of Biology Teachers) 35: (1973), 125–129, *http://www.2think.org/dobzhansky.shtml*, retrieved 2007-01-14.
21. Davis A. Young, "The Contemporary Relevance of Augustine's View of Creation," *Perspectives on Science and Christian Faith* (40:1).
22. Churches urged to challenge Intelligent Design -20/02/06
23. *Humani Generis, http://en.wikipedia.org/wiki/Humani_Generis# Evolutionism*
24. Harrison, especially Conclusion section 2 Harrison, Brian W., "Early Vatican Responses to Evolutionist Theology," *Living Tradition, Organ of the Roman Theological Forum*, May 2001.
25. Clement of Alexandria, *Stromata* Book VI, "For the creation of the world was concluded in six days" *http://www.newadvent.org/ fathers/02106.htm*
26. St. Augustine on Creation, Wikipedia http: / / en.wikipedia.org/ wiki/ Augustine_of_Hippo#Creation
27. Rafael Martinez, professor of the philosophy of science at the Santa Croce Pontifical University in Rome, in a speech reported on Catholic Ireland, net Accessed on May 26, 2009.
28. 1948 *Index* listing - for some reason the date of publication is given as 1914 not 1907
29. Quoted in Harrison
30. *See* Harrison
31. Artigas, 2,5, Artigas, Mariano; Glick, Thomas F., Martínez, Rafael A.; *Negotiating Darwin: the Vatican Confronts Evolution, 1877-1902* (JHU Press, 2006).

32. John Henry Newman, Letter to J. Walker of Scarborough, May 22, 1868, *The Letters and Diaries of John Henry Newman* (Oxford: Clarendon Press, 1973).
33. Harrison, Conclusion section 4.
34. John Paul II, Message to the Pontifical Academy of Sciences on Evolution, delivered on 22.10.1996.
35. *Ibid.*
36. Richard Owen report, *London Times* Online, accessed May 26, 2009
37. *Communion and Stewardship: Human Persons Created in the Image of God*, plenary sessions held in Rome 2000-2002, published July 2004.

# 9

# Creation in Evolution

FRANCIS P. XAVIER[1]

## Introduction

More than ever the question of 'Creation and Evolution' is much discussed now. Very often, it is discussed in a mutually exclusive sense: either creation or evolution and vice versa. In the West, it is so debated as to which theory is to be taught in the school with respect to the origin of the universe: Whether God created the universe, or, whether everything in the universe evolves (automatically / depending on 'selection rule') from lower beings. Option for the creation theory is based on the teaching of the Bible (that is, of theology) combined with the tradition of the Church and evolution is based on scientific claims. What is lacking here is a holistic view about the reality. If one can understand that both theology (religion) and science seek after truth (which is one reality), it is not difficult to see that often they are complementary in serving human beings to comprehend reality as it is. Often what science cannot believe and what faith cannot reason out culminate as a challenge to the human understanding of reality. Thus the human being becomes the integrating entity where religion and science converge and find their ultimate meaning regarding reality.

If the human being were to stand on the shores of the sea of wisdom - He/she is approached by the waves of reason originating from science as well as by waves of faith originating from religion. The key to understanding the contradiction between creation and evolution lies in accepting the basic and underlying principle, namely, God is the basic origin of reality (organic or inorganic). The question is: how does life come into the world? Whether God is at work at every emergence of higher and complex life?, (creationism) or, whether there is a built-in mechanism already in inorganic elements that in course of time explodes into life (evolution)? Even if we accept that God created the universe, the question still remains whether he created out of nothing (*creatio ex nihilo*) or he sustains the world by continual creation (*creatio continua*). It also depends on how one views the reality. One way of looking at the reality is that creation is the starting point and the continual process is the evolution. As the encyclical *Fides et Ratio* (Faith and Reason) indicates in the very beginning, faith and reason are the two wings that elevate one's spirit to reflect on reality (truth). We need a discerning mind in order to reason out and accept the theory of evolution and an understanding heart to believe that God is the origin of every reality in whom everything exists, moves and has its being as Paul would put it (Acts 17:28). After considering the various theories on either side, we shall reach at a synthesis where evolution-theory and creation-faith converge into 'creation in evolution.'

## Concept of Evolution and Creation

Evolution (from the Latin word *evolvere*) means 'to develop into something.' It is not simply just a change but development into ever complex substance leading to formation of life. In biology, evolution implies the development of plants and animals from lower basic life forms or elements. In our context it is the development of life that has the ability to become a human life (and even beyond human life, that is, after physical evolution, intellectual evolution and spiritual evolution.[2] It is understood that there was some original substance to develop into complex being. Here the time element is very important for the development of material substance into being (and further into life).

Many scientists believe that in the giant laboratory of the earth (over 4 billion years ago) elements of carbon, hydrogen, oxygen and nitrogen have combined to form complex molecules. In the process perhaps a particular combination might have triggered off the most intriguing and fascinating process called 'life.' The material basis could be a polymer, called protein, which got synthesized from simple chemical compounds like methane, ammonia and carbon dioxide. The life thus began, got further evolved through the ages till it became 'human.' The polymer could be a few billion years old but human beings are the new comers in the universe (about 1,00,000 years).[3]

On the other hand, creation means to bring out something out of nothing. Here it means the whole universe has been brought out into existence out of nothing. Here 'time' also is created - in other words 'time' began with the act of creation.[4] So time has had a beginning but it also, so to say, evolves into and merges with eternity.

In a neutral sense, creation would mean the dependent formation of the universe from an Absolute power. From a pantheistic view, the Absolute takes various forms (without, however, losing its basic identity). Here there could be the difference between the Creator and the created (creature). From the perspective of emanation, all beings flow out of the Absolute and exist formally with God's power. God exists as the power-house for the flow of life but the emanated being never becomes God.[5]

Here is the confrontation between reason and belief regarding whether life evolved from matter (with its built-in power) or was it brought into existence by an external absolute power. For a better understanding of the reality both reason and belief must go hand in hand.

## Evolution

In this section we can go over a few of the theories about evolution.

### *Cosmic Evolution*

From the time of the so called 'Big Bang' to the formation of the earth's crest was the period of cosmic evolution. During this period, a series of changes took place on the face of the universe. This can be broadly given as follows: formation of elementary particles → building up of hydrogen, deuterium and helium → formation of matter → building up of heavier elements such as magnesium, silicon, iron etc → formation of galaxies → beginning of our solar system → formation of proto-earth (about 5 billion years ago) → formation of first formidable crest of earth (about 4.2 billion years ago). This is the macro-evolution and it subsequently led the way to chemical evolution.[6]

### *Chemical Evolution*

This is also called molecular - or pre-biotic- phase. The beginning of this phase began with the organic-chemical micro molecule (combining into macro molecules) and the progress continued till the emergence of bio-cell that can live by itself. At any rate, this evolution is more a latent process in comparison with what was happening to the earth phase.[7]

### *Biotic Evolution*

Biotic evolution presupposes three factors; viz., continuous change, directional development and accumulation of information (from previous stages). Thus when evolution is talked about in a biotic sense it is a change with accumulation of (genetic) information in a developmental direction (of more complex or higher form of life or being). Based on these criteria various researches claim that the changes or development from the original basis could be identified through various stages of development of organic matter and life.[8]

In this phase the formation of bio-cell (the smallest entity that is capable of life) originates containing in itself further evolution-phase. Hence this phase is called bioevolutive process. Now begins the phase of integration resulting in various systems. Bio-cells become the building block for further more complex structure of higher system. As a result various species come into existence.[9] The evolution strategy here is the so called 'crossing-over' from lower species to higher and more complex species. This is achieved by mutation-selection-technique of chromosomes.[10] This can be further understood under two categories or models, called corridor model and spherical model.

### *Corridor Model*

This model is similar to the flat Euclidean geometry. Here the various qualities of a species are considered to be the various dimensional axes in the history of evolution. From one point of time to another, certain qualities would become better, and, certain other qualities would become worse. But we concentrate on the situation that has become better in time than the previous epoch and thus we are able to understand the better quality or even appearance of new species along the multidimensional corridor of time. According to this model, the development depends on necessary steps of mutations and probability of further success depends on the ratio of the successful mutations to the total number of mutations involved.[11]

### *Spherical Model*

In this model the quality of the evolution is compared to the spherical symmetry. The quality will be the same with respect to the concentric shells of the hyper-sphere. The quality becomes better with the spherical radius becoming shorter and shorter, thereby reaching the best quality at the centre of the sphere.[12] Thus the evolution that began in the periphery of the universe such as elements, reaches the best quality in the centre which is the crown of the universe, namely human being.

### *Psycho Evolution*

Here the evolution gets transformed into immaterial effect and achievement of organisms. It starts from the perception of signal from the environment resulting in the physical reflex and psychological reaction through instinct, consciousness, thought-pattern and even leading into cultural area. Thus the evolution becomes somewhat internal - within oneself, in the frame of society and culture.[13]

Thus material evolution becomes by and by an evolution of knowledge. It is not only mere physical evolution that can be noticed in the bodily change or development but also in the ability to reflect over life situation that becomes the end product of the evolution. Not only the human beings possess at this stage discerning knowledge (cognitive evolution) which can be established through the structure of the brain but they can also synthesize the experience and know things not only *a posteriori* but also *a priori*. This is the culmination of evolution from the physical realm to intellectual realm.[14] Further, evolution continues from the intellectual realm into the spiritual realm, namely, as noosphere, as Teilhard de Chardin would put it.

### Neo-Darwinism

The modern evolutionary theory, which is known as neo-Darwinism, is based on modern synthesis which on the one hand retains Darwin's principle of natural selection and on the other hand it includes the discoveries of population genetics, paleontology, systematic and molecular biology.[15] The causes of the synthesis-theory are,

(a) Mutation - genetic change by chance;
(b) New combination from genes by the outgoing generation;
(c) Selection through the environment (implying discarding the unnecessary genes); and
(d) Isolation due to geography or lack of contact or interaction. This also causes the change in the hereditary.[16]

In all this process, God could be postulated as transcendentally present though this idea is not welcomed by the evolutionary scientists. God might have made possible the mutation-selection-isolation-mutation cycle. In everything God, 'who is and who shall be' as revealed to Moses in the burning bush (Ex 3:14), could be the dynamic force of change and evolution.

**Phases of Evolution**

We can see two phases in the evolutionary process. The one is the natural one and the other is the supernatural transcending the natural one.

According to the physical development the physical evolution of mankind can be sub-divided into three groups (starting from about 2 million years) as ancient human, old human and modern human beings. The ancient human can be identified with *Homo erectus* who lived from about 2 million upto about 300,000 years ago. The old humans developed anatomically from the ancient human and they were similar to *Homo sapiens*. They lived from about 400,000 to about 35,000 years ago. The new human lived from about 40,000 upto 30,000 years ago. Apart from the physical development (evolution) of mankind what is important is the development of the intellect. Until about 2 million years ago, from 'animal-being' emerged the 'human-being' mainly because of the intellectual development along with the physical development. Before this change ever took place, it is estimated that about 100,000 generations might have gone by.[17]

The supernatural phase of evolution is a matter of theological speculation. This is clearly brought out by Paul in I Cor 15:42-49. In trying to answer the question of whether there will be difference in the physical body on the occasion of resurrection of the dead, Paul is trying to bring out the 'crossing-over' from the natural (worldly) physical body to the supernatural (heavenly) spiritual soul. He distinguishes between natural body and spiritual body. In this passage what is implied is that the material world with its various forms and nature will be transformed in the future. At some point in the time axes of our history the physical or material body was elevated or transformed into a body with life (or soul) which then transcends even time (as it has the spirit). The bridge to cross over between the material world and the eternal world is brought about by faith. Thus 'cross-over' is from *being* material into *becoming* (immaterial) spiritual.[18]

## Origin of Human Being

Though it is relatively easy to accept the origin of life in the universe via biological evolution, when it comes to the case of human being, it becomes more complex, even complicated and often controversial. The origin of human beings is the product of two different processes which were taking place simultaneously: on the one hand it was the bio-evolution, and on the other, it was the psycho-evolution. Under bio-evolution, due to hybridization of protein resulting in the complex nature of DNAs, human beings, as believed by many of the scientists, evolved physically through the stages of *Australopithecus africanus, Homo habilis, Homo erectus, and Homo sapiens.* But at the same time, concurrently, the psycho-evolution was also taking place. For example, *Homo habilis* possessed the ability to build up a language (mostly in the form of sounds); *Homo erectus* was able to discover fire and make use of it; and *Homo sapiens* were able to develop the language in the form of writing (symbols in the beginning) as well.[19]

The apex of the evolution is the beginning of consciousness in human being. This comes about through the formation of central nervous system consisting of various nerve cells. The communication among the nerve cells is through chemical and electrical energy transfer but the activities are coordinated from the brain. As the process becomes more and more active the experiences are stored up and thought-patterns are formed within oneself. This is called the consciousness.[20]

What is specific with human being is that each one has a soul (that other non-human beings in the universe do not possess). Now what is the origin of the soul? Does it develop with evolution?, or, is it created with each formation of human being? There are two views regarding the formation of soul:

(a) The soul emerges, so to say, into each human being when each one is biologically conceived. (This implies that evolutionary process consists of the ability to transform the consciousness as the soul. That is, soul seems to be 'immanent' in the matter).

(b) Soul is created each time by God when a human being is conceived. According to this, the biological conception is a necessary condition without which soul cannot be 'created.' God creates each soul as He created the world in the beginning or as He created the first human soul. So it is the direct act of God.

This concept of soul-formation is also understood as the process of becoming (according to Karl Rahner). Though the parents are necessary for the human birth, the formation of soul is not self-replication but it is self-transcendence. Here the parents are also the cause of the soul formation since they bring forth a new human being into the world but the soul is infused into the human being through the power of God.[21]

The standpoint of the Church regarding the evolution, as in the case of Galileo's case (Copernican revolution), has changed over the period of time. In 1950 Pope Pius XII accepted the biological evolution as a possibility but he warned that it should not be generalized especially with respect to the formation/creation of the soul. According to the Church soul is created by God in every human being. In 1996, Pope John Paul II recognized evolution as more than a simple hypothesis.

## Creation

Creation is to bring out something out of nothing. As Christians we believe that God created everything and in the beginning of Genesis we read the creation story. But we should not be surprised to encounter theories other than the simple creation story (cataloguing day by day activities of God in a time frame of six days to create the entire universe). There are a few questions to be answered in the process of making clear to ourselves how God created everything. For example, is the creation over once for all when God created everything out of nothing (*creatio ex nihilo*) or is God continuously creating things in the universe *(creatio continua)*? If God is still active in the continual creation, then all the (technical, technological, intellectual, etc.) developments (that go on even now) is creation in evolution.

### *Creationism*

Based on the first and second chapters of Genesis that God created the universe, those who believe in creation, reject that the universe could have evolved through a natural process. In 1963 a few scientists who were strongly convinced of creation as given in the book of Genesis founded the Creation-Research-Society. And today there are more than 2500 sister or daughter organizations that have come up. According to them the creation story is *scientific* and they are convinced (for example about 28% of the population in Germany) that whatever is to be known about the origin of humankind has been already said in the Bible, especially in the creation story.[22]

Assuming God, who is the fullness of perfection and goodness, has created the universe, the question remains why there is lack of perfection and goodness in the world. In the earlier days people asked the question: how can one explain, if all are created equally and created from the same origin, the existence of tyranny and slavery in the world? Did God, one tends to ask, create a terrible and arbitrary world with so much of limitations? If the origin (of matter and being) is one and the same substance/person, how can one explain the hierarchy in the various types of organisms?[23] (The existence of evil and limitations can be explained, if one accepts the concept of original sin but it is beyond the scope of this article where we try to understand the reality within the context of creation-evolution relation).

While evolution is opportunistic (natural selection), creationist view is deterministic. The nucleus of evolution theory is the complexity and diversity of species and of life. The reason given is adaptation of species, since adaptation assumes great significance when organisms are compared in the light of the theory of descent from common origin (or ancestor). This explanation of biological complexity and diversity or macroevolution, according to Riddiford and Penny, has replaced the earlier explanation proposing a divine designer.[24] According to creationists, the 'adaptive' explanations are scientifically inadequate:

(a) The terms adaptation and adaptedness are not adequately defined. Any and every morphological, physiological, and behavioural trait is termed as adaptation. Hence the term 'adaptation' is used with several different meanings. Since the environment is constantly changing, an organism's adaptedness cannot be measured absolutely.

(b) Further, the adaptive explanations are *ad hoc* and appeal to no general rule. For example, it is said that the mammals survived the period in which dinosaurs became extinct because mammals were better adapted to the increasingly cooler temperature.

(c) In the absence of knowledge about relative adaptedness and its contribution of fitness, it will be impossible to make quantitative predictions about the probability of survival of genotypes.[25]

Hence the exponents of creation theory propose that God created everything as said in the Bible. Often they believe literally whatever has been said in the Bible regarding creation.

### Theories of Creation

Even if one believes that God has created the universe with all things in it, still there are distinctions regarding how God created the universe and the things therein.

### Creation out of Nothing

The hidden grandeur of Gen 1:1-3 is that God is the absolute Lord of the world. Here the meaning 'nothing' can be interpreted in two ways as

(a) creation out of chaos; and

(b) creation out of nothing.

But creation out of nothing, according to the Christian tradition, is not to be understood in the most radical sense of a creation from absolute nothingness. 'Nothing' means simply the absence of material substance or principle apart from the fullness of God's own being. Since nothing can come out of nothing (*ex nihilo nihil fit*), creation out of nothing implies that God created out of nothing other than God's own 'fullness of being.' Though a creation out of absolute nothingness is an impossibility; a creation out of God's own 'substance' would lead to a pantheistic deification of the physical world. Creation out of nothing, therefore, signifies the theological recognition that God created a universe distinct from the divine being, not out of any preexisting matter or principle, but out of nothing other than the fullness of God's own being.[26]

This concept of 'creation out of nothing' is very much rooted in the Bible. Other than Gen 1:1-3, we find in Job 26:7 similar idea expressed in the words: God 'stretches the north over the empty place, and hangs the earth upon nothing.' Also in Maccabees 7:28 we read: 'Look at the heaven and the earth and see everything that it is them, and recognize that God did not make them out of things that existed.' In the New Testament, especially in the letters of Paul, we find reference to creation out of nothing. In Rom 4:17 it is stated: God 'gives life to the dead and calls into existence the things that do not exist.' It is more explicitly mentioned in Heb 11:3: 'By faith we understand that the world was created by the word of God, so that what is seen was made out of things which do not appear.' Again Rom 11:36 reads: 'For from him and through him and to him are all things (made).' Thus creation out of nothing, in proper sense, is very much rooted in biblical tradition.[27]

The idea of creation out of nothing has been the universal consensus of the early Fathers including Justin Martyr, Theophilus of Antioch, Irenaeus, Tertullian, Origen, etc. St. Augustine, in a classic passage in his *Confessions*, expressed a well developed doctrine of creation out of nothing. He wrote: "You, O Lord... made something in the Beginning, which is of yourself, in your Wisdom, which is born of your own substance, and you created this something out of nothing. You created heaven and earth but you did not make them out of your own substance... You... created them from nothing... for there is nothing that you cannot do... You were, and besides you nothing was. From nothing, then, you created heaven and earth."[28] The doctrine of creation out of nothing became one of the firmest parts of the general teaching of the Church concerning creation.

For Christian theology the doctrine of a creation out of nothing implies that the possibility of matter existing with God from all eternity is ruled out but God who transcends the universe can be said to have created the universe out of nothing so that it is dependent in every moment on God for its existence.[29]

### Continuing Creation

If 'creation out of nothing' implies transcendence of God, the 'continuing creation' brings in the immanence of God. But we do not consider transcendence and immanence as mutually exclusive affirmations about God. Theology has traditionally held the doctrines of creation out of nothing and continuing creation to be interrelated on the view that they are complementary aspects of God's creative involvement with the physical universe. The *creatio ex nihilo* concept was formulated and defined at a time when the universe was believed to be static. But today we believe in a dynamic universe and hence there is the need for a concept of continuing creation. Barbour, clarifies this view: Today the world as known to science is dynamic and incomplete. Ours is an unfinished universe that is still in the process of appearing. Surely the coming-to-be of life from matter can represent divine creativity as suitably as any postulated primeval production of matter 'out of nothing.' Creation occurs throughout time.[30]

But the idea of creation out of nothing in a static world need not be replaced by continuing creation in a dynamic world. These are two complementary concepts that need not substitute one for the other. Pannenberg rightly points out: "The *creatio continuata* formula presupposes the strict conception of creation as *cretaio ex nihilo* in as much as it characterizes God's preserving activity as the continuation of the creation out of nothing. For this reason alone the idea of a continuing creation cannot be set in opposition to the *creatio ex nihilo* formula."[31] Continuing creation has instead to do with God's multifaceted immanence in the world. The God who creates 'out of nothing' necessarily transcends the physical reality thus created. Yet God's transcendence does not prevent God from being present every moment and in every aspect of creation as God sustains the physical universe and the life within it in its continuous processes of dynamic flux and becoming.

Just like the *ex nihilo* concept, aspects of the affirmation of a *creatio continua* are to be found in the Bible. We read in Ps 104:24-29: "O Lord, how manifold are your works! In wisdom you have made them all; the earth is full of your creatures... When you hide your face, they are dismayed; when you take away their breath, they die and return to their dust." Similarly, the psalmist affirms the activity of the Creator in the ongoing process of our physical world when he writes in Ps 147:8-9: "(The Lord) covers the heavens with clouds, prepares rain for the earth, makes grass grow on the hills. He gives to the animals their food and to the young ravens when they cry." Perhaps the most frequently cited biblical text relating to continuing creation is found in Col 1:16-17 in which God's creative and sustaining activity through Jesus Christ is explicitated: "In him (Christ) all things in heaven and on earth were created, things visible and invisible,... all things have been created through him and for him. He himself is before all things, and in him, things hold together."

Hefner, who identifies continuing creation primarily with God's sustenance of the world, affirms that "creation...is not limited by what happened at the beginning when time was created. Creation also refers to God's ongoing sustaining of the world. Every moment of the world's existence depends upon the ongoing grace of God."[32]

## Synthesis of Creation and Evolution

The question common to creation and evolution is the formation of the universe, life from matter, and finally consciousness (culminating in the soul of human beings). This implies that the material elements have had the transcending ability to take on the form of new configuration into more complex form leading to life. Thus evolution cannot be reduced just to material dimension. On the other hand the creation has to be understood as the initial motion setting in which the creation as a whole is taken along into the future and hence it is a *creatio continua*. Thus the transcendence of God in initial creation and the immanence of God in evolution are a synergic effect which complement each other.[33]

The evolution process is seen as a process of becoming. The scheme of micro-evolution could be depicted as follows:

Gloun/quark (basic building blocks of matter) → sub-atomic particles such as proton and neutron → helium → carbon and oxygen → simple molecules such as water, ammonia, hydrogen → complex molecules such as amino acids → macromolecules such as polymers, proteins, nucleic acids → formation of simple life such as virus, bacteria → complex single cell to multi cell life → organic lives (plants, animals and fungi) → human being.

In all these we see a process of 'becoming' into higher form of 'being'. And there is a force that unites simple elements into complex molecules and ultimately bringing out a complex life-form in the form of human being which again becomes a being of consciousness and soul. In all these changes, God is present as the unifying force. The Trinity stands as the unifying force, since Trinity itself is the best example of 'becoming' and 'unification' into one Godhead. So basically the universe is creation in evolution of God which is basically getting united into the Trinity (through the unifying Spirit).[34]

Human beings, though originated from matter, have emerged, in and through the spirit, into the light of consciousness. And after Christ's salvific intrusion into human history, humankind has been lifted off from the plane of individual consciousness to that of universal consciousness. And the spirit is now at work to elevate humankind from this plane of universal consciousness to the ultimate goal of reunion with the Lord of Creation, the Omega Point. Even after the disintegration in Adam took place, the integration in the new Adam (Jesus Christ) takes place and the Spirit is now leading humankind on its course of action towards fullness in the image and likeness of God, the Creator. The Spirit of God is the unifying force that dynamically brings all to fruition ever since the creation began. But this is accomplished in and through Christ who is the ultimate point for all conscious matter-turned-life to reach, the threshold to Omega Point and for each individual this happens in the Christ-consciousness. Jesus Christ is the paradigm of God. In Jesus Christ we are not mere 'human beings' but 'human becomings' once again into the image and likeness of God.[35]

In Jesus Christ, God is working as continuous and immanent Creator. In the words of Peacoke: "The human person of Jesus is then to be seen, by virtue of his human response and openness to God, as the locus, the icon, in and through whom there is made open and explicit the nature and character of the God who has never ceased to be present continuously creating and bringing God's purposes to fruition in the order of energy-matter-space-time... So, in this sense, the 'incarnation' which occurred in Jesus the Christ may then properly be said to be the consummation of the creative and creating evolutionary process... and the significance and potentiality of all levels of creation may be said to have been unfolded in Jesus the Christ... Hence Jesus the Christ occupies in 'spiritual' history (that is, the history of the relationship of humanity with God) the place that a mutation does in biological evolution."[36]

For Teilhard de Chardin evolution is a reality and God is the driving force in the material level potentially converting it into ever more complex being. Teilhard tried to combine the evolutionary theory with belief in God's creation. Of course, it implies that one cannot take literally the Genesis account of creation. According to Teilhard, the proteins which originated from the inorganic materials should have the ability, due to the geo-chemical processes, to become the phenomenon for formation of life to emerge. The biological diversity in the universe has now ushered in the so called 'nooshphere,' that is, evolution of thoughts, which in effect is trying to bring forth a convergence. Convergence, for Teilhard, means unification of humankind to a universal personality in whom everything (though diverse and complex) in the universe meets and melts, so to say and fuses into one reality. This is the Omega Point who exists by himself as consummation of irreversible Principle. This, for Teilhard, is Jesus Christ. In Jesus Christ the transcendence of God becomes immanent. Thus in this Omega Point God is revealed as the driving force as well as the point of unification in the biological diversity. Thus God is the Prime force of evolution and evolution is the way that God does things in the universe.[37]

Human being is not only considered as a mere physical body just to eat and drink but also it is a being that is capable of love, hope, sympathy, etc. In other words human being is considered to have more than a physical body. When Wis 4:23 says that the origin of life lies in the heart, we think in terms of a soul for human being. And this soul is active along with the body. So body and soul of a human being cannot be considered as two independent entities. This is the totality of human being that transcends the visible creation as such. For example, in Ps 119:89-91, we read that the Word of Jahweh holds the firmament. But the firmament (heavens) cannot be separated from the earth. So heaven and earth together make again the totality of creation. Again Ps 148:3-6, indicates how God himself is bound with the people he created. Even if night and day fail, God will not fail in his promises, it says. It is again encouraging to see who has brought out the order and harmony in the universe as we read in Baruch 3:33-35. The 'word' of Jahweh brings out not only the order and harmony in the universe to see but also in its functions. As we read in Ps 147:15-20, each one in the universe has his/her obligation and duty to fulfill. It is this following of each one's 'dharma' so to say, that keeps the universe going as we read in Job 28:25. With this order and harmony in the universe, the human being feels joy and peace within.

From the ordinary material of the universe God creates, as we read in the Genesis, but what is important and specific and special here is that God breathes into the human being the breath of life (Gen 2:7). That is human being originates from the lower elements and organs but he/she is chosen/invited to exist in the image and likeness of God and with whom God could walk as friend and father in the garden of Eden in the cool breeze of the evening. It is true that God created human being, as he created other beings in the universe, with his powerful 'word'. And the same 'word' was the life, namely, Jesus Christ, and the Life was the light of human being (Jn 1:4). Here we find the fulcrum of the universe where the evolving earthly material world (in the form of human beings) meets the heavenly spirit. The transformation of matter into spirit takes place m Jesus through his redemptive activity (Again we are not going into the area of sin that called for redemption). This is the eschatology of the universe. As Paul says in Rom 8:19-23, the mankind takes part in the glory of God in and through his transformed creation (in Jesus Christ) and this creation, represented with human being as the apex of creation, will get into the next world (2 Pt 3:13) where God makes everything new (Rev 21:1-5).

Thus we see how God creates the material world and then brings about life from these basic elements and finally brings about human being in his own image and likeness (Col 3:10) and makes the human being capable of entering into the ongoing world of eternity (after resurrection on the so called the 'last day') - from this world of matter into the glorious world of spirit. So mankind once again becomes, as said in Eph 4:24, a new creation by becoming transformed into the resurrected Jesus and taking part in his holiness and glory in the eternal life (Jn 17:3).[38]

## Conclusion

In the process of understanding evolution and creation, we should not try to identify one with the other since they are complementary to each other. Evolution is a theory, a model explaining how beings (plants, animals, human) originate from lower form of beings. Whereas creation is a belief how human beings have been called for higher form of life - not only materialistic and physical, but intellectual and conscious as well.

We could perhaps think that God created a 'becoming-world' with open-space and possibility to develop itself. And this is called evolution by natural scientists. Both evolution and creation are processes; the former, on the physical level explaining how one being becomes a higher being, whereas the latter stating where the dynamic force for becoming comes from. God is the initial dynamic force that set the evolutionary process in motion, as he created time, and He still continues the work in the universe - and this process we understand as evolution.

God who created the universe out of nothing is still at work as the God of immanence creating continually. So it is a creation in evolution. The Spirit that was hovering over the emptiness in the beginning of time entered the matter and through its creative evolution brought out life from the matter. Once life came in, based on experience, the Spirit brought in consciousness, leading to the final form of Christ's Abba-consciousness. The same spirit is still hovering over the universe sanctifying and converging everything, even the opposing principles, to fruition in and through Christ. Thus in the process of matter becoming human beings, humans becoming Christ-conscious and finally converging in God, it is the Spirit that plays the vital role. It is the same Spirit that makes each one of us call God 'Abba, Father' (Rom 8: 15) and thereby uniting all of humankind as one family and thereby the entire universe into the fold of God's Trinity.[39] This is then creation which has taken the ongoing dynamic force of evolution.

## Notes and References

1. Francis P. Xavier is a scientist with specialization in botany, based in Chennai.
2. U. Kull, *Evolution* (Stuttgart: Metzler, 1987), p. 1.
3. V. R. Gowariker, N.V. Viswanathan and J. Sreedhar, *Polymer Science* (New Delhi: New Age International, 1986), p. 1.
4. R. Kolterman, *Grundzuege der modernen Natur-Philosophie* (Frankfurt/M: Knecht, 1994), p. 78.
5. Kolterman, 1994, p. 79
6. H. K. Erben, *Evolution* (Stuttgart: Enke, 1990), p. 18.

7. Erben, p. 19.
8. L. Kaempfe (ed.), *Evolution and Stammesgeschichte der Organismen* (Jena: Fischer, 1992), p. 26.
9. Erben, p. 19
10. I. Rechenberg, *Evolutionsstrategie* (Stuttgart: Friedrich Frommann, 1973), p. 91.
11. Rechenberg, pp. 103 ff.
12. Rechenberg, p. 115.
13. Erben, p. 20.
14. Erben, p. 136.
15. J. W. Pollard (ed.), *Evolutionary Theory* (Chichester: John Wiley, 1984), p. 3.
16. Koltermann, 1994, p. 173.
17. Kaempfe, pp. 477-485.
18. A. Hulsbosch, *Die Schoepfung Gottes* (Wien: Herder, 1965), pp. 21ff.
19. Erben, pp. 145-150.
20. S. N. Bosshard, "Evolution and Shoepfung," in *Christiliclier Glaube in moderner Gesellschaft* (Vol.3) (Freiburg I. B: Herder, 1981), pp. 98-104.
21. Koltermann, 1994, pp. 238 ff.
22. Koltermann, 1990.
23. E. Meyr, *Und Darwin hat doch rech* (Muenchen: Piper, 1994), pp. 28-33.
24. Pollard, p. 26.
25. Pollard, pp. 27-30.
26. M. W. Worthing, *God, Creation and contemporary Physics* (Minneapolis: Fortress, 1996), pp. 73 f.
27. Worthing, pp. 74 f.
28. Worthing, pp. 76 f.
29. Worthing, p. 77.
30. Worthing, p. 112.
31. Cited in Worthing, pp. 112 ff.

32. Worthing, pp. 112-115.
33. Bosshard, pp. 121 f.
34. K. Schmitz-Moormann (Ed), *Schoepfung und Evolution* (Duesseldorf: Patmos, 1992), pp. 115-130.
35. Francis P. Xavier, Vaiharai, I (1996), pp. 123-133. Xavier, 1998.
36. A. Peacoke, *God and Science* (London: SCM Press, 1996), pp. 81-88.
37. Erben, pp. 110 f.
38. Hulsbosch, pp. 60-77.
39. Francis P. Xavier, Vaiharai, 3 (1998), pp. 168-187.

# Creationism: Neither Science, Nor Theology!

10

BINOY PICHALAKKATTU[1]

## Introduction

Creationism covers a spectrum of beliefs. It has more than one meaning. At its most basic, Creationism is the belief that the universe was created by a deity of some sort. At a broad level, a creationist is someone who believes in a God who is absolute creator of heaven and earth, out of nothing, by an act of free will.[2] Such a deity is generally thought to be constantly involved in the creation, ready to intervene as necessary, and without whose constant concern the creation would cease or disappear. Christians, Jews, and Muslims are all Creationists to some extent in this sense. Generally they are known as 'theists,' distinguishing them from 'deists,' that is, those who believe that there is a designer who does not interfere once the designing act is finished.

In this paper we start with different types of creationism. We focus in detail on the latest sense of creationism, known as Intelligent Design Creationism (IDC) which explicates the cosmological, astronomical, mathematical, evolutionary and chaotic models of divine design. In the process of explanation we show that creationism is non-scientific, especially that the IDC is a methodological error from a scientific perspective. Finally we address the methodological concerns in creationism to affirm that the claims of creationism are not anything scientific, but faith formulations which are unfounded theologically and exegetically.

## Types of Creationism[3]

There are different types of creationism and may be classified into Christian and non-Christian creationism.

### *Christian Creationism*

Christian Creationism consists of Scientific Creationism, Flat Earth creationism, Geocentric Creationism, Young Earth Creationism, Old Earth Creationism Progressive Creationism and Evolutionary Creationism.[3]

#### *Scientific Creationism*

Scientific creationism is the fundamentalist version of creationism which is biblical in essence. This creationism (usually called Creation Science) involves a literal interpretation of the Bible that is incompatible with evolution as well as with much other science and history, but which fundamentalists attempt to harmonize with scientific investigations of nature. Creation science is the attempt to present scientific evidence interpreted with Genesis axioms that support the claims of creationism.

#### *Flat Earthers' and Geocentrists' Creationism*

Flat Earthers believe that the Earth is flat rather than round. The sky above is a dome or "firmament". This position is most commonly based upon a literal reading of the Bible, for example references to the "four corners of the earth" and the "circle of the earth." Although some believe that all Christians used to think that the Earth is flat, that isn't the case. Geocentrists accept a spherical earth but deny that the sun is the center of the solar system or that the earth moves. Both flat-earthers and geocentrists reflect the cosmological views of ancient Hebrews.

### *Young Earth Creationism*

Young Earth Creationists (YEC) rely upon the most literal interpretation of the Bible in comparison to other forms of special creationism. At its heart, the Young Earth Creationist movement is a movement of conservative Christians. Young Earth Creationists (YEC) is founded on a literal interpretation of the Bible. They believe that the earth is 6000 to 10,000 years old, that all life was created in six literal days, that death and decay came as a result of Fall, and that geology must be interpreted in terms of Noah's Flood. However, they accept a spherical earth and heliocentric solar system. It is rare to find a Young Earth Creationist making a case either for creationism or against evolutionism without doing so from a deliberately religious and, usually, fundamentalist Christian position.

### *Old Earth Creationism*

The Old Earth Creationism accepts the existence of an "old earth," such that an ancient earth is accepted, but not evolution itself. This requires rejecting a completely literal interpretation of Genesis, but not abandoning it wholly and not simply reading it as metaphorical in the manner of Theistic Evolutionists. Jewish and Christian Old Earth Creationists (OEC) take a number of different paths on Genesis.

### *Progressive Creationism*

Progressive Creationism is the most common Old-Earth Creationism view today. It accepts most of modern physical science, even viewing the Big Bang as evidence of the creative power of God, but rejects much of modern biology. Progressive Creationists generally believe that God created "kinds" of organisms sequentially, in the order seen in the fossil record, but say that the newer kinds are specially created, not genetically related to older kinds.

### *Theistic Evolution and Evolutionary Creationism*

Creationism does not have to be incompatible with evolution; there are many who believe in creator god(s) and who also accept evolution. They may have deistic beliefs and still believe that God started everything then let it run without interference. Theistic Evolution encompasses theism, some system of traditional religious beliefs, and the idea that a god or gods used evolution to develop life on earth. Theistic Evolution says that God creates through evolution. Theistic Evolutionists vary in beliefs about how much God intervenes in the process. It accepts most or all of modern science, but it invokes God for some things outside the realm of science, such as the creation of the human soul.

Evolutionary Creationism differs from Theistic Evolution only in its theology, not in its science. It says that God operates not in the gaps, but that nature has no existence independent of His will. It allows interpretations consistent with both a literal Genesis and objective science, allowing, for example, that the events of creation occurred, but not in time as we know it, and that Adam was not the first biological human but the first spiritually conscious being.

### Intelligent Design Creationism

Intelligent Design is the most recent form of creationism to develop, but its roots go much back in history. Intelligent Design (ID) is the claim that "certain features of the universe and of living things are best explained by an intelligent cause, not an undirected process such as natural selection."[5] Fundamentally speaking, Intelligent Design is based upon the idea that the existence of God could be deduced from the existence of intricate design in the universe. The Intelligent Design movement began with the work of Charles Thaxton, Walter Bradley, Michel Denton, Dean Kenyon and Philip Johnson.[6] This movement says that the kind of information inherent in the universe, and in biological evolution in particular, cannot be generated by purposeless, random causation. It holds that certain features of the universe and of living things are best explained by an intelligent cause rather than by an undirected process. Intelligent design is a scientific disagreement with the core claim of evolutionary theory that the apparent design of living systems is random. They bring out evidences for design from molecular biology and information sciences.[7] They also highlight the cosmological, astronomical, mathematical, evolutionary and chaotic models to substantiate their claim of divine design. For them the number of stars and the planetary orbits, the rotation period of the earth and the surface gravity, the magnetic field of the earth and the gravitational interaction with moon, the oxygen to hydrogen ratio and the ozone level in atmosphere, the seismic activity, the atmospheric electric discharge rate, etc., are really the divine marvels to look at.

Though the promoters of Intelligent Design Creationism do away with the Big Bang theory and the theory of evolution, they try to look at the design in the cosmos in the light of contemporary scientific theories in cosmology, astronomy, astrophysics, mathematics, evolutionary biology, quantum mechanics, etc.

### *Evolutionary Design: The Theory of Evolution*

The contemporary evolutionary worldview in science has its origin in the work of Charles Darwin (1809-1882). The publication of Darwin's *On the Origin of Species* in 1859 marked the beginning of a new era in our understanding of the universe and of us. The book deals with the evolutionary changes in the living and non-living beings of the universe. Darwin proposed that evolutionary changes in organisms occur not through the passing of acquired characteristics but through the passing of inherited characteristics. He argued that some inherited variations give an edge in successful adaptation to new environments. Darwin proposed this process as "natural selection". Natural selection is "the favouring of survival and reproduction of organisms those possessing traits adapting them to a particular environmental situation at a particular time and the elimination of organisms that do not possess those traits in the same environment."[8] What Darwin offered was a way of understanding how biological life is also governed by natural laws. The diversity of organisms, the origin of species, including the origin of human beings, could now begin to be explained by an orderly process of change governed by laws that science could articulate and describe.[9] Darwin's theory proposed that even the emergence of finely tuned organisms could be explained as the result of a natural process, i.e., natural selection. Natural selection could explain functional design without needing to appeal to an external divine designer. With natural selection, it was argued, the origin and adaptive nature of living organisms could be accounted for in terms of natural laws that operated within entirely natural processes.

At the heart of Darwin's theory is the insight that inherited variations result in some creatures being better adapted than others to their environment and therefore more likely to leave more offspring. Darwin understood natural selection as the preservation of favourable variations and the rejection of injurious variations.[10] He saw that some variations confer advantage in adapting to a particular environment and therefore to the possibility of survival. These advantageous variations would be transmitted to future generations more frequently on average than their alternatives. In time, favourable variations would be preserved and those that were not useful for adapting to a particular environment would be eliminated. Darwin's theory suffered in that he had no way of accounting for the rise of inherited variations. Heredity was not well understood at that time. But at the turn of the 19th century, scientists began to absorb and adopt the insights on heredity that had already been developed by Gregor Mendel (1882-1884). It became clear that the inherited characteristics are transmitted across generations in units known as genes, and that these genes are inherited in a predictable fashion. It was discovered that changes in genes, called mutations, appeared to occur randomly. These mutations were now seen to be the source of novelty, which created the possibility of evolutionary change.[11] Gradually it became clear that mutation and natural selection are both necessary to explain evolutionary change. In the 1930s genetics and Darwinian natural selection were brought together in a satisfying synthesis, which Julian

Huxley in 1942 named "the Modern Synthesis".[12] In spite of various developments in paleontology, molecular biology and bio-chemistry, a majority of the scientists understand the evolutionary worldview as consistent with a form of neo-Darwinism, in which genetic variation and natural selection are understood to be major factors in evolutionary change. The inner dynamism and the innate potential of the living and non-living beings underline the inherent design within the cosmos.

### *Cosmological Design: The Fine-Tuning*

According to cosmologists the extraordinary subtle balance of the four forces of the universe - strong nuclear force, weak nuclear force, electromagnetic force and gravitational force - has made the emergence of life and consciousness possible.[13] For the contemporary astrophysicists and cosmologists, the universe is expanding and the expansion rate of the universe requires a delicate and precise balancing.[14] If the strong nuclear force that binds the nuclei of various elements were slightly weaker, we would have only hydrogen in the whole of the universe. If the same force were slightly stronger, all the hydrogen would have been converted to helium. In either case heavy elements and chemical compounds would not have been formed. It is calculated that for every billion antiprotons in the beginning of the universe, there were just one billion and one protons. The billion pairs annihilated each other to produce radiation with just one proton left over. A greater or smaller number of survivors would have made our kind of material world impossible. Can such a fine-tuning of the universe, formation of elements and the particle anti-particle ratio be considered the fingerprints of God? Is it an invitation to observe the protecting hands of God immanent in the creation of the universe?

### *Astronomical Design: The Life Giving Explosion*

"The universe is the sacred temple of God. The astronomers are priests of Almighty", said Johannas Kepler.[15] For 300,000 years after the Big Bang the universe was in a process of cooling down.[16] During this period there was a sea of hydrogen and helium nuclei, photons and free electrons all around space in a state of constant interaction. When the temperature of the universe was cooled down to about 3000 degree Kelvin, the electrons and atomic nuclei were combined to form ordinary atoms, mostly hydrogen. As the photons suddenly lacked energy required to separate electrons from the nuclei, the particles were combined to form neutral atoms. By then the sea of photons had no further interactions with matter. The hydrogen and helium atoms were then free to collapse under the influence of gravity. This collapse produced galaxies. The birth of galaxies was accompanied by the birth of stars. Stars were formed within molecular clouds which are aggregations of molecular gas residing in galactic disks. The astronomical theories reveal that we originated in the catastrophic collapse of an aging star.

Should we perceive the hand of God in the process of the formation of stars as well as in the supernova explosion, equivalent to the explosion of hundreds of millions of hydrogen bombs per second, causing the formation of black holes, neutron stars and other elements? Life is dependent on the initial physical conditions of those explosions, for had the proportion of hydrogen to helium been different there would either have been no water, or the heavy elements would have been locked up inside the stars. If the nuclear forces that hold the atoms together had been stronger, then carbon, essential for life, would have been converted to oxygen as it formed. The importance of such initial conditions has given rise to the anthropic principle which says the natural laws of the universe are fine-tuned so that our own existence becomes a possibility. Is this design by an external mind?[17]

### *Mathematical Design: Harmony*

Mathematics is necessary to discuss intelligently the material aspect of the great universe. "Nature's great book is written in mathematics," said Galileo.[18] The harmony and the common mathematical pattern of nature reveal the fingerprints of God! There are many mathematical models for the growth of living organisms and other patterns commonly found in nature. The

Italian mathematician Leonardo of Pisa invented a sequence, namely, *Fibonacci Series* (1,1,2,3,5,8,13,21,34,55,89...) which could very well be applied to the cell growth of living organism.[19] Jay Hambidge in 1926 developed the Golden section or the Golden ratio phi (1.618033).[20] The Golden section is observed in nature with respect to proportions of insect body, flower-body dimensions, leafing pattern in trees, arrangement and the width of human teeth. For a perfectly proportional human body, the ratio of the total height to the height of the navel is equal to the Golden section. The DNA molecule with 34 angstroms length by 21 angstroms width is also based on the Golden section. It is interesting to observe some other common mathematical patterns of the human body. Our heart beats around 100,000 times every day, our blood is on a 96,000 km journey, our lungs inhale over two million litres of air everyday and we give birth to 100 billion red cells every day.[21] All of us have five senses, twenty-seven bones and thirty-two permanent teeth. Is the mathematical harmony of the nature and the human beings an invitation to wonder at the works of the divine mathematician?

### *Chaotic Design: The Chaos Theory*

The theory of Chaos is about explaining apparent disorder and ultimate order in the universe. It states that things are random, and complex and order emerges out of disorder.[22] The Chaos theory indicates that we live in an unpredictable, open-ended world.[23] Most natural processes are chaotic systems. For example the sea is a chaotic system driven by a finite amount of inputs such as wind, sun, tides, landmasses, etc. The Changes in a chaotic system can have different levels of impact. Each event has a constantly different amount of effect on the next step. The famous example is the hypothetical 'butterfly effect' coined by Edward Lorence.[24] The Flapping of the wings of a butterfly can, at a given time, effect the direction of a hurricane on the other side of the planet. Or it may have no effect at all. Thus the Chaos theory is about patterns in chaos and chaos in pattern. The chaos refers to an underlying interconnectedness that exists in apparently random events.

A new branch of geometry has been developed to explore the chaotic matters, which are called 'fractals.'[25] The mathematician Benoit Mandelbrot coined the word fractal to refer to the traces, tracks, marks, and forms made by the chaotic dynamic systems. They vary from the formation of galaxies to rugged coastlines, from unpredictable weather currents to flow of blood in the human body. The theory of chaos and the fractals highlight that every part of the universe is intimately related to the whole while remaining itself. Further the chaos theory calls us to accept the contingency, uncertainty and complexity in nature and human life. It accommodates even the natural disasters of tsunami, earthquakes and landslides as different steps of the cosmic-divine dance. Is such a dancer a balancing, dynamic and dialogical God who delights in the diversity of creation? Is such a creator one who participates in the play of the world, who partakes in the creativity of the cosmos? Can the interplay of order and openness, operating at the edge of chaos; be seen as 'the hands of God.'[26]

## Intelligent Design Creationism as a Methodological Error

Having seen the cosmological, astronomical, mathematical, evolutionary and chaotic models of divine design, we address the methodological validity of Intelligent Design Creationism. Scientifically, Intelligent Design is limited in two ways: it can neither identify all things that are designed, nor can it tell us with certainty that a particular thing is not designed.[27] For me, the scientific claim of intelligent design is a methodological error. Because the advocates of intelligent design assume that the biblical truth and scientific truth belong to the same domain. It is true that the leap of faith is reasonable as far as the domain of faith is concerned, but making a scientific claim on faith matters is irrational. They argue that God fixed distinct kind of organisms at the point of original creation. Such a claim is not itself a strictly scientific claim, but instead a belief about science. It is rooted in the belief system known as scientific creationism. It is not a product of scientific inquiry, but gratuitous assumptions that arise from religious preferences that have nothing to do with science. It is never permissible to mix science with a particular belief system. Although one cannot do science without having some background beliefs about reality, these beliefs should not become part of science itself.

## Creationism as a Non-scientific Language

Creationism is a religious metaphysical belief which claims that a supernatural being created the universe. Creation science is not science but pseudoscience. It is a religious dogma masquerading as scientific theory. Creation science is put forth as being absolutely certain and unchangeable. It assumes that the world must conform to its understanding of the Bible. Where creation science differs from creationism in general is on the assumption that once the Bible is interpreted to mean something, no evidence can be allowed to change that interpretation. Instead, the evidence must be refuted.

Creationism in a way is not necessarily connected to any particular religion. Millions of Christians and non-Christians believe there is a Creator of the universe and that scientific theories such as the theory of evolution do not conflict with belief in a Creator. However, those Christians calling themselves 'creation scientists' have co-opted the term 'creationism', making it difficult to refer to creationism without being understood as referring to "Scientific Creationism." Thus, it is commonly assumed that creationists are Christians who believe that the account of the creation of the universe as presented in *Genesis* is literally true in its basic claims about Adam and Eve, the six days of creation, making day and night on the first day even though He didn't make the sun and moon until the fourth day, making whales and other animals that live in the water or have feathers and fly on the fifth day, and making cattle and things that creep on the earth on the sixth day, etc.

Creation scientists claim that *Genesis* is the word of God and thus infallibly true. They also claim that *Genesis* contradicts the Big Bang theory and the theory of evolution. Thus, those theories are false and scientists who advocate such theories are ignorant of the truth about the origins of the universe and life on Earth. They also claim that creationism is a scientific theory and should be taught in our science curriculum as a competitor to the theory of evolution.

The following aspects of creationism make it non-scientific. First, the creation scientists are willing to argue their case in the arena of science, not biblical authority. They assume that the biblical truth and scientific truth belong to the same domain. They argue that the book of Genesis is itself a theory which tells us how the world was physically created: God fixed distinct kind of organisms at the point of original creation. They did not evolve. For them geological and biological truth attest to biblical truth. With regard to the theological commitments, scientific creationists affirm the creation of the world out of nothing, the insufficiency of mutation and natural selection to explain the process of evolution and the relatively recent formation of the earth, about six to ten thousand years ago.[28]

Second, certain fundamentalist creationists hold the view that the Bible is inerrant, without error. It tells the truth about everything it mentions. It is right about nature, the universe, the origin of human beings, the reproduction of species, and so on. All of its historical claims are true. The miracle stories happened just the way the Bible says. There is to be no compromise of biblical truth. The Bible is the Word of God in a full, complete, total manner and in all respects. Hence, if the Bible teaches that Adam and Eve were literal people living in a garden somewhere on earth that we could locate on earth, then that story is just true. If evolution teaches something contrary to what the right interpretation of Scripture requires, then it is wrong. True science is in harmony with the Bible. Whatever contradicts the Bible is bad science. Some conservatives have made a variety of accommodations to science with respect to biblical cosmology, the age of the earth, and even evolution. Some even venture to distinguish between matters of science not essential to religious truth and matters of faith in which the Bible is without any error at all. Thus Biblical literalism is at the opposite end of scientific materialism. It is based on the literal understanding of the infallible scripture.[29] Both ideologies represent the misuse of science. Scientific materialist starts from science but ends by making broad philosophical claims. The biblical literalist moves from theology to make claims about scientific matters. In scientific materialism science swallows religion. In biblical literalism religion swallows science. Both schools need to respect the difference between two disciplines.

Third, the Ecclesiastical Authoritarianism is another defensive tactic followed by some Creation Scientists who perceive science and scientism as a threat.[30] Presuming a two-step route to truth in which natural reason is followed by divine revelation, theological dogma is here granted authority over science on the grounds that science is founded on God's revelation. In 1864, Pope Pius IX promulgated the syllabus of errors, wherein item 57 stated it to be an error to think that science and philosophy could withdraw from ecclesiastical authority. However a century later, the Second Vatican Council dropped the defences by declaring the natural sciences to be free from ecclesiastical authority and called them 'autonomous' disciplines.[31]

## Methodological Concerns in Creationism

Creationism is to be treated as a sort of faith formulation which is not founded on sound exegesis or sound theology. On the other hand, evolution is a scientific language. Basically the difference between faith language and scientific language lie in the approach. A theologian and a scientist approach the reality differently.[32] Science is based on careful observation of events and experiments conducted; then on the construction of suitable and self-consistent theories. But there is a possibility to adopt a new approach based on different experiences, since no amount of positive observation can prove a theory. Rather, a single observation can prove the contrary, as evidenced by Copernican astronomy.

The apparent contradictions between faith and science are only complementary. The common factor between theology (creationism!) and science (evolutionism!) is the search for truth.[33] The reality which each seeks after is the same but the approach and understanding are different for the scientist and the theologian. Science seeks knowledge but the religious quest is for wisdom. Knowledge and wisdom are neither coextensive nor mutually exclusive. But they overlap, in this sense, religion reveals but science explains; science informs, but religion reforms. Science is a study of causes and religion is an inquiry into meaning.[34] Science operates in an *I - It* mode, while religion involves, the *I - Thou* mode. So science and religion are like different sorts of maps, and both help us to get around in the world because each in its own way represents that world/ reality more or less faithfully. Science and theology are two sides of reality and they complement each other.[35] For example, science could tell us how the universe functions but science could not say why there should be this universe. Whereas theology or religion would tell us that the universe is the expression of God's love and the ultimate purpose of the universe is to merge in God, the Almighty. Science describes the reality of existence whereas religion inspires the meaning of its existence. Hence science and theology together make the meaning of reality understandable. Both being complementary to each other, gives us the comprehensive view and understanding of the reality. The opposition between science and theology is often a struggle to clarify, to what extent causal explanations are compatible with real meaning and actual reality.[36] Neither science nor religion arrives at certainties. They at best predict probabilities; but religion is looser than science and often can predict only a range of possibilities. Religion is fully operational for religion has its own value system which permits the translation of principles into conduct, whereas any scientific system is parasitic on some value system before it can become operational in life.[37] Neither provides us with a complete or absolute description of reality. While science gives information about the actual physical world, theology gives insight into our life in and with God. Hence both together give us a more authentic glimpse of what reality is like.[38] It does not call for a mixing up of faith language and scientific language as in Evolutionary Creationism but a constructive interface between faith and reason based on a criterion of reasonableness. It also calls for the possibility of drawing analogical and metaphorical parallels from science to enhance one's faith.

Both science (evolutionism!) and theology (creationism!) employ metaphorical languages and models which may eventually be combined into higher conceptual themes such as theories or doctrines. A model in science is a systematic analogy postulated between a phenomenon whose laws are already known and the one under investigation. Metaphors arise when we speak on the basis of models. The metaphorical nature of scientific knowledge entails an acceptance of a world only partially and imperfectly understood. For Barbour, metaphor plays a wider role in religious than in scientific language.[39] The metaphors of theological models that explicate religious experience can refer to and can depict reality and they share this character with scientific models of the natural world.

One major difference between the way models are deployed in science and theology is that in the latter, models have a strong affective function evoking moral and spiritual response. The metaphors of theological models that explicate religious experience can refer to and can depict reality and they share this character with scientific models of the natural world. Both disciplines organize observation and experience through models that are analogical, extensible, coherent, and symbolic and are expressed through metaphors. However there are important differences between them. The type of "data" found in religion differs from those found in science.[40] Religion serves non-cognitive functions missing in science, such as eliciting attitudes, personal involvement and transformation. It includes story, rituals and historical revelation. On the other hand science contains both higher-level laws and lower-level laws. Consensus is formed in religion very differently from how it is formed in science. One must be aware of this dynamic tension between these similarities and dissimilarities.

However there are some problems in this way of relating religious belief (creationism!) with science (evolutionism!). The basic clash underlying the claims and counter-claims of traditional and modern sciences has been a clash of moralities.[41] The scientific attitude makes only the ethical demand that every progress in knowledge must be made by the advancement of critical evidence for or against the present reigning theories, methods and paradigms. Though science is a theory laden enterprise, it is clearly more objective than religion. The kinds of data from which creationism draws are radically different from those in science and the possibility of testing religious belief is limited. One major difference between the way models are deployed in science and theology is that in the latter models have a strong affective function evoking moral and spiritual response. In an attempt to legitimate religion in an age of science, it is tempting to dwell on similarities and pass over differences. By treating religion as an intellectual system and talking only about religious beliefs, one may distort the diverse characteristics of religion as a way of life. So the consideration of an adequate methodology, based on the criterion of reasonableness, is still an important task in the dialogue between science (evolution) and theology (creation). If theology is at its best a reflective enterprise that can develop and grow, it can be open to new insights, including those derived from the theories of science.

## Towards a Criterion of Reasonableness

The test for creationism today is to use the criterion of reasonableness in its methodology. For any language to be authentic, it has to satisfy an adequate criterion. For any faith language to be believable, it will have to satisfy the criterion of reasonableness that lead us to infer the best explanation of the broader features of the natural world and of what humans believe to be their experiences of God.[42] Truths that are claimed to be revealed cannot disregard the criterion of reasonableness, for they cannot be at the same time self-warranting and convincing. According to St. Anslem, the view of the theological enterprise is faith seeking understanding. Thus conceived, theology is reflection upon religious experience, the attempt to bring our rational and ordering faculties to bear upon a particular part of our interaction with the way things are. A.N. Whitehead wrote: "The dogmas of religion are the attempts to formulate in precise terms the truths disclosed to the religious experience of mankind. In exactly the same way the dogmas of physical sciences are the attempt to formulate in precise terms the truths discovered by the sense perceptions of mankind".[43] It brings out an analogy between the activities of religion and science in that both are concerned with the criterion of reasonableness.

Religious faith involves the use of reason and without reason faith becomes a blind submission. 'Faith seeking understanding' seems to imply that faith by itself is devoid of understanding, since it 'seeks' it. But obviously the human act that is faith, besides being a divine gift, is not devoid of some understanding. From a Christian point of view, the claims that we are created in God's image, fallen but redeemable through Christ, are not demonstrable by reason. The proper response to these claims is indeed faith but only after we have recognized with our minds the incomprehensibility of our nature and our own wretchedness. Then we can see by reason the coherent picture of ourselves which Christian theology gives us as it enables us to understand those paradoxes which left us in our wretchedness. Even though faith is not produced by reason, our faith is reasonable because Christian claims illumine the mind on matters that otherwise baffle us.[44] Without such illumination faith is improper. The nature of faith and its relation to reason are often misunderstood as leap of faith. That means when all the available evidences falls short of establishing the truth of religious faith, we must leap the gap between evidence and truth. This is to treat truth and reason belonging to the same order. But religious faith is not a leap within the order of the intellect, a leap which violates the very essence of that order. The leap of faith is a leap from the order of the intellect to the order of the heart.[45] We leap because we recognize the reality of the domain of the heart, not because there is a shortage of evidence. We recognize the reality of the order of the heart when we realize that we cannot achieve the well-being we seek from possessing the order of the body or the order of the intellect. The desire for our well-being, when purified with the desire for earthly prosperity and worldly success, points toward an order that is above the order of the intellect. Thus there is a leap (chasm) between the orders of the body, and the intellect and the order of the heart. The criterion of reasonableness is rooted in this awareness. For me, the transcendent notion of creation (creationism) and the immanent notion of evolution (ongoing creation) together give a holistic understanding of reality. Though one can make use of the scientific terminologies to comprehend the theological mysteries, one should not be making any scientific claim over one's faith vision as contemporary Creationists do, which is a methodological error as far as the science-religion encounter is concerned.

## Conclusion

In this paper we started with different types of creationism. We focused in detail on Intelligent Design Creationism and explicated the cosmological, astronomical, mathematical, evolutionary and chaotic models of divine design. We argued that creationism is non-scientific, and it is a methodological error from the scientific and theological perspectives. Finally we addressed the methodological concerns in Creationism and affirmed that Creationism is to be treated as not anything scientific but as a sort of faith formulation which itself cannot claim to be founded on authentic biblical exegesis. Hence the test for creationism is to use the criterion of reasonableness.

### *Notes and References*

1. See Creationism, Wikipedia The Free Encyclopedia in *http://en.wikipedia.org/wiki/*Creationism, accessed on 08-02-2010.
2. Jurie van den Heever, "Creationism in the Colonies: Science, Religion and the Legacy of Apartheid in South Africa," ed. Cornel W du Toit, The Evolutionary Roots of Religion: Cultivate, Mutate or Eliminate, Proceedings of the 14th conference of the South African Science and Religion Forum of the Research Institute for Theology and Religion held at the University of South Africa, vol. 13, Pretoria, 2008, p. 156.
3. See Creationism, Stanford Encyclopedia of Philosophy in *http://plato.stanford.edu/entries/creationism/*, accessed on 05-03-2010.
4. See P. K. Singh, "Intelligent Design, Fine Tuning and Evolution Theory: A Synopsis of Competent Rational Theory," in Thoughts on Synthesis of Science and Religion, eds. T.D. Singh and

Samaresh Bandyopadhyay (Calcutta: The Bhakti Vedanta Institute, 2001), p. 229.

5. *Ibid.*, p.230.
6. *Ibid.*
7. See Lazarus Walter Macior, "Critical Scientific Concepts in the Creation/Evolution Controversy," in Creation and Evolution: Proceedings of the Institute for Theological Encounter with Science and Technology (ITEST) Workshop, October, 1997 (Missouri: ITEST Faith/science Press, Missouri, 1997), p. 33.
8. See Francisco J. Ayala, "Darwin's Revolution," in Creative Evolution? eds. John H. Campbell and J. William Schopf (Boston: Jones & Bartlett, 1994), pp.1-17.
9. See Charles Darwin, On the Origin of Species (London: Unit Library, 1902), p. 76.
10. For details See Augustine Pamplany, Theological Mysteries in Scientific Perspective (TMSP) (Bangalore: Asian Trading Corporation, 2005), p. 95.
11. Refer Denis Edwards, The God of Evolution: A Trinitarian Theology (New York: Paulist Press, 1999), p. 6.
12. See Fritjof Capra, The Tao of Physics: An Exploration of the Parallels between Modern Physics and Eastern Mysticism (Flamingo: 1990), p. 253. Hereafter the book will be abbreviated as TP. Also see John Polkinghorne, Science and the Trinity: The Christian Encounter with Reality (New Haven and London: Yale University Press, 2004), p. 68.
13. Refer Robert J. Spitzer, "Indications of Creation in Contemporary Astrophysics," in Ultimate Reality and Meaning, vol. 24, no.1, September 2001, p. 217. According to Spitzer the very fact that the entropy of the universe is increasing implies the universe is expanding. According to Stephen Hawking the expansion rate of the universe which depends on the initial explosive energy during the Big Bang, the mass of the universe and the strength of the gravitational force requires a delicate and precise balancing for the formation of this universe. See Kuruvilla Pandikattu, The Bliss of Being Human: Science and Religion for Self-Realization (Pune: Jnanam, 2004), p. 55. Hereafter the book will be abbreviated as BBH. Also see P.J. Mc Laughlin, Modern Science and God (Dublin: Clonmore & Reynolds Ltd., 2000), p. 77.

14. As cited in Job Kozhamthadam, "The Changing Face of Science Christianity Dialogue," p. 4.
15. For details refer Fred Adams and Greg Lauglin, The Five Ages of the Universe: Inside the Physics of Eternity (New York: A Touch Stone Book, 1999), pp. 23-24.
16. See Jean Dorricott, Jean. SCM Study Guide to Science and Religion (London: SCM Press, 2005), p.7. Hereafter the book will be abbreviated as SGSR.

    17 See "Math Equation Quotations," in *http://iae-pedia.org/ Math_Education_Quotations,* accessed on 27-02-2010.
18. See "Phi and Fibonacci Series," in http://goldennumber.net/ fibonser.htm, accessed on 23-02-2010. In the 12th century, Leonardo Fibonacci discovered a simple numerical series that is the foundation for an incredible mathematical relationship behind phi. Starting with 0 and 1, each new number in the series is simply the sum of the two before it. 0, 1, 1, 2, 3, 5, 8, 13, 21, 34, 55, 89, 144, . . .The ratio of each successive pair of numbers in the series approximates phi (1.618. . .), as 5 divided by 3 is 1.666..., and 8 divided by 5 is 1.60.
19. The Golden Section is also known as the Golden Mean, Golden Ratio and Divine Proportion. It is a ratio or proportion defined by the number Phi (= 1.618033988749895... ). For details see "The Golden Section Ratio Based on a Phi," in *http://goldennumber.net/ goldsect.htm,* accessed on 23-02-2010.
20. Roger V. Jean, "Impressions of Synthesis from Ancient Egyptian Theology," in TSSR, p. 311.
21. Refer Ziaeddin, Surdar and Iwona Abram, Introducing Chaos (Cambridge: Icon Books, 1999), p. 6. Hereafter this book will be abbreviated as IC.
22. See Dorricott, SGSR, p.15.
23. See Pandikkattu, BBH, 47, 50. Also see Dorricott, SGSR, pp. 15-16.
24. Surdar Ziaeddin, and Iwona Abram, IC, pp.7-8.
25. See E. Osborn, Irenaeus of Lyons (Cambridge: Cambridge University Press, 2001), pp. 89-93.
26. See P.K. Singh, "Intelligent Design, Fine Tuning and Evolution Theory: A Synopsis of Competent Rational Theory," in TSSR, pp. 229-30.

27. As cited in Ted Peters, Science, Theology and Ethics (Burlington: Ashgate, 2003), pp.17-18. Hereafter the book will be abbreviated as STE.
28. See John F. Haught, Responses to 101 Questions on God and Evolution (New York: Paulist Press, 2001), p. 85. Hereafter the book will be abbreviated as RQGE.
29. See Ted Peters, STE, p. 17.
30. Vatican II, Gaudium et Spes: Pastoral Constitution on the Church in the Modern World, December 1965, no. 59.
31. See Ted Peters, STE, p. 4.
32. *Ibid.*
33. *Ibid.*, p. 8.
34. *Ibid.*, p. 42.
35. *Ibid.*, p. 6.
36. *Ibid.*
37. *Ibid.*, p. 22.
38. See Arthur Peacock, Theology for A Scientific Age: Being and Becoming Natural, Divine and Human (Minneapolis: Fortress Press, 1993), p. 12. Hereafter this book will be abbreviated as TSA.
39. See Ian Barbour, Issues in Science and Religion (New York: Harper and Row, 1971), p. 158. Hereafter the book will be abbreviated as ISR.
40. See Van A. Harvey, The Historian and the Believer: The Morality of Historical Knowledge and Christian Belief (New York: Macmillan, 1966), p. 65. For details refer pp.50-100 of the same.
41. Refer Peacock, TSA, pp. 16-17.
42. Refer Whitehead, Religion in the Making (Cambridge: Cambridge University Press, 1926), p. 57.
43. Refer Diogenes Allen, Christian Belief in a Post-Modern World: The Full Wealth of Conviction (Kentucky: Fox Point, 1989), p.145.
44. *Ibid.*, p. 148.

# 11

# Transdisciplinarity, Psychology and Primary Theories of Origin

CHRIS MONTOYA, DAVID MONTOYA & GRAEME MACKAY[1]

Science does not exist without the scientist as religion does not exist without the believer. Both endeavors are human constructions and as such both methods of knowing are inextricably bound in a quagmire of self-interest, emotion and faith. A better understanding of the psychology behind how and why humans are driven to create primary theories of existence, ostensibly apart from organized religion, is critical to future scientific progress concerning origins. In this paper primary views concerning ontogeny, phylogeny and cosmology are examined. It is argued that building primary theories with an eye on the transdisciplinary perspective highlights distortions caused by sub-conscious mechanisms. Finally, in contrast to popular thought, bringing subconscious distortions into conscious appreciation demonstrates that science and religion are currently in alignment with respect to these three primary views of origin.

Until someone builds a time machine mankind will never know how things really began. With this in mind, primary theories of everything as creative endeavors may be seen as symptoms of "mental illness", a modern form of ancient Greek mythology where Sisyphus was eternally tasked by the gods to perform an impossible endeavor.[2] At what point does a theory become a driving force to create justification for psychopathology? Manifestations of the pathology can range from the neurotic to psychotic breaks from reality as the stricken repress, distort, deny and rationalize in a veiled attempt to make social reality intelligible from their egocentric perspectives.[3] The more intelligent the patient the more rational the theory appears and the more the contagion spreads.[4] Many exceptionally creative scientists and artists have had these predispositions. In the 18$^{th}$ century Hegel labeled all God reverencing scientists as irrational. Real or imagined threats, such as these, cause the mind to respond with fear. Fear in the predisposed mind releases defense mechanisms to protect the ego, but in addition these same mechanisms also distort reality invisibly, in light of the "creative illness."[5] In rational-emotive therapy individuals become aware of subconscious distortions. This awareness will facilitate and delimit areas of agreement between scientific and Judeo-Christian religious worldviews at three levels of transdisciplinary harmonization. A soft fusion at the level of ontogeny, a moderate fusion at the level of phylogeny and a hard fusion at the level of cosmology will be discussed. Further and armed with the knowledge of "creative scientific illnesses" we will, from a different parallax, re-evaluate Darwin's Theory of Evolution exploring the eclectic nature of our reality in light of our apparent human cognitive and emotional limitations.

**Theories of Origin – A Soft Fusion (Ontogeny)**

Theories of human ontogeny consider both the biological-genetic as well as the socio-cultural aspects of development. Religion appears neutral or in agreement with the various aspects with some exceptions. We will use the "fact" of when human life begins as an apparent exception between the perspectives, to highlight subconscious distortions that are a hindrance to scientific and religious harmonization. In the current world-view, pro-life vs. pro-choice is seen as a battle between religion and science. Pro-lifers are represented as irrational and religious claiming human life begins at conception, whereas, pro-choicers are represented as scientific rational thinkers choosing not to suppose when human life begins. Is this an accurate representation of the world or is it merely a psychological distortion? Viewing the conflict from statistics, another discipline, may bring reality into focus. The religious belief as to when human life begins is limited to a restricted number of "non-scientific cognitive frames," and although pro-lifers claim life begins at conception the exact time is not Biblically defined. Rational scientists, on the other hand, whose data appear to be invariant across a number of different "cognitive frames," are also blindsided. Contrary to the current worldview, university level Lifespan Development textbooks across North America define the human life span as beginning at conception and ending at death.[6] Human lifespan appears, at least on the surface, to be a simple, rational and adequate definition.

From conception lifespan data are then collected, collated and tallied. This methodology appears straightforward and may seem to be a proper way for developmental sciences to operate. Ego defense mechanisms, however, create unconscious pitfalls that cause developmental scientists from the best universities to misreport the leading cause of death in Canada. In 2001, heart disease caused 74,824 deaths followed closely by cancer at 65,205 deaths. Abortion occurs post conception and claimed over 112,000 Canadian lives in 2001.[7] The subconscious distortion in this case may take the form of not wanting to be stigmatized for saying that North Americans kill more humans than are taken naturally or to be threatened by the label "irrational" for merely appearing to support a religious perspective. Data like 4 out of 10 women in North America have had an abortion come from the religious right. Isn't this correct? Or is data data? With some distortions revealed, a new worldview emerges. Developmental science and religion are ostensibly reporting the same findings. Life begins at conception and any other line that is drawn after we receive our genetic code is arbitrary. Yet the current worldview does not reflect this. Even today if you ask well-read people about abortion and when human life begins the prominent reply one hears is Roe vs. Wade. Yet Roe vs. Wade is considered a privacy issue not an ontogeny issue. Once we as intellectuals can see past the ego defense distortions, a unity of conscious thought leads us to a general confluence where a soft transdisciplinary fusion is possible. Soft fusion is basic face validity: a nominal agreement "metaphorically" that life begins at conception.

### Theories of Origin - A Moderate Fusion (Phylogeny)

Theories of phylogeny span from God created the species (Creationist), to something created the species (Intelligent Design) to Darwin (Evolution). The current worldview concerning Charles Darwin, we feel, is best stated in the words of the Oxford University Press, "Darwin...argued for a material, not divine, origin of the species."[8] As recently as June 2005 the Harris Poll released information stating that 55% of North Americans believe that Creationism, Intelligent Design Theory, and Darwinian Evolution should all be taught together in public schools under the rubric of science.[9] Have scientists and theologians accurately defined the various phylogenic positions? Defense mechanisms at the personal level and groupthink at the psychosocial transpersonal level have again caused considerable distortion.

Specifically, in the *Origin of the Species*, in the chapter titled Recapitulation and Conclusion, Darwin clearly writes, *"Therefore I would infer from analogy that probably all the organic beings which have ever lived on this earth have descended from some one primordial form, into which life was first breathed by the Creator...To my mind it accords better with what we know of the laws impressed on matter by the Creator, that the production and extinction of the past and present inhabitants of the world should have been due to secondary causes."* Darwin concluded in the last paragraph of the *Origin of the Species, "There is grandeur in this view of life with its several powers, having been originally breathed by the Creator into a few forms or into one..."* Breathed life into of course, given Darwin's Christian roots comes from the God of Genesis where.

God reportedly did just that when creating humans. Darwin takes poetic liberties as to the style and timing. Darwin further writes in his Difficulties in Theory Chapter, *"Have we any right to assume that the Creator works by intellectual powers like those of man?"*

Darwin was a deist creationist at the writing of his theory of evolution. In the current worldview, evolution stands on the shoulders of Darwin. Therefore, what is currently taught around the world is Intelligent Design. High school, College and University instructors should feel free then to teach "Traditional Darwinian Evolution" not as it has been misconstrued through fear-based subconscious mechanisms and groupthink as Godless, but as the intelligent design science it was written to be. Eleven years after the publication of *The Origin of the Species* Darwin, before his death, published *The Descent of Man*. It was in this latter work Darwin again reiterated, *"the idea of a Creator and Ruler of the Universe had been answered in the affirmative."*[10] Yet again the current worldview does not reflect this.

Although both Darwinian Evolution and Christianity demonstrate convergent validity, in that both narratives appear under one rubric of intelligent design, more is needed for a statistically based moderate transdisciplinary fusion. Given 15 items in any storyline there would be over 1 trillion ways of combining them into your creation story. Fifteen ways to choose the first element, times fourteen ways to choose the second element, times thirteen ways to choose the third element, etc. If there were only one correct order the odds would be 1 trillion to one that you would randomly select the right order. The Bible narrative and scientific narrative demonstrate an excellent 4$^{th}$ dimensional alignment: One, before the Big Bang God set things up for explosion/ expansion.[11] Two, God says let there be light and bang! Three, light escapes from the event horizon. Four, the heavenly firmament forms i.e. the disk of the Milky Way forms.[12] Five, the Earth cools and water appears. Six, life appears first in water. Seven, life appears next on land. Eight, plant life appears first.[13] Nine, animal life appears next. Ten, birds appear next. Eleven, mammals appear next. Twelve man appears last.[14] Thirteen, man was naked first, then was clothed in animal skins. Fourteen, man was first a farmer. Fifteen, man was then a keeper of animals.[15] There is a definite and ordinal transgression of boundaries and knowledge coherence.[16] Once ego defense mechanisms and groupthink are exposed by psychological insight, scientists can envision the invisible: a general overarching confluence between phylogeny and a Creation narrative forming a moderate transdisciplinary fusion.

**Theories of Origin (Cosmology)**

Theories of cosmology ostensibly span from Einstein and the Big Bang to a steady state universe. Hypotheses concerning quantum foam, string theory and various other theories of everything are being published. On the street, however, the worldview revolves around the big bang, the cosmological constant and whether there will be a big crunch or continued expansion. Since the Big Bang Theory became dominant and displaced the constant state theory of the universe most cosmologists believe that if there was a beginning then there had to be a beginner, starter or Creator. The secularists apparently had lost the battle of God in cosmology because they could not get around the mathematics of Einstein. Math, in addition to humor, it seems is a way around unconscious defense mechanisms. Some day quantum physics may be joined mathematically to concepts in general relativity in a grand theory of everything.[17] However, even with a theory of everything, the paradox over God cosmology, general relativity and quantum physics will continue. Cosmology and religion are currently sharing a common narrative: because there was a start, there was a Creator or starter of the cosmos.

## A Hard Transdisciplinary Fusion of Primary Theories of Origin

For an elegant fusion to occur at this level a basic tenet must be that there was truth in the Bible and there was factual probabilistic accuracy in the physical sciences. In addition, convergent validity with an exact mathematically defined interval or ratio interface between disciplines was required.[18] Specifically, what occurred was a point-by-point temporal linking of the Creation narrative with hard scientific data concerning the temporal unfolding of the universe. The authorized King James Edition (Ben Asher text) of the Bible was used.[19] Only the descriptions of days 3, 4, 5, 6 and 13 of Creation were used from the Bible because they could be literally linked to cosmological, geologic, fossil and historical data. Older, time tested scientific paleontology compilations were used for the correlation. Days in the Bible narrative were linked to scientific observations in the following fashion. From Genesis the span of the 3rd day was mapped onto scientific data from the creation of the solid planet to the appearance of seed bearing plants termed angiosperms. The span of day three was calculated as 4.46 billon years by subtracting 4.6 billion years (oldest estimated age of the earth) from 136 million years, the approximate arrival date of true seed-bearing plants. In a similar fashion on day 4 God said, "Let there be lights in the firmament of heaven to divide day from night; and let them be for signs and for seasons, and for days and for years." This epoch has been estimated scientifically as the time it took for our atmosphere to turn from opaque, to translucent, to transparent. This span took approximately 1 billion years spanning from 1.75 billion years ago to 750 million years ago.[20] In a similar fashion on day 5 God said, "Let the waters bring forth abundant moving creatures." Day 5 then spanned all the way to birds. From a scientific perspective this span included early jellyfish-like creatures termed coelenterates to the first birds. This span took approximately 305,000,000 years. The dates spanned from 500 million years ago to 195 million years ago. In a similar fashion on day 6 God created modern mammals and cattle were mentioned. Modern mammals came on the scene 53,000,000 years ago. (It is important to note that archaic mammals and water mammals were created earlier). Day 6 ended with the appearance of man. The earliest hominids with tools (Homo Habilis) appeared approximately 3 million years ago in Africa (although more recent evidence could place it earlier). The time span for day 6 therefore was approximately 50,000,000 years.[21]

Using a different methodology, on day 13 fourteen hundred years BC, Moses wrote, "For a thousand years in Thy sight are as yesterday..." The inspired time dilation circa day 13 therefore was 1000 years to one day. The time span of day 13 was 1000 years (Psalm 90:4). In fourth-dimensional curvilinear calculations of the appropriate day, the day selected was the one where the date falls closest to the midpoint of the span on graph 1.

**Temporal Overlap Pattern**
**Years from the Present**

**Present Time = Moses Star of Day 1**

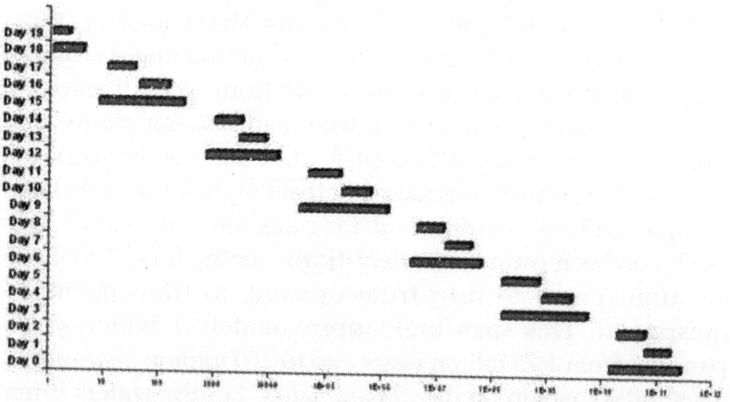


**Figure 1:** *Graphically illustrates the temporal overlap pattern created by applying the literal translation of the Holy Bible to the extant fossil and geologic records. Note at the end of Day 0, approximately 12.5 billion years from the present time, the so called Big Bang occurred. The time of Moses is marked by a four pointed star on Day 13. Finally, we come into temporal synchrony with our distant hypothetical observer 6.66 epochs from the creative process that started long before the big bang.*

The original five data points were plotted in standard psychophysical log-linear formats.[22] The data points were then analyzed using a Pearson Product Moment Correlation. A t-test to assess the significance of the correlation coefficient was calculated. Finally, the linear regression of Y on X for ungrouped data was calculated for the original five data points.

The correlation from the hard fusion of the 5 plotted points wasr = -. 9969. The temporal correlation was significant $t_{(3)} = -21.9$, $p < .001$. The interpolated line is described by the linear equation: $Y' = -.7567(x) + 15.34$. It is apparent that temporal duration, as psychophysically described from a transdisciplinary perspective, correlating cosmological, geologic, fossil and historic records with the Bible narrative is curvilinear and predictable. Figure 1 graphically illustrates that the epochs present themselves in 6.66 overarching triplets. The length of all the other non-data point days was extrapolated from the linear regression (See Figure 2). It is also clear that our universal time, compared to our distant hypothetical observer, is decelerating (see Figure 2). The length of each of the 5 epochs is predictably shorter on each of the original 5 selected days following Creation.[23] Of some interdisciplinary interest is the fact that in the Brahma religion the first heart beat of the earth (day after its creation) was approximately 4 ½ billion years in length, which matches our data.[24] In addition, the Mayan calendar, which started around the time of the ten

**Temporal Slowdown Since Big Bang**

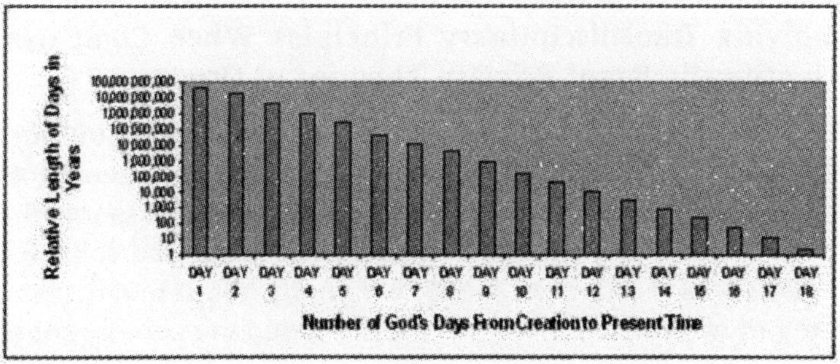


**Figure 2**

commandments (J. Eric S. Thompson determined that 0.0.0.0.0 Mayan Time corresponded to the Julian date 584283, which equaled August 11th, 3114 B.C. in our Gregorian calendar) ends in the same decade that our transdisciplinary data reaches temporal synchrony with our distant hypothetical observer some 5125 years later on December 21st, 2012 A.D.[25]

### Conclusions about Origins

The books of the Bible are divinely inspired human constructions dealing in faith and truth, whereas the books of science are human constructions dealing in the senses and probabilistic fact. The authors are convinced that theologians and scientists are well-meaning, moral people who diligently search their areas of expertise for meaning and purpose. However, the narratives extrapolated from the truth of the Bible or the hard data of science about our origins, by their very psychological nature, should not be considered immediately logical or consistent. On the other hand, time-tested Biblical interpretations and time-tested scientific theories should be confluent. The negative impact of ego defense mechanisms summated through social psychology at the transpersonal level via the mechanism of groupthink over time can be best detected using a broad transdisciplinary lens. This initial nexus is but a seminal step toward a seamless transition bridging interdisciplinary research into multidisciplinary designs and transdisciplinary awareness: an awareness that both science and religion will require to function in the new millennium.

### Applying Transdisciplinary Principles When Comparing Scientifically Based Primary Theories of Origin

Further and penultimate to our purpose, the following question is posited: should our ultimate hypothesis be that there is one single best origin narrative? In addition, are we to assume that origin issues will simply be solved by the continued collection and analysis of data? Or, should we finally admit that there are many nontrivial distinct scientifically based yet equally sound ways of describing origin, whether speaking to the ontogeny, phylogeny or cosmology of the precept. That is to say, given the current numerous theories and narratives can competent seekers of knowledge be anything but eclectic in our questioning, methodologies and visions? To this general purpose we will in a transdisciplinary manner re-evaluate Darwin's initial observations, this time remaining within the scientific arena to emphasize just one of many potential nontrivial distinct scientifically based alternate ways of describing origin data given the available objective scientific evidence.

Whereas many published articles cite the need for merging disparate areas of scientific investigation via transdisciplinary techniques[26], no articles to date, however, have attempted to lay down specific and simple, statistically-based methodologies for eliminating or modifying extant mono-disciplinary theories into "best fit" transdisciplinary models. Utilizing a transparent and simple transdisciplinary statistically- based method we significantly reduced a number of divergent validity problems currently encountered with traditional Darwinian evolution ($p < .001$). In addition, to align the current interpretation of the fossil record with other disparate scientific communities, mutation as the driving force behind species change was de-emphasized. Instead an emphasis on an over-arching trans-species phenotypic expression proceeding from an infinite variety of similar and competing genetic ancestors was adopted.

## A Transdisciplinary View of Darwin's Grand Theory

Dennett, Dawkins, and Mayr, ostensibly claim that since 1859 the basic precepts, of Darwin's Theory of Evolution, have remained virtually untouched. Much like Freudian Theory, Darwin's Theory of Evolution has existed in a safe mono-disciplinary cocoon. Beyond biology, and indeed, the instant Darwin's Theory was introduced into a "transdisciplinary" public school system, the war has raged. Battles were fought in the courtrooms, not lecture theatres and journals. Male oriented white scientific communities of the time, still entangled in Christian traditions, saw this war as "good science". Male domination whether sexual, colonial or scientific, given Darwin's Victorian roots seemed the order of the day, and the order was religiously followed: An order formed as much out of politics, religion and history as scientific observation and documentation. The question now remains, have we, as a species, learned anything from our past century of behavior? Freud and Darwin would argue an emphatic and resounding no! If mankind were totally controlled by unseen subconscious forces and genetic determinism might not all man-made theories be forever distorted, twisted and yet last for millennia?[27]

If there were another lens, however, to view distant scientific vistas, one with a self-correcting filter, allowing for a clearer synthesis and thesis would we employ it? If this new telescopic lens highlighted subconscious and indeed conscious distortions, other more accurate and objective scientific explanations might restructure older so called "special" theories via Popper's classical disconfirmation philosophy?[28] Transdisciplinarity and its emerging methodologies have the ability to create such a telescopic lens and filter. Based on the concept of meta-theoretical convergent validity, transdisciplinarity is emerging as the current scientific methodology. What this broad new lens has and will continue to reveal is that the data was and is and will always be correct, however, the human process and the human interpretation was, can, and will continue to be flawed. Acknowledging this very human actuality allows for a better objective separation of form from flow from flaw.

## Creationist Data from a Victorian

Since Darwin, scientists have, in an inter-disciplinary fashion, actively argued evolved genetic speciation based on fossil evidence. Genetic speciation involves micro and macro-adaptation caused by environmental pressures that change organisms genetically over immense periods of time. When once similar organisms can no longer produce viable offspring, due to genetic differences, a new genetic creature had evolved. Genetic change, via mutation, was the underlying principle of Darwin's gradualism.

As mentioned previously although Charles Darwin named his book 'Origin of Species,' the only statements about the arrival of species concerned are the following. In his *Origin of the Species*, in the chapter titled Recapitulation and Conclusion, Darwin wrote, *"Therefore I would infer from analogy that probably all the organic beings which have ever lived on this earth have descended from some one primordial form, into which life was first breathed by the Creator... the laws impressed on matter by the Creator, that the production and extinction of the past and present inhabitants of the world should have been due to secondary causes...There is grandeur in this view of life with its several powers, having been originally breathed by the Creator into a few forms or into one..."* As reiterated previously breathed life into given Darwin's Christian roots comes from the God of Genesis where God reportedly did just that when creating humans. Darwin further writes in his Difficulties in Theory Chapter, *"Have we any right to assume that the Creator works by intellectual powers like those of man?"* Then eleven years later, in *The Descent of Man* Darwin stated, *"... the idea of a Creator and Ruler of the Universe had been answered in the affirmative."* We argue that Darwin's Christian- based theory fuels the religious ideal that we, as a species, are somehow swimming up a stream against the laws of physical entropy from simple to complex, from manhood toward godhood.

Attempts to eviscerate Darwin's Original Theory by taking out the Creator gave evolution a statistically untenable random base and left us with concepts like Social Darwinism, the selfish gene and man as a simple "top of the food chain omnivore." Many social scientists resisted this type of simplistic reductionism. As over 90% of the world's population believes in God and all major world religions claim Him or Her as theirs, could it be that Darwin in his original premise was correct and what we see is intelligent design? This is a question science will never, and can never, answer because it transcends the limits of our philosophy of science as argued by Popper. Many well-meaning scientists begin their theories starting with a non-observable intelligent designer. By starting origin theories in this fashion, they begin and finish in the metaphysical arena without ever once setting foot into a truly scientific one. In a similar fashion, Darwin's theory spun a yarn where a simple beginning leads to a complex end. Objectively we simply do not see non-sentient organisms moving towards Darwin's godhood.

To make his god-building theory work, Darwin believed that environmental influences were coded by somatic cells and transmitted to progeny via germ cells. Mendel's Laws of Heredity proved Darwin conclusively wrong. Darwin's theory of change, towards godhood via natural selection, was then to be further supported by De Vries's unlikely Theory of Mutation. De Vries's theory assumed that mutations produced progressive change. When mutations, however, consistently produced retrogression, micro-mutations were proposed. Since the lack of intermediate fossils was an insurmountable objection, S. J. Gould and others proposed a "Punctuated Equilibrium Theory" and hopeful monsters emerged.[29] Modern punctuated evolution pressured Darwinian evolution as the fossil record appeared to support punctuated evolution more closely, but the hopeful monster was still moving against the pull of universal entropy toward godhood driven by the artificial engine of natural selection. Moving past evolution's pseudo-scientific beginnings no current scientist or theologian denies that natural selection improves stock within existing species. We argue, however, that natural selection has never been observed to produce new species.

Some feel that Darwin actually needed God to get things started. After all, what are the odds that life could evolve from inanimate matter randomly on its own? From a multidisciplinary perspective, Hoyle the English astronomer who first coined the term the Big Bang eloquently stated, "The odds of life beginning randomly from innate matter anywhere in the Universe was, 1 chance in $10^{40,000}$." To put it in numbers we can appreciate, if we were to pack the known universe full of electrons the number would only be $10^{130}$ electrons.[30] Let's say we marked one of these electrons. If you were then blind folded and allowed to randomly walk anywhere in our universe looking for the one marked electron, you would have a much better chance of finding it than the odds of life spontaneously generating from inorganic material. So from this physics and mathematics transdisciplinary perspective it is functionally impossible that life could have randomly occurred. This was not Darwin's fault in the beginning. Darwin created an intelligent design theory but was emotionally powerless to stop what was intellectually happening to his theory.

Darwin in his "The Origin of the Species" argued that all life came from possibly one primordial organism. An organism so formed he argued could be pre-programmed to change given environmental pressures by the hand of the Creator. The idea that one life form could genetically mutate randomly, however, into the abundance of life seen around us is statistically inconceivable given the 4.5 billion year time frame we are working with. Punctuated evolution with its multiple starts is also statistically highly improbable. Take for example the following example from biology.

> A gene group, PAX-6, is a key regulator in the development of eyes in all vertebrates. It's analog has been found to control the development of the visual systems of mollusks, insects, flatworms, and nemerteans (ribbon worms). These represent 5 of the 6 phyla that have eyes. The molecular similarity is nothing less than astounding. The paired domain of the gene contains 130 amino acids. The match of the amino acids between insects and humans is 94%! Between zebra fish and humans the match is 97%!
>
> Could five genetically separate phyla have evolved these similar genes individually by random chance? There are twenty different amino acids available to fill each of the 130 spaces on the gene. This means there are $20^{130}$ or $10^{170}$ possible combinations. The number far exceeds the number of particles in the entire universe.
>
> Any combination is possible one time. Getting the same or even similar combinations a second, third, fourth and fifth time is the statistical problem. The likelihood that random mutations would cause the same combination five times is $10^{170}$ raised to the fifth power. There is no way this same gene could have evolved independently in each of the five phyla. The gene that controls the development of the eye must have

been programmed at a level below the Cambrian. That level is either the amorphous sponge-like Ediacarans or the one-cell protozoa, but neither had eyes. Evolution is not random. In addition, morphological constraint is evident in complex body organs, when very different phyla of animals develop very similar organs to satisfy similar needs. Being different phyla, they have been genetically separated since the inception of multi-cellular life. Hence they had to develop these similar solutions independently. The astounding similarity between octopus, squid and human eyes makes it so statistically improbable as to be functionally impossible that they evolved from different organs and converged.[31]

Since life as perceived from a multidisciplinary perspective could not have started from one or even five mutating phyla what probably happened? There is indeed a more elegant, multi-disciplinary explanation of the fossil evidence than either Darwinian or punctuated evolution and an elegant mathematical procedure to investigate the ability of transdisciplinary theories to describe the extant data.[32]

## The Migratory Theory of Genetic Fitness: A Transdisciplinary Primary Theory of Origin

It is a fact that environmental changes that lead to creating new gene pools have never been scientifically demonstrated in living organisms that leave fossil evidence. According to the philosophy of science laid down by Popper an explanation is needed that does not rely on a genetic change over time that we cannot observe or religious explanations as originally proffered. Such speculative non-observable explanations are pseudoscientific and irrational. So what can we observe? Or more importantly, what do we observe and what explanation can be proffered as the current best-fit scientific model given our new transdisciplinary lens and telescope?

The Migratory Theory of Genetic Fitness (MTGF) is a transdisciplinary model that re-interprets and re-evaluates the current evolutionary account of mankind's origins. Whereas Darwin argued that all life forms originally evolved from a few or even one primordial genetic code, The Migratory Theory of Genetic Fitness predicts just the opposite. It stands to reason, that when life first appeared, our planet spawned an infinite variety of very similar, 4 base pair, organisms all at once. Some organisms terminated immediately and some patterns never lived at all. There was no one single terrestrial organism that all other life came from, trillions of similar yet distinct patterns began the journey. Following the principle of survival of the fittest, these hardy primordial gene pools are still competing for survival today. Nothing has changed from the beginning of life on our planet but their number, which is ever decreasing via the process of extinction. Over the eons it has been "involution not evolution" that shaped our biosphere. To date no one has demonstrated how life began on Earth, from the inanimate to the animate, and indeed as there could be, yet to be discovered multiple trajectories we may never know. The transdisciplinary approach, however, gives us a broader field of view from which to reach a stable objective and testable consensus. The Migratory Theory of Genetic Fitness, based on the fossil record, is an outwardly observable phenotypic exposition rather than a non-observable unnecessary inward genotypic mutation. The MTGF involves simple mass migrations of many similar genetically stable organisms as climate patterns changed. As global climates slowly oscillated the mass extinction of millions of competing genetically similar organisms was inevitable. The MTGF predicts, in fact, just the opposite of what the current theory of punctuated evolution predicts. Instead of new genetic organisms arising via mutations to their genetic codes in response to varied environmental pressures, (genetic changes that are so statistically improbable "as to be functionally impossible") the fossil record clearly and plausibly indicates a high degree of phenotypic plasticity coupled with total stunning silence concerning genetic plasticity and mutation.

The current evolutionary approach cannot simply and clearly explain the apparent explosion of life at various epochs. Yet there is a straightforward and extremely parsimonious explanation. The MTGF suggests that the conditions needed to fossilize bones were not available in all areas and at all times on earth. The reason for the "apparent and misinterpreted" sudden explosions of new species in certain temporal epochs was that large groups of similar species migrated into fossil producing areas while adapting to climate change and those that could not phenotypically adapt quickly enough left their fossil traces behind layer after similar but slightly different phenotypic layer. These clear phenotypic variations observed across temporal epochs and rock strata have been misinterpreted as "unobservable" genetic mutations brought on by environmental pressure within a common ancestor leading to phenotypic change. The creation of an unobservable genetically based construct is unnecessary and statistically cumbersome.

In the past, origin scientists have speculated as to what they could not objectively and directly observe and have fit their speculations into a pre-existing theory/model. We feel a better methodology is to objectively and directly observe what is currently occurring and first assume that this was the past pattern and then create a theory model from the data. Following this methodology, currently we do not observe viable "genetically new" (non-man made) species that would leave fossil remains spontaneously occurring today. However, what we continue to observe is genetic erosion occurring through the bio-entropic mechanism of extinction. Using this new more appropriate methodology the MTGF clears up some more of evolution's external validity and multi-disciplinary problems. The MTGF clearly demonstrates that terrestrial life follows the physics based universal entropy principle. With billions of genetically similar organisms in competition, the principle of survival of the fittest has been eliminating countless unsuccessful but similar organisms for eons. Primordial gene pools have always survived by phenotypic adaptation and migrating into new and better territories. In addition to diversity created by reshuffling via sexual reproduction, environmental stress can also cause major phenotypic changes. For example, asexual eukaryotes (sponges) fuse two haploid cells to create a diploid zygote when stressed. Indeed similar mechanisms may transform cell colonies into aggregates and then into multi-cellular organisms.[33] As is plainly observed, major structural phenotypic adaptation does not have to equal transformation or mutation into "a new genetic species." As similar more fit species competed more successfully, they made extinct similar less fit organisms. The less fit similar but different organisms left their fossil residue behind layer after layer. The MTGF Theory argues that the terminal extinction trajectories of unsuccessful primordial organisms have been misinterpreted, in evolutionary theory, as a common ancestor branching into distinct new species and that this belief is held firmly in the face of contradictory statistical evidence.

Finally, it is also well documented that most, if not all, genetic mutations are lethal. It makes more sense, therefore, to assume that such lethal combinations were eliminated long ago and that today we are left with only the most genetically fit gene pools. The MTGF predicts that in modern times we will not observe gene pools spontaneously evolving contrary to the universal principle of entropy. All possible genetic combinations were randomly attempted at the beginning of time.

In conclusion then, and not to put too fine a point on it: Darwin in his "The Origin of the Species" argued that all life came from possibly one organism and then mutated into the abundance of life we observe around us today. One life form could not genetically mutate into the abundance of life seen around us today given the 4.5 billion year time frame we are working with. Punctuated evolution with its multiple starts is also statistically highly improbable. The current genetically based theory of evolution is cumbersome, unnecessary and insufficient to explain the current bio-diversity observed on our small planet. The MTGF is a phenotypic theory. Extremes in phenotypic plasticity that result from an interaction between the internal genetic code and the external environment have been overlooked for too long a period.

**Transdisciplinary Improvements with the MTGF**

There are a number of other a trans-disciplinary improvements with the MTGF.

1. The MTGF theory is immediately and directly testable and therefore refutable within our lifetime. The Darwinian Model would take millions of years to

replicate and refute. Putting into practice the "what you can currently observe principle," the MTGF clearly predicted and demonstrated with current observable data that changes in gravity, pressure, $CO_2$ levels, radiation (indeed anything that induces stress) can create impressive phenotypic structural changes in a variety of genetically stable species within short periods of time. In support of the MTGF, plants and animals raised in outer space with lower gravity change their phenotypic expression in one generation.[34] We have also seen that background radiation can have a profound effect on offspring.[35] In addition, simple pressure changes can have a dramatic effect on the phenotypic expression in plants. [36]

2. By not creating unobservable constructs the MTGF, from Popper's Logic of Scientific Discovery as a theoretical model, is more parsimonious. The theory does not have to predict things we cannot see. The MTGF simply assumes that what we see today, the extinction level event of 100s of species a year, has been going on from the beginning of time.
3. The MTGF is also helpful at the inter-disciplinary level. For years scientists have found discrepancies in the fossil records i.e. supposed older-appearing fossils occurring after newer ones. Because small pockets of biosphere can be sheltered while others have increased changes, the MTGF would predict different overlapping phenotypic trajectories. Based on abnormal gravitation, gas levels, radiation sources, or even sound vibrations phenotypic expressions could have been prematurely triggered or conversely maintained for many generations.[37]
4. The ontogeny replicates phylogeny principle is viewed differently from the MTGF parallax. First we ask the question, could a mutated species still go through these types of developmentally ordinal and appropriate phylogenetic stages? The MTGF model suggests that

the ontogeny replicates phylogeny principle is simply a developmental record of the response of a stable gene pool to environmental stressors. Just how plastic a phenotypic response can be, given a stable gene pool and a stressful environment, is unbelievable yet all around us. Imagine identical genes that on one hand give us an aerodynamic butterfly maneuvering in 3 dimensional gaseous space with more precision than a modern helicopter, while on the other hand with identical DNA genes can create a totally different phenotype: the slow moving clumsy terrestrial caterpillar.

5. One of the most astounding pieces of evidence to proceed out of the human genome project is that we seem NOT to need approximately 95% of the genes in our DNA. Dormant junk genes do what exactly? Are our junk genes simply a defense against viral infections or have we burned through 95% of our species iterations? Taking the ontogeny replicates phylogeny principle to a new vista, what if the reverse is also true? Again using the "what you can currently observe principle" Since there is a limited number of divisions for our human cells at the ontogeny level, is there also a limited number of iterations for our entire species?[38] Maybe what killed off the dinosaurs was not an extraterrestrial comet but the simple fact they came to the end of their natural generational iterations.

In conclusion, the MTGF predicts that the phenotypic expression of a unique gene pool is far more plastic than we had ever imagined. In one hundred years of non-random quasi-experimentation we have horses that range in size from 24 inches to over 8 feet, Beefalo and Ligers, midgets and giants. Instead of multiple vague definitions of species as the current evolutionary theory uses, the MTGF has only one definition of a sexually reproducing species. If organisms can produce viable offspring they are from the same seminal gene pool that occurred in primordial times. If they cannot interbreed they are a different primordial species. To wit, primordial species adapt in a highly plastic phenotypic fashion; they do not evolve by genetic mutation. Our purpose in proposing the MTGF was two fold. One was to honor Darwin's original observations of macro-adaptation, natural selection and extinction and secondly to propose a more elegant trans-disciplinary explanation of the fossil record with Darwin in mind. We feel we have achieved our purpose.

## A Simple and Elegant Statistical Comparison between Two Competing Transdisciplinary Theories

We do not have to reinvent the mathematical wheel to consider the transdisciplinary statistical improvements that the MTGF has over Darwin's evolutionary theory. Disciplines like paleontology, history, scientific philosophy, and statistics as well as Popper's criterion for theory testing i.e. parsimonious (including simple definitions of things like species), directly testable, directly observable, directly manipulatable etc. can be seen as comparable categories. The scientist/statistician can also easily compare one theory category to another. For example: Yes theory A is more parsimonious than theory B or No theory A is not as directly testable as theory B. A statistic that deals with categories like Chi Square ($X^2$) can be easily adapted. Work by Camilli and Hopkins indicates that $X^2$ for both random and mixed models provides reasonably accurate estimates of Type I error, without correction, for N e" 8.[39] The Montoya & Mackay Transdisciplinary Method states that to adequately compare transdisciplinary theories across multi-disciplinary borders you need at least 7 degrees of freedom (N-1 = 7). That is 8 transdisciplinary category areas will be needed for a minimum transdisciplinary comparison. All theories are expected to have at least one transdisciplinary peccadillo. As science deals in probability not truth, we can expect to eventually disconfirm or modify every theory no matter how grand. All scientists are required to criticize their own theory in at least one area compared to other theories that it is being compared with. For example the MTGF gives little to nothing as an explanation of how life began whereas Darwin stated that the "Creator" created everything in the beginning.

Using this simple methodology let's categorically compare Darwin's Theory and the MTGF. We use 9 category areas.

**A Chi Square Categorical Comparison of Two Primary Theories of Origin**

| | *Darwin* | *MTGF* |
|---|---|---|
| Non-Creationist Theory | No | Yes |
| More Parsimonious | No | Yes |
| In Line with Universal Entropy | No | Yes |
| Directly Manipulatable | No | Yes |
| Directly Refutable | No | Yes |
| Directly Observable | No | Yes |
| Life Statistically Probable | Yes | No |
| Non-mutation Based Highly Probable | No | Yes |
| Simple Definition of Species | No | Yes |

For each theoretical point an advantage (A) i.e. better transdisciplinary fit for example with the philosophy of science directly refutable or disadvantage (D) i.e. a weaker transdisciplinary fit for example with statistics life highly improbable, is awarded to each theory.

$$X^2 = \frac{\Sigma (O-E)^2}{E}$$

| | *Advantage* | *Disadvantage* | *Margin Totals* |
|---|---|---|---|
| Darwin | 1 | 8 | 9 |
| MTGF | 8 | 1 | 9 |
| Margin Totals | 9 | 9 | 18 |

Expected cell 1 value 9 x 9 / 18 = 4.5
Expected cell 2 value 9 x 9 / 18 = 4.5
Expected cell 3 value 9 x 9 / 18 = 4.5
Expected cell 4 value 9 x 9 / 18 = 4.5

| *Observed* | *Expected* | *O – E* | *(O-E)* $^2$ | *(O – E)* $^2$*/E* |
|---|---|---|---|---|
| 1 | 4.5 | -3.5 | 12.25 | 2.722 |
| 8 | 4.5 | +3.5 | 12.25 | 2.722 |
| 8 | 4.5 | +3.5 | 12.25 | 2.722 |
| 1 | 4,5 | -3.5 | 12.25 | 2.722 |
| Total | | | $X^2_{(1)} = 10.888, p < .001$ | |

It is clear that the MTGF provides us with a statistically significant transdisciplinary improvement over Darwin's Theory of Evolution. This type of straightforward statistical maneuver can be used with soft, moderate or hard fusion comparisons and should become the benchmark for objectively and straightforwardly comparing all transdisciplinary theories in the future.

## Other Scientifically Based Non-Darwinian Theories of Evolution: New Directions

The current worldview is that Darwin's theory of evolution is the only scientific theory that explains the evolution of the animal kingdom. In fact, however, several other theories have been proposed in addition to the MTGF. Professor Stuart Kauffman a proponent of Complexity Theory states, "Darwin's natural selection captivates us all. But is it right? Better, is it adequate? I believe it is not."[40] Indeed many aspects of evolution in the animal kingdom can better be explained by Complexity Theory, and this leads Kauffman and others to conclude that Darwin's Theory is not the correct explanation for the evolution of the animal kingdom.[41] In complete contrast to Darwin's Theory the Neutral Theory of Molecular Evolution, championed by Professor Motoo Kimura, of the National Institute of Genetics in Japan, holds that new mutated genes are neither more or less advantageous than the genes they replace. Variability in species, according to this theory, is not caused by selection but by random drift of mutant genes. This model is as statistically viable as Darwin's theory but also suffers from the same malaise.[42] The Acquiring Genomes Theory, argued by Margulis and Sagan highlights the fact that "Mutation accumulation does not lead to new species or even to new organs or new tissues." What does lead to new species is termed symbiogenesis. Symbiogenesis according to this theory occurs when one organism absorbs genetic material from another species via a process of incomplete digestion. This new genetic material changes the aggressors genetic code directly e.g. photosynthetic animals.[43] Finally the Impact Theory posits that some extinction level events have nothing to do with genetics at all, but can be due to non-local phenomena.[44] Dr. Professor Nathan Aviezer gives an excellent review of non-Darwinian scientifically based theories in his book Fossils and Faith.[45] In agreement with Kauffman and Kimura, it is patently clear that large portions of Darwin's Theory of evolution (synthetic or not) are neither necessary nor sufficient to explain the bio-diversity on our planet. Therefore in the future we propose that a transdisciplinary comparison be performed, as outlined in this paper, of all viable "scientifically based" primary theories of how life came to be on Earth. We believe it is only by clearly seeing our past mistakes that our future may be more properly envisioned and prepared for. In the words of Sir Fredrick Hoyle, "The Darwinian Theory is wrong, and the continued adherence to it is an impediment to discovering the correct evolutionary (or involution) theory."[46] In conclusion, transdisciplinary mathematical methodology, as previously outlined, is our best, and indeed perhaps only hope of quickly and successfully sorting through best-fit primary models of origin.

### Notes and References

1. Dr. Chris Montoya is currently a tenured professor at Tompson Rivers University British Columbia Canada. David Montoya graduated in Psychology from Thompson Rivers University British Columbia Canada and Graeme Mackay is a graduate in Physics at the University of British Columbia, Canada.

2. See, e.g., N. C. Andreason, "Creativity and Mental Illness: Prevalence Rates in Writers and Their 1st Degree Relatives," in *American Journal of Psychiatry*, 144 (1987), pp. 1288 - 1292. K. R. Jamison, "Manic Depressive Illness and Accomplishment: Creativity, Leadership and Social Class", In F. K. Goodwin & K. R. Jamison (Eds.), *Manic Depressive Illness*, (Oxford England: Oxford University Press, 1988). R. Prentky, "Creativity and psychopathology: Gambling at the seat of madness", In J. A. Glover, R. R. Ronning & C. R. Reynolds (Eds.), *Handbook of Creativity*, (New York, Plenum, 1989). A. Rothenberg, *Creativity and madness: New findings and old stereotypes* (Baltimore, Johns Hopkins University Press, 1990).

3. S. Freud, "The Psychopathology of Everyday Life", In J. Strachey (Ed.), *The Standard Edition of the Complete Works of Sigmund Freud,* Vol. 6, (London, Hogarth, 1901/1960).
4. J. E. Alcock, *A Textbook of Social Psychology*, 6th edition (Pearson Prentice Hall, Toronto, 2005), pp. 404-410.
5. H. Ellenberger, *The Discovery of the Unconscious* (New York, Basic Books, 1970).
6. See, e.g., J. S. Turner, and D. B. Helms, *Life Span Development*, 5th Edition, (Toronto, Harcourt Brace College Publishers, Library of Congress # 93 - 80877, 1995), p. 3 and 378. K. S. Berger, *The Developing Person Through the Lifespan*, 4th edition, (New York, Worth Publishers, 1998), p. 65. J. W. Santrock, Mackenzie-Rivers, A., K. H. Leung, and T. Malcomson, *Lifespan Development*, 2nd Canadian edition (Toronto, McGraw-Hill Ryerson, 2005), pp. 535-536.
7. Statistics Canada 2006, *http://www40.statcan.ca/cbin/fl/cstprintflag.cgi*. MacKenzie-Rivers Santrock, Leung & Malcomson, *Life-Span Development*, 1st Canadian Edition (Toronto, McGraw-Hill Ryerson, 2003).
8. C. Darwin, *The Origin of the Species* (Oxford, Oxford University Press, 1996), pp. 391-396.
9. Harris Poll # 52, "Harris Poll Explores Beliefs about Evolution, Creationism, and Intelligent Design," *Skeptical Inquirer*, 29 (December 2005), pp. 56-58.
10. See e.g., C. Darwin, *The Decent of Man*, (Chicago, Great Books, Encyclopedia Britannica Inc., 1996), p. 302. Charles Darwin, *On the Origin of Species* (Cambridge, Mass.: Harvard University Press, 1964), pp. 82-87.
11. L., M. Krauss, *Atom, An Odyssey from the Big Bang to Life on Earth…and Beyond*, (New York, Little, Brown and Company, 2001), pp. 69-70 & 279. J. Silk, *The Big Bang*, 3rd Edition (New York, W. H. Freeman and Company, 2001), pp. 73, 376,455 & 108.
12. G. Kane, *The Particle Garden* (Addison, Wesley Publishing Company, 1995), pp. 154-157.
13. Harold C. Bold, *The Plant Kingdom*, 4th edition (New Jersey, Prentice Hall Inc. Publisher, Englewood Cliffs, Library of Congress, QK48.B59 1977), pp. 296-297.
14. Robert, T. Orr, *Vertebrate Biology*, (Saunders Co. Publisher, Library of Congress QL605 075v, 1976), pp. 10-11.

15. See, e.g., J. D. Mcdougall, "Fission-Track Dating", *Scientific American*, 235/6, (1976), pp. 114-122. S. Fleming, *Dating in Archaeology: A Guide to Scientific Techniques* (New York, St. Martin's Press, 1977). F. E. Johnston, and H. Shelby, *Anthropology the Biocultural View*, (Dubuque, Wm. C. Brown Company Publishers, Iowa, Library of Congress #77 - 77077, 1978), pp. 194-195. M. Harris, *Culture, People, Nature, An Introduction to General Anthropolgy*, 3rd Edition, (Harper and Row Publishers Inc. 1980), ppp. 50 & 102. E. Stashi, & J. Marks, *Evolutionary Anthropology, An Introduction to Physical Anthropology and Archeology*, (New York, Harcourt Brace Jovanovich College Publishers, 1992), pp. 504-528. S. Jones, R. Martin, and Pilbeam, *The Cambridge Encyclopedia of Human Evolution* (UK, Cambridge University Press, 1994), pp. 383-385.
16. R. J. Lawrence, and C. Despres, "Futures of Transdisciplinarity", doi, 10.1016/ j.futures, Elsevier, *wwwsciencedirect.com*, Futures 36, 2004, pp. 397–405.
17. See e.g., D. Freedman, "Parallel Universes: The New Reality, From Harvard's Wildest Physicist", *Discover Magazine*, 1990, p. 52. M. Kaku, *Hyperspace* (Oxford, Oxford University Press, 1994), p. 245. K. S. Thorne, *Black Holes and Time Warps, Einstein's Outrageous Legacy* (New York, W.W. Norton and Company, 1994), pp. 96-120 & 483-512. D. L. Schacter, *Memory Distortion: How Minds, Brains, and Societies Reconstruct The Past* (Cambridge, Massachusetts, Harvard University Press, 1995). M. Drosnin, *The Bible Code* (New York, Simon and Schuster, Rockefeller Center, 1997), pp. 76 & 123. B. R. Greene, D. R. Morrison, & J. Polchinski, "StringTheory", *The National Academy of Sciences*, Vol. 95 (1998), pp. 11039 -11040. E. O. Wilson, *Consilence the Unity of Knowledge* (Vintage Edition, Random House, 1999). J. E. Lidsey, *The Bigger Bang* (Cambridge, Cambridge University Press, 2000), pp. 1-2. J. C. Wheeler, Cosmic *Catastrophes, Supernovae, Gamma-Ray Bursts, and Adventures in Hyperspace* (Cambridge, Cambridge University Press, 2000), pp. 218-220. S. W. Hawkings, *The Universe in a Nutshell* (Bantam Books 2001), pp. 30-33 & 148-153. Michio, Kaku, *A Theory of Everything*? A net paper/presentation by a professor of Theoretical Physics, City College of Yew York (2001). S. Strogatz, *How Order Emerges from Chaos in SYNC The Universe, Nature and Daily Life* (New York, Hyperion Books, 2003). B. Greene, *The Fabric of the Cosmos Space Time and the Texture of Reality* (Vintage Books Edition, Random House, 2005).

"The Story of the Great Attractor", University of Illinois (*HTTP:/ /archive.ncsa.uiuc.edu /Cyberia/Cosmos/GtAtractor.html*). Day M., 2005.

18. G. Furguson, and V. Takane, *Statistical Analysis in Psychology and Education*, 6th edition (New York, McGraw Hill, 1989).
19. *The Holy Bible*, Self Pronouncing Edition, Conformable to the 1611 King James Edition (New York, The World Publishing Company, 1935).
20. G.L. Schroeder, *The Science of God* (Broadway Books, Dell Publishing Group Inc. 1997), pp. 60 & 67.
21. See e.g., Harold, C. Bold, *The Plant Kingdom*, 4th edition (New Jersey, Prentice Hall Inc. Publisher, Englewood Cliffs, Library of Congress, QK48.B59, 1977), pp.296-297. Robert, T. Orr, *Vertebrate Biology*, op cit., pp. 10-11. W. Harland, R. Armstrong, A., Craig, L. Cox, A. Smith, and D. Smith, *A Geologic Time Scale*, (New York, Cambridge University Press (1989). O. Jensen, McGill University (*HTTP://travesti.eps.McGill.ca/*~oliva / terrestial_planets / lecture-4.pdf), 2002-01-13. N. A. Campbell, J. B. Reece, L. G. Mitchell, *Biology* (New York, Addison Wesley Longman Inc. 1999), pp. 446-450.
22. G. T. Fechner, *Elemente der psychophysik* (Leipzig: Breitkopf & Hartel, English Translation of Volume 1 by H. E. Alder, New York (Holt, Rhinehart and Winston, 1966). S. S. Stevens, "The Surprising Simplicity of Sensory Metrics", *American Psychologist*, 17 (1962), pp. 29-39.
23. C. P. Montoya, and G. Mackay, *Quantum Logging*, a mini-Lecture, Sponsored by the University College of the Cariboo Cultural Events Committee (2000). C. P. Montoya, and G. Mackay, *The Unified Primary Perspective*, a miniseries connecting science and religion, sponsored by the Office of Chaplain, University College of the Cariboo (2003/2004). D. E. Montoya, G. Mackay, & C. P. Montoya, *The Migratory Theory of Genetic Fitness: Re-worked Darwinian Evolution*, sponsored by the Office of the Chaplin, Thompson Rivers University (2005).
24. T. Ashley-Farrand, *Ancient Power of Sanskrit Mantra and Ceremony*, Volumes 1–3, *duf@earthlink.net*, India (2000).
25. See e.g., Calendrics Mayan, Dolphin Software. 48 Shattuck Square #147 Berkeley, CA. 94704 (1989 &1993). Jean Meeus, *Astronomical Tables of the Sun, Moon and Planets*, (Richmond, VA., Willmann-

Bell Publishers. 1983). Neil F. Michelsen, *The American Ephemeris for the 21st Century* (San Diego, CA, ACS Publications, 1982, 1988). Ian Ridpath (ed.), *Norton's 2000.0: Star Atlas and Reference Handbook* (Longman Group UK Limited, 1989). Linda Schele, and David Freidel, *A Forest of Kings: The Untold Story of the Ancient Maya* (New York, William Morrow and Company Inc., 1990). Linda Schele, David Freidel, Joy Parker, *Maya Cosmos: Three Thousand Years on the Shaman's Path* (New York, William Morrow and Company Inc., 1993). Dennis Tedlock, *The Popol Vuh: The Definitive Edition of the Mayan Book of the Dawn of Life and the Glories of Gods and Kings* (New York, Simon & Schuster, 1985).

26. See e.g., J. L. Lawrence, and C. Despres, "Futures of Transdisciplinarity", *Futures* 36 (2004), pp. 397-405. A. Max-Neef Manfred, "Foundations of Transdisciplinarity", *Ecological Economics* 53, Elsevier (2005), pp. 5-16. M. E. Renato, Sabbatini and S. H. Cardoso, *Interdisciplinary Science Reviews*, Vol. 27, No. 4/I (M Communications Ltd. 2002), pp. 303-311. D. J. Rapport, "Transdisciplinarity Education: Where, When, How?" *Ecosystem Health*, 4/2 (Blackwell Science Inc., 1998), pp. 79-80. T. Horlick-Jones, and J. Sime, "Living in the Border: knowledge, risk and Transdisciplinarity", *Futures* 36 (Elsevier, 2004), pp. 441-456. E. Hamberger, "Transdisciplinarity: A Scientific Essential", *Annals New York Academy of Sciences*, 1028 (2004), pp. 487-496. D. Senghaas, "Peace Research and the Analysis of the Causes of Social Violence: Transdisciplinarity", *Bulletin of peace Proposals*, 7/1 (1976), pp. 64-70. T. W. Valente, P. Gallaher, and M. Mouttapa, "Using Social Networks to Understand and Prevent Substance Use: A Transdisciplinary Perspective", *Substance Use & Misuse*, 39/10–12 (2004), pp. 1685-1712.

27. G. Wald, "The Origin of Life," *Scientific American*, (August 1954), pp. 19-21. C. Folsome, "Life: Origin and Evolution", *Scientific American Special Publication* (1979), p. 38. W. Dember, N. and J. S. Warm, *Psychology of Perception*, 2nd Edition (New York, Holt, Rhinehart and Winston, 1979), p. 25. F. E. Mosedale, *Philosophy and Science, The Wide Range of Interaction* (New Jersey, Prentice-Hall Inc., Englewood Cliffs, 1979), p. 7. B. Kolb, & I.Q. Whishaw, *Fundamentals of Human Neuropsychology*, 1st Edition (Francisco, W. H. Freeman and Co. San, 1980), p. 16. R. Quiring, U. Kloter, W. Gehring, "Homology of the eyeless gene in Drosophilia to the small eye gene in mice and Aniridia in Humans," *Science* 265 (1994) pp. 785-789. B. M. Fagan, *People of the Earth, An Introduction*

*to Pre-history* (New York, Lindbar Corporation, 1998), pp. 40 & 115-129. "The Undiscovered and Undiscoverable Essence: Species and Religion after Darwin", *The Journal of Religion* 22, pp. 12-20.

28. K. R. Popper, *The Logic of Scientific Discovery* (New York: Basic Books, 1959).
29. L. Mendis, *Reason's for Head and Heart* (Sri Lanka, Dr. Lalith Mendis Publisher, 1995).
30. F. Hoyle, C. Wickramasinghe, *Evolution from Space: A Theory of Cosmic Creation*, ISBN - 0 - 671 - 49263 - 2 (1981). F. Hoyle, C. Wickramasinghe, "The Case for Life as a Cosmic Phenomena," in *Nature*, 322 (1986), pp. 509-511.
31. R. Quiring, U. Kloter, W. Gehring, *op cit.*, pp. 785-789. G. L. Schroeder, *The Science of God* (Broadway Books, Dell Publishing Group Inc., 1997), pp. 60 & 67.
32. C. P. Montoya, "Transdisciplinarity, psychology and primary theories of origin: Putting Science and Religion in its Place: New Visions of Nature," An International Symposium with the University of California Santa Barbara, Ian Ramsey Centre, St. Anne's College, University of Oxford, 13th–16th July 2006. D.E. Montoya, and C.P. Montoya, "The Migratory Theory of Genetic Fitness: Putting Science and Religion in its Place: New Visions of Nature," Ian Ramsey Centre, St. Anne's College, University of Oxford, 13th–16th July 2006. This original research paper was included in the oral symposium presentation: Transdisciplinarity, psychology and primary theories of origin, for contrast purposes and the paper was distributed at the conference.
33. G. B. Johnson, *The Living World*, 2nd Edition (USA, McGraw Hill, 2000), pp. 304-307.
34. A. Paul, A.C. Schuerger, M.P. Popp, J.T. Richards, M.S. Manak, and R.J. Ferl, "Hypobaric Biology: Arabidopsis Gene Expression at Low Atmospheric Pressure", *Plant Physiology*, 134 (2004), pp. 215-223. S. McCarthy, "Space Farm", *The Canadian Foundation for Innovation's Electronic Magazine*, 16 (May/June 2006).
35. K. S. Berger, *The Developing Person Through the Life Span*, 4th Edition (Worth Publishers, 1998) pp. 102-103.
36. H. Koichibara, "Tomatomation," *Unesco Courier* (March 1987). E. Gilmore, "Sunflower over Tokyo," in *Popula* (1988), p. 75.
37. D. Carlson, "Sonic Creation Illustrated," 7/2 (2000), pp. 24-31.

38. B. Sykes, *A Future Without Men: Adam's Curse* (New York, Norton and Company, 2004), pp. 294-296.

39. G. Camilli, K. D. Hopkins, "Applicability of Chi Square to 2 X 2 Contingency Tables with Small Expected Cell Frequencies," in *Psychological Bulletin*, 88 (1978), pp. 163-167.

40. S. A. Kauffman, *At Home in the Universe: The Laws of Self-Organization and Complexity* (Oxford: Oxford university Press, 1995), pp. vii-viii.

41. P. Bak, C. Tang, and K. Weisenfeld, *Physical Review Letters*, vol. 59 (1987), pp. 381-384.

42. M. Kimura, *Nature* (1968), pp. 624-626.

43. L. Margulis, & D. Sagan, *Acquiring Genomes a Theory of the Origins of the Species* (New York, Basic Books, 2002).

44. L. Alvarez, & W. Alvarez, *Science*, 208 (1980), pp. 1095-1108.

45. Aviezer, N. 1980, *Fossils & Faith, Understanding Torah and Science* (New Jersey, KTAV Publishing House, Inc., Hoboken, 2001), pp. 221-238.

46. F. Hoyle, *Mathematics of Evolution* (Memphis, Tennessee, Acorn Enterprises, LLC, 1999).

# Index

M



N

## U



## V



## W



## Y



## Z